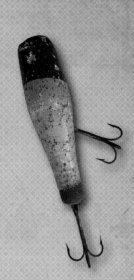

The LIFE *of the* LAKES

A GUIDE TO THE GREAT LAKES FISHERY

WALLEYE
Sander vitreus

© EMILY S. DAMSTRA

Brandon C. Schroeder, Dan M. O'Keefe, and Shari L. Dann

MICHIGAN SEA GRANT COLLEGE PROGRAM

LURE PHOTOS: BOB RASHID, ELIZABETH LAPORTE AND BRANDON SCHROEDER, MISG

Copyright © 2019 by Michigan Sea Grant, Regents of the University of Michigan

First edition, 1993. Second edition, 2003. Third edition, 2012. Fourth edition, 2019.

Published in the United States of America by the University of Michigan Press

Manufactured in Korea

Printed on acid-free paper

Fourth edition first published April 2019

A CIP catalog record for this book is available from the British Library.

Library of Congress Cataloging-in-Publication data has been applied for.

ISBN 978-0-472-03721-6 (paper : alk. paper)

ISBN 978-0-472-12386-5 (e-book)

The Life of the Lakes, A Guide to the Great Lakes Fishery

The production of this edition of *The Life of the Lakes* was supported by the National Oceanic and Atmospheric Administration Great Lakes Regional Fisheries Extension Enhancement Regional Coordination project, grant number NA05OAR4171045, the Michigan Sea Grant College Program, the University of Michigan, and Michigan State University Extension.

Michigan Sea Grant College Program, a cooperative program of the University of Michigan and Michigan State University, supports Great Lakes research and education.

The University of Michigan (UM) and Michigan State University (MSU) are equal opportunity/affirmative action institutions. UM and MSU Extension programs and materials are open to all without regard to race, color, national origin, gender, religion, age, disability, political beliefs, sexual orientation, marital status, or family status.

Michigan Sea Grant, 520 E. Liberty St., Suite 310, Ann Arbor, MI 48104-2210
msgpubs@umich.edu | (734) 763-1437 | michiganseagrant.org

CONTENTS

"*A lake is the landscape's most beautiful and expressive feature. It is earth's eye; looking into which the beholder measures the depth of his own nature.*"

— Henry David Thoreau

FOREWORD

Indigenous peoples of North America have been fishing the Great Lakes for 5000 years; European settlers from the days they arrived. The colonizers learned what the native people knew: the Great Lakes would provide, in the words of Michilimackinac commandant Antoine Cadillac, a "daily manna that never fails."

But the daily manna did fail. Survey after survey, starting in the 1860s, showed species once seen as limitless were fished out. The first to go was Atlantic salmon, and many other kinds of fish, like sturgeon and whitefish, were also decimated by the time of the Great Depression. By the mid-twentieth century, because of commercial over-fishing and habitat loss, the fishery was a shell of what it once was.

The sea lamprey was the death blow. After sea lampreys invaded Lake Erie and above (around 1920), lake trout was extirpated from four of the five Great Lakes, whitefish fell to historic lows, and several species of ciscoes were gone for good. Sea lampreys changed a way of life in the region and the once-thriving fishing towns faced existential crises; some did not make it through intact.

Science, cooperative management, and sea lamprey control have saved the Great Lakes fishery. The 1954 Convention on Great Lakes Fisheries between Canada and the United States started a sea lamprey control program that continues to this day and saves 100 million pounds of fish each year. The convention also ended a parochial approach to management that contributed as much to fishery loss as the sea lamprey. The formation of "lake committees" in 1965 created a place for managers to exchange data and information, and the 1981 Joint Strategic Plan for Management of Great Lakes Fisheries committed the managers to actively work toward their shared goals. Thanks to these measures, the Great Lakes fishery has improved steadily—today generating at least $7 billion annually.

The Life of the Lakes, now in its fourth edition, chronicles our fishery's rich history. Readers will gain an understanding of ecology and management, the fish—then and now—that make up various fisheries, and the future of the resource that so many of us depend upon for food, income, subsistence, and recreation. The story of our region plays on in the pages of *The Life of the Lakes*!

ROBERT LAMBE, EXECUTIVE SECRETARY
Great Lakes Fishery Commission

UP NORTH MEMORIES

FISHING NETS — NAUBINWAY, MICH. — A-1859

INTRODUCTION

From the earliest days, people have been drawn to the beauty, resources and way of life found in the Great Lakes—first native peoples, then European explorers and immigrant settlers and now, us, the current residents and students of the region. It is no secret why. The lakes are incredible in every sense of the word.

The people and these inland seas have been intricately intertwined, one influencing the other, throughout history. Perhaps the most dynamic relationship in that history has been with the Great Lakes fishery.

Through studying the Great Lakes fishery, we learn about the people and cultures that have depended on the productivity of the lakes. The story of the fishery also reflects the story of aquatic ecosystems, biodiversity, water quality, and environmental change, degradation, and rehabilitation. The Great Lakes fishery is the thread running through all these aspects, serving as the gauge of resource sustainability and quality of life for people in the region.

In this fourth edition of *The Life of the Lakes*, we have continued to focus on the Great Lakes fishery of the past; to outline the current status of the Great Lakes fishery today; and to discuss fisheries issues expected in the future. We have also provided a brief overview of ecology and management, as it applies to the Great Lakes and freshwater aquatic systems. The same comprehensive information found in earlier versions of this book is included here.

However, since the Great Lakes are dynamic and ever-changing, our approach to covering them should be too. More graphics and pictures have been added to help illustrate the colorful culture of the Great Lakes. For example, a new quick-reference section includes maps of each lake and its watershed along with an overview of the ecology, fisheries, and socioeconomics of the region. The main sections have been streamlined, sidebars and breakouts have been added, and this edition is in full color.

We hope you find *The Life of the Lakes* to be a valuable, educational and interesting source on the Great Lakes fishery— one that serves as your guide to exploring the vibrant Great Lakes that you return to through the years.

Great Lakes fisheries are defined as intricate webs of fish populations, their aquatic environments, and the people who use and enjoy them. These fisheries are important parts of the life of the lakes.

Terms used to describe the Great Lakes fishery are shown in **bold** throughout this publication and appear with definitions in the **Glossary**.

LAKE
SUPERIOR

Ontario

Minnesota

Duluth

Thunder Bay

Royale
Basin

Apostle Basin

Duluth Basin

Keweenaw
Basin

Deepest Sounding
1332 ft. (406 m)

Marquette

Sault Ste

Ontar

Michigan

Escanaba

Green Bay

Wisconsin

Marinette

Green Bay

Traverse City

Deepest Sounding
925 ft. (282 m)

Chippewa
Basin

Two Rivers

Oshkosh

Sheboygan

Minnesota

LAKE
MICHIGAN

Michigan

Mid-Lake
Plateau

Muskegon

Madison

Milwaukee

Iowa

Racine

South
Chippewa
Basin

Lansing

Dubuque

Illinois

Evanston

Benton Harbor

Chicago

Gary

Indiana

Ohio

miles 0   80   160

km 0   100   200   300

2

-410 -300 -250 -225 -200 -175 -150 -125 -100 -75 -50 -30 -10 0 200 400 500 700 900 1200 1500

Elevation in Meters

THE GREAT LAKES BASIN

The maps and descriptions in this section are new to the fourth edition of *The Life of the Lakes*. They serve as a quick reference for information about the ecology, fisheries, and species diversity of each lake, as well as the socioeconomic and physical attributes of the lakes and their connecting channels.

The maps show major cities and the extent of each lake's watershed—or the area of land wherein all of the precipitation eventually flows into the lake.

It is important to remember that healthy watersheds reduce flood risk, support crops, filter pollutants, mitigate effects of climate change, and boost human well-being, and that actions upstream have impacts downstream.

Each lake has features that define its character, the region that surrounds it, and the fishery it supports. Look to this section to get an overview of the lakes and to see how features of a lake affect the communities in its watershed and how, in turn, those communities affect the lake.

North Channel

Quebec

Manitoulin Basin

Georgian Basin

Parry Sound

Deepest Sounding 750 ft. (229 m)

Alpena

Midland

Alpena - Amberley Ridge

Ontario

Canada

United States

Bay City Basin

Peterborough

Kingston

Belleville

LAKE HURON

Saginaw Basin

Goderich Basin

Sarnia Basin

Bay City

Toronto

Niagara Basin

Mississauga Basin

Scotch Bonnet Ridge

Deepest Sounding 802 ft. (244 m)

Rochester Basin

Oswego

aginaw

Goderich

Hamilton

United States

Canada

LAKE ONTARIO

Rochester

New York

Syracuse

Port Huron

Sarnia

Niagara Falls

United States

Canada

Ontario

Nanticoke

Buffalo

Detroit

Lake St. Clair

Deepest Sounding 210 ft. (64 m)

Dunkirk

Ithaca

Windsor

Eastern Erie Basin

ann Arbor

Leamington

Central Erie Basin

The Great Lakes Basin Bathymetry Map

Erie

Mercator Projection, Scale 1:1,500,000

NOAA Great Lakes Environmental Research Laboratory

Base map compiled by the NOAA National Geophysical Data Center

LAKE ERIE

Western Erie Basin

Ashtabula

Pennsylvania

Toledo

Sandusky

Cleveland

ECOLOGY

Lake Michigan's main basin contains cold, clear, nutrient-poor water. This provides good habitat for trout, salmon, whitefish, and other cold-water species, but the amount of food available in open water has dropped in recent years. Open-water prey fish such as alewife and bloater have declined dramatically since the 1980s.

Large rivers and associated inland lakes formed by drowned river mouths provide important habitat connections and nutrient inputs. In certain areas, excess nutrients create blooms of algae that die off and decompose, creating oxygen-deprived "dead zones." Green Bay, considered the world's largest freshwater estuary, is particularly vulnerable to these events. In shallow, rocky areas of the lake, excess nutrients can fuel the growth of bottom-dwelling algae that wash ashore and foul beaches. The rotting algal muck can also harbor bacteria implicated in die-offs of fish and waterfowl in northern Lake Michigan.

Spawning fish often move into rivers or use rocky reefs in Lake Michigan's main basin. Dam removal and management efforts have improved conditions for spawning fish in many rivers. Many rivers in the northeastern part of the basin support naturally reproducing runs of introduced salmon.

FISHERIES

Though 136 fish species appear in the Lake Michigan watershed, only 68 are found in the lake itself. Five types of deepwater cisco disappeared from the lake due to overfishing and invasive species. Native strains of lake trout were also extirpated by the mid-1950s. Harvest limits, habitat restoration, water quality regulations, and stocking programs have aided in partial recovery of some species, including lake trout, cisco, lake sturgeon, and Great Lakes muskellunge.

Lake Michigan is the birthplace of the Great Lakes salmon fishery. Coho salmon were successfully stocked in the Platte River in 1966, and Chinook salmon followed in 1967. Recreational salmon and trout fisheries have fluctuated over the past 50 years, but Lake Michigan still supports a large charter-fishing fleet that primarily targets the "big five" salmonines: Chinook salmon, coho salmon, steelhead (rainbow trout), brown trout, and lake trout.

Some bays and drowned river mouth lakes offer excellent fishing for other species, including walleye and smallmouth bass. Lake whitefish continues to be the most popular and valuable commercial species on Lake Michigan, although catches have declined in recent years. State-licensed commercial fishers operate in Wisconsin and Michigan waters, and tribal commercial and subsistence fisheries operate in 1836 treaty waters of northern Lake Michigan. In Illinois and Indiana, commercial fisheries for yellow perch closed in 1997.

SOCIOECONOMICS

After Lake Erie, the Lake Michigan basin has the second highest population. Major urban centers include Chicago (Illinois), Milwaukee (Wisconsin), and Green Bay (Wisconsin), each relying on the lake for shipping, municipal, and industrial water use. Chicago also uses canals and water control structures to drain up to 2.1 billion gallons of Lake Michigan water per day into the Mississippi River. Originally designed for wastewater management, the canals also affect invasive species introductions, navigation, and flood control.

The basin is a mix of residential, agricultural, and forested land, with the majority of undeveloped land found in the northern part. Many popular vacation destinations attract tourists to the Lake Michigan shoreline. The rocky points, islands, and protected bays of northern Lake Michigan are a draw for communities along Wisconsin's Door Peninsula and Michigan resort towns like Petoskey and Traverse City. Sandy beaches and dunes stretch along most of Lake Michigan's eastern shore from Indiana Dunes National Lakeshore in the south to Sleeping Bear Dunes National Lakeshore in the north.

ECOLOGY

In northern Lake Huron, features such as the North Channel, lower St. Marys River, and Les Cheneaux Islands provide varied habitats ranging from deep, cold channels to shallow, vegetated bays. These areas and high-quality tributary streams provide spawning and nursery habitat for many native and introduced fish species.

Farther south, Saginaw Bay is shallow, warm, and nutrient-rich compared to the lake's main basin. Saginaw Bay tributaries include the Saginaw, Tittabawassee, and Flint rivers. Although these rivers have a history of industrial and agricultural pollution, they provide spawning habitat for important fish species such as walleye.

After the late 1990s, diminishing nutrient levels and booming populations of invasive mussels contributed to declines in plankton, bottom-dwelling invertebrates, and prey fish. Natural reproduction of introduced Chinook salmon in Canadian tributaries of Georgian Bay also led to high numbers of predatory fish in Lake Huron during the early 2000s. Dwindling prey fish could not sustain high salmon numbers, and both salmon and their primary prey (invasive alewife) collapsed by 2004.

FISHERIES

After the collapse of alewife and Chinook salmon, Lake Huron charter fishing dropped by half, and recreational fishing declined dramatically. However, native walleye and lake trout rebounded in the absence of alewife, and walleye fishing became popular in Saginaw Bay.

Lake Huron now offers quality mixed-bag fisheries in addition to offshore lake trout fishing. In the northern part of the lake, it is possible to catch Atlantic salmon, lake trout, rainbow trout, Chinook salmon, coho salmon, pink salmon, and walleye on the same trip. Some nearshore areas also provide good fishing for northern pike, yellow perch, smallmouth bass, and cisco.

Lake Huron's commercial fisheries include lake whitefish trap net fisheries in addition to multispecies fishing operations in Saginaw Bay and Canadian waters. Bloater "chubs" are also targeted with gill nets set in deep water.

SOCIOECONOMICS

Northern Lake Huron is largely rural and forested with mining and minor agricultural industries. Relatively undeveloped coastlines, islands, and rocky formations are popular tourist destinations, such as the Les Cheneaux Islands in northern Michigan and the Manitoulin Islands in Ontario. Northern Lake Huron sees significant tribal fishing activities under a 1836 treaty agreement.

The Saginaw Bay region contains the largest populations and the geographically largest watershed, which feeds the Saginaw River and Bay. This region's urban and rural landscapes are dominated by agriculture and industry. Michigan's southern "thumb" region is mostly rural, with population centers in Port Huron (United States) and Sarnia (Canada) at Lake Huron's southernmost point. Other major population centers along the Lake Huron coastline include Alpena and Bay City (United States) and Owen Sound (Canada).

Past forestry, mining, agriculture, and industrial activities have contributed to Lake Huron's ongoing water quality and contamination problems, particularly in the Saginaw River and Bay. Dams providing hydroelectric power also restrict fish passage on major tributaries such as the Cheboygan, Thunder Bay, and Au Sable Rivers.

Recreational fishing is a major economic driver for small Lake Huron communities. Many businesses struggled as Chinook salmon numbers dropped during recent decades; meanwhile, others benefited from resurging native Saginaw Bay walleye populations. Saginaw Bay's fisheries—particularly perch and walleye—represent more than 75 percent of Lake Huron's total fishing participation. Lake Huron also contributes 10 percent of the total Great Lakes commercial harvest, largely driven by lake whitefish. Commercial fishing and aquaculture are prevalent in Canadian waters of Lake Huron.

ECOLOGY

Lake Erie is the shallowest, warmest, and most productive of the Great Lakes. Three distinct basins provide a variety of offshore habitats. The Detroit River, Maumee River, and smaller tributaries drain into the western basin, which averages 24 feet deep and contains extremely nutrient-rich water. The central basin lies east of Point Pelee, Ontario, and the Lake Erie Islands. This basin averages 60 feet deep and is slightly less productive. The eastern basin, which lies to the east of Erie, Pennsylvania, and Long Point, Ontario, is the deepest and least productive of the three basins. Here, water up to 210 feet deep provides colder conditions for fish that cannot tolerate warm summer temperatures elsewhere in the lake.

Harmful algal blooms regularly plague Lake Erie. The western basin's warm, shallow water and nutrient-rich agricultural runoff create perfect conditions for toxin-producing blue-green algae. Invasive zebra mussels and quagga mussels worsen the situation by filtering out desirable types of algae and leaving the harmful blue-greens. Otherwise, the effects of invasive mussels on Lake Erie's fisheries and ecology are subtle; water clarity, zooplankton density, and prey fish biomass haven't changed since the invasion.

Coastal wetlands serve as nursery habitat for fish and waterfowl. Birdwatching is a major springtime attraction at Point Pelee and Long Point, where migrating birds rest after crossing the open lake.

FISHERIES

Lake Erie has the largest commercial fishery of any Great Lake, with most of the fish being harvested from Canadian waters. Yellow perch and walleye make up most of the Canadian commercial harvest, while those species dominate U.S. recreational and charter catches.

Thanks to its habitat diversity, Lake Erie supports more fish species than any other Great Lake. The Lake Erie basin supports several native and invasive fish species not found in other Great Lakes watersheds. The Sandusky River also has the dubious distinction of being the first known breeding habitat in the region for an Asian carp species; grass carp eggs were first collected there in 2015.

Due to pollution, habitat degradation, invasive species, and overfishing, some once-prolific fish species have disappeared. Ciscoes, once the most common commercial catch in Lake Erie, are now absent from the lake. The lake sturgeon has been making a comeback in nearby Lake St. Clair, but despite the abundance of habitat for adult sturgeon in Lake Erie they have not been able to reproduce in significant numbers for many decades.

SOCIOECONOMICS

Lake Erie's is the most densely populated Great Lake basin, with large metropolitan areas like Detroit, Toledo, Cleveland, and Buffalo. Lake Erie's basin includes the largest percentage of agricultural land in the Great Lakes, particularly along Erie's western and northern shores. The automobile industry dominates the economy, along with natural gas, salt mining, and the world's largest sandstone quarry. Lake Erie's shores also boast several major commercial shipping ports.

Lake Erie features popular coastal tourism destinations like Point Pelee National Park in Canada and designated scenic byways along the U.S. shore. Walleye and yellow perch are the foundation of Lake Erie's productive commercial and popular recreational fisheries.

For decades, Lake Erie has been a focal point for critical water quality concerns. Social movements leading to the Clean Water Act in 1972 rallied, in part, to address pollution issues that caused algal blooms and dead zones in Lake Erie and even the infamous Cuyahoga River fires. Today, the Cuyahoga River is one of nine federally designated areas of concern for Lake Erie, and a resurgence of harmful algal blooms in western Lake Erie remains at the center of water quality, ecosystem, and human health concerns for the region.

ECOLOGY

All of the Great Lakes ultimately drain into Lake Ontario. The Niagara River carries nutrient-rich water from Lake Erie to the western end of Lake Ontario. At its eastern end, Lake Ontario drains into the St. Lawrence River, which ferries Great Lakes freshwater to the Atlantic Ocean. Before construction of the Erie Canal, Welland Canal, and St. Lawrence Seaway, natural barriers such as river rapids and Niagara Falls prevented or restricted the movement of both fish and boats into the upper Great Lakes.

Being the farthest downstream, Lake Ontario was the first to be colonized by Atlantic Ocean invaders such as the sea lamprey and alewife. These species devastated native fish in much the same way as they did in Lake Michigan and Lake Huron. Non-native baitfish still dominate Lake Ontario's offshore forage base.

Bays formed by drowned river mouths provide ideal nursery habitat for many fish species. These freshwater estuaries also support abundant waterfowl and other wildlife.

The offshore waters of Lake Ontario are less productive than nutrient-rich Lake Erie but considerably more productive than the upper lakes. Water clarity has been increasing since the invasion of zebra and quagga mussels, but baitfish, trout, and salmon have been slowly declining since the early 1980s, years before invasive mussels took hold.

FISHERIES

Lake Ontario has the smallest commercial fishery of any Great Lake and accounts for only 1 percent of commercial landings in Great Lakes waters. Recreational and charter anglers commonly seek non-native Chinook salmon, coho salmon, steelhead, and brown trout, along with native lake trout and Atlantic salmon.

Once home to several unique Great Lakes species, Lake Ontario now has more extirpated (locally extinct) species than any other Great Lake. Two relatives of the walleye (blue pike and sauger) were lost from Lake Ontario along with bigeye chub, lake trout, Atlantic salmon, and four types of deepwater cisco.

The Atlantic salmon is native to Lake Ontario but was not historically found in the other Great Lakes. Native salmon were wiped out by overfishing and destruction of stream habitat by the late 1800s. Stocking programs have attempted to reestablish Atlantic salmon in Lake Ontario and its tributaries. In 2014, researchers found evidence of natural reproduction of Atlantic salmon in the Salmon River for the first time in over a century.

The cisco (also called lake herring) managed to survive overfishing, environmental changes, and invasive species that wiped out its close relatives. Ciscoes are now increasing in the Bay of Quinte, but remain at a low level relative to historic abundance. The bloater, one of the deepwater ciscoes, has been the subject of recent stocking efforts.

SOCIOECONOMICS

Lake Ontario is surrounded by a largely rural landscape, with forest covering nearly half of the basin. Development on the U.S. side leans heavily toward agriculture, while the Canadian shore sports more industrial areas and urban centers like Toronto, Ontario's largest city. The lake's link to the Atlantic Ocean drives activity at 13 major commercial shipping ports.

Recreation and tourism are vital economic drivers, thanks to Niagara Falls and various state, provincial, and national parks. Commercial fisheries, primarily for whitefish, and recreational fisheries targeting trout and salmon also support the economy.

Wetland loss and water quality are two of Lake Ontario's environmental threats. Lake Ontario has three federally listed areas of concern.

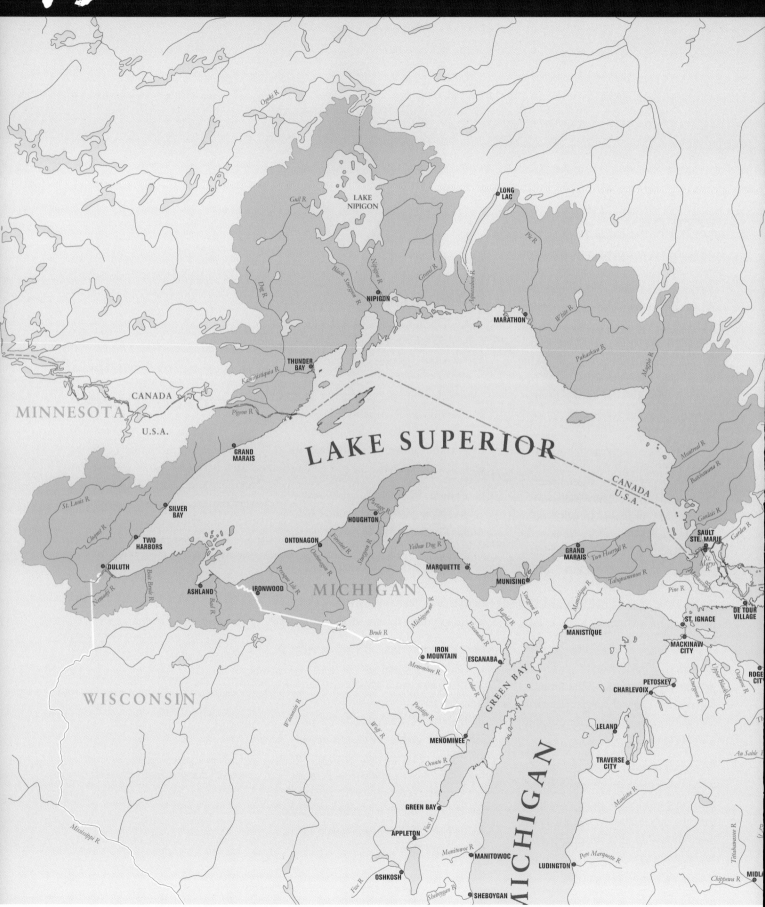

ECOLOGY

Known for its sparkling waves and rugged shorelines, Lake Superior contains more water than the other Great Lakes combined. Superior is the northernmost lake and the least affected by invasive species, habitat degradation, and other human-driven changes. The deepest and coldest Great Lake, Superior's nutrient-poor waters have allowed native cold-water fishes to flourish.

The watershed is dominated by the Canadian Shield, noted for its ancient rocky outcroppings and thin, nutrient-poor soil. The Canadian Shield does not include the limestone bedrock common in watersheds to the south. Without the steady weathering of limestone, Lake Superior's waters are too calcium-poor to sustain a large population of invasive quagga mussels, which build their shells with calcium carbonate dissolved in lake water.

FISHERIES

Lake Superior's cold, clear water is ideal for native ciscoes and lake trout. Lake Superior supports 52 fish species, fewer than any other Great Lake, in part because other lakes offer more diverse temperatures and habitats.

Unlike other lakes, Lake Superior's native species retain the upper hand over invasive and introduced species. Ciscoes

and their relatives provide an important link between zooplankton and predatory fish. The only abundant, invasive, plankton-eating fish is the rainbow smelt.

Lean lake trout are the backbone of recreational fisheries in offshore waters of Lake Superior. Bold anglers can find huge lake trout near sunken islands and rock reefs. Stannard Rock, north of Marquette, Michigan, is one such destination that has produced fish weighing over 60 pounds. While trolling is typically the preferred method of lake trout fishing in the Great Lakes, Lake Superior also offers good opportunities for jigging.

Harbor areas and protected bays like Duluth Harbor and Tahquamenon Bay offer some opportunities for cool-water fish like pike, walleye, and perch. Introduced coho salmon and steelhead also provide fisheries near river mouths. Although these species were originally stocked, natural reproduction in Lake Superior rivers is now high enough to sustain populations.

Lake Superior's commercial fisheries target lake whitefish, lake trout, and ciscoes. The largest market for cisco (also called lake herring) is for roe (eggs) that is exported to Scandinavian countries. Cisco and bloater are also sold as "smoked chubs" at many roadside fish markets around Lake Superior.

SOCIOECONOMICS

Lake Superior's mostly rural communities are spread across a forested and largely undeveloped landscape. Timber and mining industries are important economic drivers, notably copper mining in the Keweenaw Peninsula. The lingering environmental effects of mining operations continue to cause water quality and community development problems.

Duluth, Minnesota, is an important commercial shipping port for exporting agricultural products from the interior United States. Duluth and other commercial ports are often unintentional introduction points for invasive species carried in cargo ship ballast water.

Other major community centers include Marquette, Michigan, and Sault Ste. Marie (Michigan and Ontario, Canada), where the St. Marys River connects Lake Superior with Lake Huron. A sizable Native American community fishes in Lake Superior under treaty agreements; commercial fishing by the tribal fleet and other vessels plays an important economic role in the region. Recreational fishing and tourism also draw dollars to Lake Superior.

Flowing from Lake Superior to Lake Huron, the St. Marys River, like all of the Great Lakes' connecting channels, forms part of the U.S.-Canadian border. Flow between the lakes is regulated by a 16-gate compensating works structure that is controlled by the International Lake Superior Board of Control, which was established by the International Joint Commission. The IJC is a binational agency that regulates shared water uses and investigates and recommends solutions for transboundary issues between the United States and Canada.

Over its 70 miles, the St. Marys falls an average of 22 feet depending on lake levels. Most of the elevation change takes place at the St. Marys rapids in the northern portion of the river. First bypassed by a lock in 1797, the rapids have since been modified by locks and canals to facilitate shipping and hydropower.

The Soo Locks at Sault Ste. Marie, Michigan, are operated by the U.S. Army Corps of Engineers and have approximately 80 million tons of commercial commodities passing through them each year. The locks are in the process of being updated. At the same time, the river's remaining rapids are being restored as habitat for the river's unique fishery.

The St. Marys River supports a diverse fishery that includes walleye, yellow perch, smallmouth bass, and cisco. There are also runs of Atlantic salmon, Chinook salmon, pink salmon, and rainbow trout (steelhead), and the region is famous for northern pike and muskellunge as well.

Cold, clear water from Lake Huron drains south into the St. Clair River. The river is better described as a strait—a narrow waterway that connects two larger bodies of water. Nevertheless, the St. Clair River flows swiftly and shares many characteristics with rivers, including a delta at its southern end. The St. Clair Flats is a maze of channels, backwaters, wetlands, and islands formed by sediment from the St. Clair River, which settled out over millennia as water from the strait entered the calm water of Lake St. Clair. The delta provides excellent wildlife habitat along with spawning and nursery habitat for many fish species.

Lake St. Clair is sometimes called the "Heart of the Great Lakes" due to the heart-like shape of its main basin and Anchor Bay to the north. The lake is very shallow (mostly under 25 feet deep), and Anchor Bay is particularly shallow

and weedy. Since the invasion of zebra mussels, clear water has stimulated aquatic plant growth throughout the lake. Lake St. Clair is known as a world-class recreational fishing destination for smallmouth bass and muskellunge.

Water flowing from Lake St. Clair forms the Detroit River, also a strait. The Detroit River supports an excellent spring recreational fishery for walleye. The International Wildlife Refuge and islands such as Belle Isle and Grosse Ile provide wetland habitat, but much of the Detroit River waterfront has been developed and lined with seawalls. The straits' natural rapids were destroyed to create a navigation channel that extends north into Lake St. Clair and the St. Clair River.

Despite radical habitat changes and historical industrial pollution, the fisheries of the St. Clair-Detroit River System have proven resilient. One of the

world's largest lake sturgeon populations spawns in the St. Clair River and feeds in Lake St. Clair and connected waterways. In recent decades, restoration projects have created spawning reefs, rebuilt wetlands, and removed contaminated river sediments.

The St. Clair-Detroit River System provides an example of an extremely productive fishery adjacent to major population centers. On the U.S. side, metro Detroit is home to nearly 4.3 million people. On the Canadian side, agricultural land and cities like Sarnia and Windsor are common. The influx of clean water from Lake Huron boosts water quality in this heavily settled region, although combined sewer overflows contribute to beach closings, and some fish species are highly contaminated with mercury and other pollutants.

HUDSON BAY

CANADA

U.S.A.

THUNDER BAY

LAKE SUPERIOR

DULUTH

SAULT STE. MARIE

LAKE MICHIGAN

LAKE HURON

MILWAUKEE

CHICAGO

DETROIT

WINDSOR

U.S.A.

CANADA

LAKE ERIE

CLEVELAND

TORONTO

LAKE ONTARIO

BUFFALO

QUEBEC CITY

CA

U.S.A.

St. Lawrence River

MONTREAL

OTTAWA

BURLINGTON

PORTLAND

BOSTON

NEW YORK

PHILADELPHIA

WASHINGTON D.C.

GULF OF ST. LAWRENCE

ATLANTIC OCEAN

PATRICE AUDET

The St. Lawrence River and Seaway flows approximately 800 miles between Lake Ontario and the Atlantic Ocean. Part of the river forms the U.S.-Canadian border. The river can be divided into three sections. A freshwater portion stretches between Lake Ontario and Quebec City. At Quebec City, the ocean's influence transforms the river into an estuary. The estuary stretches approximately to Anticosti Island, where it widens to become the Gulf of St. Lawrence.

Between 1954 and 1959, the U.S. and Canadian governments created the St. Lawrence Seaway by deepening and widening portions of the river to allow navigation of deep-draft vessels between the Atlantic Ocean and the Great Lakes. Besides shipping, the river also provides hydroelectric power, tourism opportunities, and a diverse fishery.

Anglers in the St. Lawrence River catch large sport fish, panfish, and other species. Some of the bays and slower-flowing areas hold northern pike, walleye, and yellow perch that can often be accessed year-round on open water or through ice. Smallmouth bass—now a predator of invasive round goby—can be found near structures like points, islands, and rocky areas.

Restoration efforts are underway in and around the river to bolster the population of lake sturgeon, which are among the largest freshwater fish in the world. Another St. Lawrence denizen is the muskellunge. The river holds muskellunge well over 50 inches long that weigh up to 70 pounds.

ECOLOGY

and

MANAGEMENT

Why do we study ecology? What does it tell us? How does ecology influence effective resource management? This section provides an overview of the life found in the Great Lakes, the ecosystems and their basic functions, and the factors related to responsible management of the aquatic ecosystems within the lakes.

The study of ecology helps us understand how natural systems work and better predict their responses to change. On the surface, we study these interactions because we are curious about the world around us. Delving deeper, we have a responsibility to understand our world because our actions can have a profound effect on many natural systems. Another reason we explore the world around us is because nature and natural systems can be great teachers; examining how issues have been solved in the natural world helps us develop creative solutions to man-made problems. Ultimately, we study ecology because it is in our best interest. Since water is essential to life, identifying how a system functions when it is healthy can help us restore key ecological systems, sustaining our survival.

Because the Great Lakes system holds about 20 percent of the world's surface freshwater, and because the region and the country rely on the lakes for many things, it is especially important to study and understand these ecological systems. Fish and aquatic systems serve as valuable gauges of environmental change and environmental health. The fisheries serve as an indicator of resource sustainability. Understanding the fisheries helps us better manage and protect the Great Lakes in ways that enhance quality of life

ECOLOGY

SHAPING THE BASIN

The Great Lakes are a geologically young system compared to the world's oceans, which are billions of years old. The lakes as we know them today began to form 15,000 to 18,000 years ago. Around 9,000 years ago, glaciers last retreated from the region, leaving a relatively short time for fish to evolve or move

into the region's lakes. As the glaciers receded, the Great Lakes shorelines changed greatly. Water levels fluctuated as the land rebounded (lifted up) when the heavy glaciers retreated northward. As the shorelines and rivers around the Great Lakes changed over thousands of years, the paths for fish to move into and throughout the region also developed.

Some parts of the Great Lakes region are cold and are far north—meaning the climate provides a shorter growing season. Other parts of the region are warmer and have longer growing seasons. In spite of sometimes harsh surroundings, the Great Lakes are productive. They form the largest surface freshwater system in the world and are recognizable even from space. Covering more than 94,000 square miles and draining more than twice as much land, the Great Lakes hold an estimated 6 quadrillion gallons (22.7 quadrillion

GREAT LAKES SYSTEM PROFILE

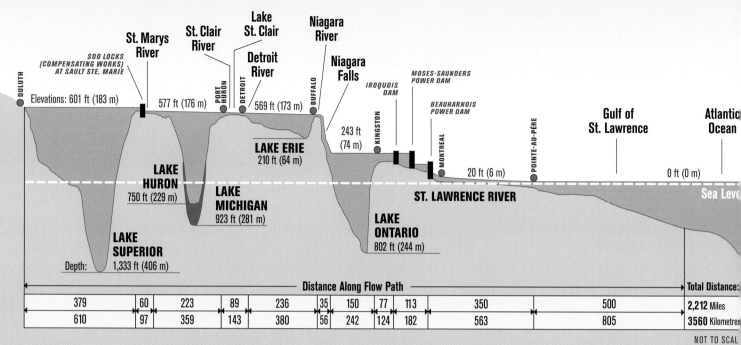

Distance Along Flow Path

| 379 | 60 | 223 | 89 | 236 | 35 | 150 | 77 | 113 | 350 | 500 | **2,212** Miles |
| 610 | 97 | 359 | 143 | 380 | 56 | 242 | 124 | 182 | 563 | 805 | **3560** Kilometres |

NOT TO SCAL

ILLUSTRATION: MICHIGAN SEA GRAN

WHAT MAKES THE GREAT LAKES "GREAT"?

Size, Length, and Volume

❖ Total length of Great Lakes shoreline, including islands: 11,000 miles.

❖ World's supply of surface freshwater in the Great Lakes: about 20 percent.

❖ Combined surface area of all the Great Lakes: 94,000 square miles (244,000 square kilometers).

❖ The surface area of the lakes is larger than Connecticut, Massachusetts, New Hampshire, New Jersey, New York, Rhode Island, and Vermont—combined.

❖ Gallons of freshwater: 6 quadrillion (22.7 quadrillion liters).

Key Facts

❖ Approximately 37 million people in the United States and Canada live in the Great Lakes basin—8 percent of the U.S. population and about 32 percent of Canada's population.

❖ More than 3,500 species of plants and animals live in the Great Lakes basin, including approximately 180 species of fish.

❖ The Great Lakes are among the world's 15 largest lakes.

❖ A geologically young system compared to the world's oceans, the Great Lakes began to take their present shape about 10,000–15,000 years ago.

	Huron	Ontario	Michigan	Erie	Superior
Length	206 mi / 332 km	193 mi / 311 km	307 mi / 494 km	241 mi/ 388 km	350 mi / 563 km
Breadth	183 mi / 295 km	53 mi / 85 km	118 mi / 190 km	57 mi / 92 km	160 mi / 257 km
Depth	Avg: 195 ft / 59 m Max: 750 ft / 229 m	Avg: 283 ft / 86 m Max: 802 ft / 244 m	Avg: 279 ft / 85 m Max: 923 ft / 281 m	Avg: 62 ft / 19 m Max: 210 ft / 64 m	Avg: 483 ft / 147 m Max: 1,330 ft / 406 m
Elevation	577.5 ft / 176 m	243.3 ft / 74.2 m	577.5 ft / 176 m	569.2 ft / 173.5 m	600 ft / 183 m
Volume	849 mi³ / 3,538 km³	393 mi³ / 1,639 km³	1,180 mi³ / 4,918 km³	116 mi³ / 483 km³	2,900 mi³ / 12,100 km³
Surface area	23,000 mi² / 59,565 km²	7,340 mi² / 19,009 km²	22,300 mi² / 57,753 km²	9,910 mi² / 25,655 km²	31,700 mi² / 82,100 km²
Drainage basin	51,700 mi² / 134,100 km²	24,720 mi² / 64,030 km²	45,600 mi² / 118,095 km²	30,140 mi² / 78,000 km²	49,300 mi² / 127,700 km²
Shoreline length (including islands)	3,830 mi / 6,164 km	712 mi / 1,146 km	1,640 mi / 2,639 km	871 mi / 1,402 km	2,726 mi / 4,385 km
Outlet	St. Clair River to Lake Erie	St. Lawrence River to the Atlantic Ocean	Straits of Mackinac to Lake Huron	Niagara River and Welland Canal	St. Marys River to Lake Huron
Replacement time	22 years	6 years	99 years	2.6 years	191 years

liters) of water, about one-fifth of the world's fresh surface water supply and nine-tenths of the U.S. supply. Their sheer size means that these bodies of water can support an abundance of life.

CONNECTIONS

The channels that connect the Great Lakes are an important part of the system. The following are significant linkages within the system:

❖ The St. Marys River in the north is a 60-mile waterway flowing from Lake Superior down to Lake Huron.

❖ At the St. Marys rapids, the Soo Locks bypass the rough waters, providing safe transport for ships.

❖ The St. Clair and Detroit Rivers—and Lake St. Clair between them—form an 89-mile-long channel connecting Lake Huron with Lake Erie.

❖ The 35-mile Niagara River links Lakes Erie and Ontario, and sends

NUMBER OF FISH SPECIES FOUND IN THE GREAT LAKES BASIN*

Basin	Number of fish species
Erie	129
Ontario	119
Huron	117
Michigan	136
Superior	83
Lake Nipigon	39
St. Lawrence River	105
Total 5 lakes and tributaries	172
Total basin	179

Source: Coon 1999 in Taylor and Ferreri 1999   *Includes tributaries

approximately 50,000 to 100,000 cubic feet of water per second over Niagara Falls.

❖ The man-made Welland Canal also links the two lakes, providing a detour around the falls.

❖ From Lake Ontario, the water from the Great Lakes flows through the St. Lawrence River.

❖ Water in the Great Lakes flows through these passages and journeys 2,212 miles from Lake Superior out to the Atlantic Ocean.

A DIVERSITY OF LIFE AND HABITATS

The Great Lakes support an abundance and diversity of life, including fish, plants, birds, and other organisms. Each lake's fish **community** is closely tied to the whole set of living and nonliving lake components—collectively called the **ecosystem**. The **abiotic** (nonliving) features of the lakes interact with the **biotic** (living) organisms to affect the amount and type of life that can be supported. Ecology is the study of the interaction between abiotic and biotic factors. Because of their size and varied geography, geology, and ecology, the Great Lakes include subregions that vary in climate, sunlight, temperature, depth, nutrients, chemical composition (such as oxygen concentrations), water movements, shoreline, and other physical and biological characteristics. This variation means that some areas of the lakes are more productive than others.

HABITATS AND ZONES

The Great Lakes provide a variety of habitats, or areas where fish can find their

ILLUSTRATION:
MICHIGAN SEA GRANT

WHAT IS A WATERSHED?

Watersheds are often referred to as drainage or catchment basins and are defined as the land area that drains—or sheds—water to a particular river, stream, or body of water. High points in the landscape determine watershed boundaries.

Wetlands, bays, rocky reefs and areas around islands provide the shallows that many fish depend upon at some time in their lives.

life requirements of water, food, shelter, and space. **Habitats** differ in the amount of sunlight they receive, the amount of nutrients present, and water temperature. Generally, a lake can be divided into offshore, nearshore, and lake bottom zones. These zones sometimes interact with extensive and diverse habitats of the coastal shoreline and inland waterways. That is to say, while there are designated zones within aquatic systems, they often overlap and influence each other.

COAST

The Great Lakes coastline is as diverse as it is long. Sandy beaches and ranging dunes are intermingled with vegetated coastal wetlands, rocky cobble shorelines, and other rare and unique habitats. The diverse habitats of Great Lakes coastlines provide invaluable ecological functions. For example, bays, rocky **reefs**, and the sheltered areas around islands provide the shallows that many fish depend upon at different points in their life cycles.

Inland streams, rivers, and wetlands within the basin drain more than 295,000 square miles (767,000 square kilometers) of the heart of North America, forming the Great Lakes **watershed**. Many different fish migrate to the tributaries, rivers, and streams flowing into the Great Lakes to **spawn** (reproduce). Species such as walleye, lake sturgeon, coaster brook

trout, and various suckers (e.g., white, longnose, and redhorse) are just a few examples of the native fish that use these waterways for migration and spawning. Additionally, **non-native** species such as salmon, steelhead, rainbow smelt, and the invasive sea lamprey are migrating fish that use Great Lakes waterways.

WETLANDS

Coastal wetlands represent some of the most productive and biologically diverse ecosystems in the Great Lakes. **Wetlands**—with their warm, shallow, nutrient-rich waters—support a lush growth of aquatic plants, which in turn harbor small, aquatic life. These conditions provide food and shelter for fish. Wetlands may include inland marshes that fish access by way of migrating up river systems, or coastal wetlands located along Great Lakes shorelines, such as coastal marshes or embayments. Coastal wetlands are also essential as breeding, nesting, and feeding areas for a wide array of native and migratory birds. Wetlands are home to a variety of smaller organisms that act as food and that perform nutrient cycling roles in these ecosystems.

NEARSHORE AND OFFSHORE

Life in the nearshore and the offshore waters of the Great Lakes is dynamically and essentially linked. Waves and

currents carry nutrients and energy from coastal wetlands and embayments into offshore areas, enriching them enough to support more life. Nutrients cyclically flow or "spiral" down river from inland waterways, feeding life along the way out to the lakes. In turn, adult fish may return up rivers to spawn—returning nutrients inland through their eggs, young, or sometimes dying in the river themselves and returning the nutrients of their own bodies through decomposition. These processes contribute to world-class fishing opportunities in the Great Lakes, particularly where anglers gain access to Great Lakes fish migrating and moving among inland, nearshore, and offshore water habitats.

LIFE ZONES IN FRESHWATER

Sunlight and nutrients are fundamental drivers of life in the Great Lakes; the availability of both determines the productivity of life—starting with plant life—in various areas or habitats of the lakes. The aquatic life present in the Great Lakes depends upon the amount of sunlight reaching portions of these large bodies of water. The degree of light penetration into the water varies greatly among lakes, among regions within a lake, and seasonally. **Algae**, **plankton**, and **turbidity**, for example, may reduce

Continued on page 24

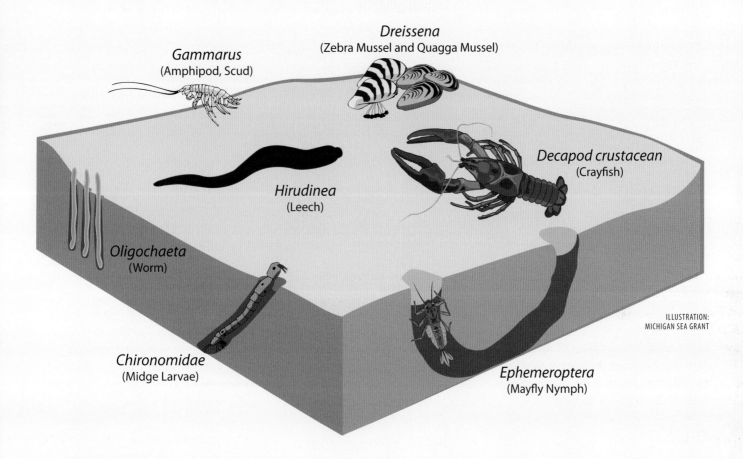

Gammarus
(Amphipod, Scud)

Dreissena
(Zebra Mussel and Quagga Mussel)

Hirudinea
(Leech)

Decapod crustacean
(Crayfish)

Oligochaeta
(Worm)

Chironomidae
(Midge Larvae)

Ephemeroptera
(Mayfly Nymph)

ILLUSTRATION:
MICHIGAN SEA GRANT

BENTHIC ORGANISMS

Description: Microscopic to small animals that live on the lake bottom. Includes animals from the following groups:

❖ **Anelida:** Oligochaetes (aquatic "mud" worms) and leeches (*Hirudinea*)—members of segmented worm group; most under 5 cm.

❖ **Crustaceans:** Decapods (crayfish)—cylinder-shaped body with heavy shell and five pairs of walking legs; claws.

❖ **Amphipods (including *Diporeia spp.*):** Sometimes called freshwater shrimp, scuds, or sideswimmers; no shell, gills at base of legs, slightly compressed (flattened side-to-side). Note: *Diporeia* was called *Pontoporeia* until the 1980s.

❖ **Native Mollusks:** Mussels, clams, fingernail clams, snails, etc.—majority have a shell covering internal organs,

such as mouth and digestive tract, gills, or lung, and a muscular "foot" used for locomotion.

❖ **Insect Larvae:** Chironomids (midge larvae)—long, cylinder-shaped; some have anal gills. *Hexagenia* (mayfly nymph)—long, slender body with feather-like gills along sides of abdomen; three tails at posterior and a pair of tusks at mouth.

❖ **Aquatic Adult Insects:** Limited to the nearshore (littoral) zones.

Adult Diet: Scavengers/omnivores—decaying plant and animal debris (**detritus**), bacteria, algae; some feed on crustaceans or insect larvae; crayfish and midge larvae mainly herbivorous, but also **detritivores**.

Habitat/Behavior: Many **benthic** organisms build burrows or seek cover under rocks or debris.

Oligochaetes build tubes and bury themselves head first, leaving the tail end with gills up in the water.

Midge larvae may construct small tubes of algae, silt, or sand.

Mayfly nymphs of the genus *Hexagenia* burrow into soft **sediment** in areas high in oxygen.

Diporeia is historically the most important of the benthic organisms in the diet of Great Lakes fish. During the day it lives close to or even buried in the sediments; by night it migrates toward the surface.

LIFE ZONES: PELAGIC, BENTHIC, AND LITTORAL

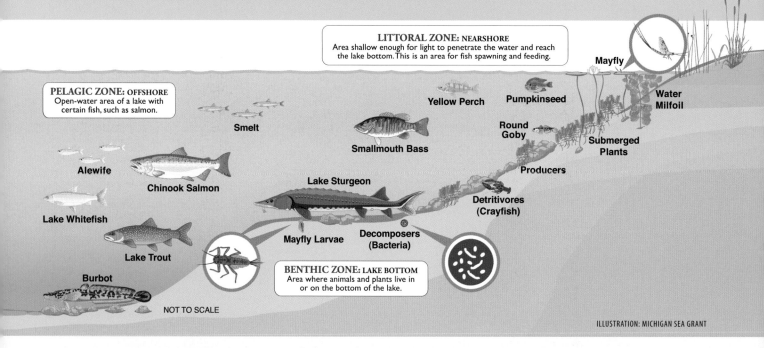

LITTORAL ZONE: NEARSHORE
Area shallow enough for light to penetrate the water and reach the lake bottom. This is an area for fish spawning and feeding.

PELAGIC ZONE: OFFSHORE
Open-water area of a lake with certain fish, such as salmon.

Mayfly

Water Milfoil

Yellow Perch

Pumpkinseed

Smelt

Round Goby

Smallmouth Bass

Submerged Plants

Alewife

Producers

Chinook Salmon

Lake Sturgeon

Detritivores (Crayfish)

Lake Whitefish

Mayfly Larvae

Decomposers (Bacteria)

Lake Trout

BENTHIC ZONE: LAKE BOTTOM
Area where animals and plants live in or on the bottom of the lake.

Burbot

NOT TO SCALE

ILLUSTRATION: MICHIGAN SEA GRANT

A lake can be characterized into distinct zones based on its physical structure and the life supported. For example, most lakes have pelagic, benthic, and littoral zones.

The pelagic zone is the open-water, offshore area of a lake. The benthic zone encompasses the lake bottom. The littoral zone is the nearshore area that is shallow enough for light to reach the lake bottom and that allows rooted plants to grow.

While some fish species seek out the characteristics of one zone, many fish readily move between offshore benthic, pelagic, and nearshore areas, pursuing life necessities such as oxygen, food, optimum water temperatures, and spawning habitat.

Lakes can also be categorized into other zones based on factors such as levels of dissolved oxygen, light penetration, and temperature.

how far light can penetrate the water column. The different depths where light reaches into the water are referred to as life zones.

Generally speaking, the part of a lake where light can penetrate is called the **limnetic** or **photic zone**. In contrast, the depth of the lake, where light energy cannot penetrate, is called the **profundal** or the **aphotic zone**.

LITTORAL ZONE

The **littoral zone** refers to the part of a sea, lake, or river that is close to the shore. These nearshore habitats closest to the edge of the lake are shallow enough so that light can penetrate the water, reach the bottom, and support the growth of rooted vegetation. Given proximity to land, this area also receives

the most direct runoff (e.g., sediment and nutrients) from the watershed.

This combination of light and nutrient input ensures that these nearshore littoral areas are extremely productive zones rich with aquatic life. In protected areas, rooted plants provide shelter and habitat for fish and other life. Vegetated zones are not commonly found along windswept shores in Great Lakes proper, but are common in protected bays, connecting waters, and drowned river mouths. Additional life is supported by **phytoplankton** or microscopic plant life free-floating in the water. Due to this abundant productivity, the littoral zones, which include coastal wetlands, are very valuable for Great Lakes fisheries because they provide areas for spawning and feeding.

PELAGIC ZONE

The **pelagic** zone is the offshore, open-water area of a lake. In the pelagic zone, the uppermost portion of the water is within the limnetic zone, where light can penetrate and foster growth of algae and other forms of microscopic open-water plants and life. The amount of nutrients in depths of these offshore areas largely depends on productivity or aquatic life that filters down from light-rich pelagic areas closer to the water surface. Waves and currents also transport nutrients and energy from nearshore to offshore zones, enriching them and supporting more life.

Each zone or area of the lake has very different habitat characteristics and therefore different assemblages of aquatic life. Fish species such as sunfish, smallmouth bass, perch, and walleye prefer to spend their lives in the slightly warmer littoral (nearshore) zones. Some adult fish, such as salmon and cisco, spend much of their time in the colder regions of the pelagic (offshore) zone. Other species, such as lake trout, burbot, and deepwater sculpin may similarly be found in offshore waters but prefer deeper, benthic areas. In reality, many of these offshore species move readily between offshore benthic and pelagic, and even nearshore areas, seeking life necessities such as oxygen, food, optimum water temperatures, and spawning habitats.

BENTHIC ZONE

The **benthic** zone includes the entire bottom of the lake. The Great Lakes have a wide variety of bottom types, or substrates, including mud, silt, sand, rock, and gravel. In nearshore areas and some offshore areas, benthic life benefits from light that reaches bottom. However, in some of the deeper, offshore areas, benthic zones are aphotic, meaning they receive little to no light.

In those areas where light does not penetrate, energy exchange with other zones is critical. For example, dead organisms and other detritus from the pelagic zone can float down to the benthos—the flora and fauna at the bottom of a lake—supporting life in the deep. Benthic organisms live in the sediments or among the different bottom materials. Benthic organisms, including some bacteria and invertebrates, are detritivores that feed on decomposing dead plants and animals. Some fish, such as lake sturgeon or many of the sucker species, eat small benthic organisms like worms and insect larvae.

PHYSICAL AND CHEMICAL PROCESSES

Physical and chemical properties and processes of the lakes are closely linked with life in the lakes. The nutrient and chemical composition of the Great Lakes can vary tremendously by location and over time. Large areas of the Great Lakes are considered **oligotrophic**, or low in nutrients. Those areas tend to be deep and cold. Other areas are **eutrophic**, much warmer and richer in nutrients than the oligotrophic areas. **Mesotrophic** regions have moderate amounts of nutrients and, therefore, moderate biological productivity. The nutrient levels found in Great Lakes habitats affect both the number and the type of fish and other aquatic organisms.

Water temperature is extremely important to a fish's survival, growth, and reproduction. Fish are often described and classified as cold-, cool-, or warm-water species, depending on their respective temperature preferences and tolerances. Each species of fish in the Great Lakes has a preferred range of water temperature and other water conditions. Fish may spawn or grow better at different temperatures. Some species, such as salmon and lake trout, are cold-water fish, generally found in deep waters. Others, such as walleye and perch, are cool-water fish and thrive in waters that are slightly shallower and warmer. Still others, such as bowfin or gar, can be considered warm-water fish. They have developed **adaptations** and an ability to tolerate and even thrive in warmer water with lower oxygen levels.

OXYGEN IN THE WATER

Since fish are cold-blooded animals, water temperature affects their respiration, metabolism, and growth rates—when water is colder, these processes are generally slower, and when

DEAD ZONES

In the late 1960s, Lake Erie was declared "dead." It was devoid of much fish life due to overenrichment (or human-induced *eutrophication*) of water as a result of nutrient runoff from land. These "dead zones" are *hypoxic* (water with dissolved oxygen levels below 2 mg/l) or anoxic (water that does not contain dissolved oxygen at all) areas without enough dissolved oxygen to support fish or other aquatic animal life.

Increased organic matter from both internal inputs (e.g., nutrients increasing algae production) and external inputs (e.g., sewage) can create excessive biological oxygen demands on an aquatic habitat. This demand can create dead zones by quickly using up the available oxygen in the water.

Dead zones again resurfaced in Lake Erie in the early 21st century. However, new factors causing these low- or no-oxygen zones may be linked with low water levels and the presence of invasive zebra and quagga mussel populations, in addition to excessive nutrient loading as in the past. Regardless, dead zones are actually the result of some areas of the lakes being too alive!

A view from space of a harmful algal bloom on Lake Erie.

WATER TEMPERATURE

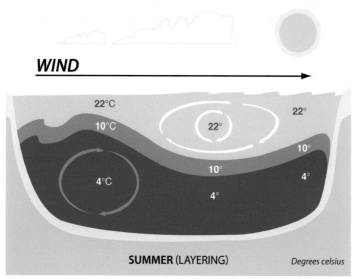

WIND

22°C
10°C
22°
22°
10°
10°
4°C
4°
4°

SUMMER (LAYERING)   *Degrees celsius*

ILLUSTRATION: MICHIGAN SEA GRANT

EPILIMNION

The surface layer of water that is constantly mixed by wind and waves and is warmed by the sun, from late spring to late fall.

METALIMNION

The middle layer characterized by a steep gradient in temperature and demarcated by the regions above (epilimnion) and below (hypolimnion). The metalimnion is the barrier that prevents mixing and heat exchange between the epilimnion and hypolimnion.

HYPOLIMNION

The deepest layer of uniformly cold water that does not mix with the upper layers and has low circulation. The colder water within the hypolimnion is at its maximum density at a temperature of 39.2° F (4° C).

THERMAL STRATIFICATION

Thermal stratification is a seasonal phenomenon that occurs from late spring to late fall in temperate regions. In the summer, the upper layer of water in the Great Lakes (epilimnion) is warmed significantly by the sun. Cooler water separates, forming two additional layers (metalimnion and hypolimnion) that are heavier or denser. During the winter, there is no stratification as the lake cools, and the overall temperature of the lake is more uniform.

it is warmer they are faster. Temperature also affects the amount of oxygen that is typically available in a fish's environment because cold water can hold more oxygen than warm water. For example, a trout (requiring more oxygen) benefits from living in a cold-water environment because that environment is likely to hold more oxygen. Conversely, a warm-water fish might have a higher tolerance for surviving in low-oxygen conditions. Oxygen levels in water habitats can be influenced by nutrient inputs and biological life. Seasonal changes also affect fish habitats. In the summer, portions of the lakes undergo **thermal stratification**—a process that results in layers of water with different temperatures, oxygen saturation, and nutrients.

❖ Warm water near the surface forms the **epilimnion**.
❖ Colder water on the bottom forms the **hypolimnion**.
❖ The two layers are separated by a thin **metalimnion** (the thermocline occurs here), in which the water temperature drops markedly.

At certain times of the year shallow, nearshore water can warm more rapidly than the deeper portions of a lake. This can create a thin, vertical transition zone, called a thermal bar, sandwiched between the warmer nearshore and colder offshore waters. Although a temporary seasonal feature, the thermal bar plays an important role in lake ecology by restricting mixing between coastal and offshore waters. This role is particularly evident during the spring runoff period when the retention of water near the

coast may benefit aquatic organisms by providing warmer water temperatures and elevated nutrient concentrations, or may threaten coastal environments by retaining **pollutants**.

SEASONAL TURNOVER

In the spring and fall, the Great Lakes experience what is known as seasonal turnover. That happens when surface waters warm or cool toward 39.2° F (4° C), the point at which water is densest and heaviest. The dense top waters sink and "mix" up the lake layers. For example, in the fall as Great Lakes surface waters cool and become denser, they sink; the cooler top water mixes with the less dense water below. In spring, frozen or cold surface water is heated by the sun and, as it approaches 39.2° F, it sinks and turnover (mixing) occurs once again.

PHOTOS: SHAWN SITAR

WHAT'S IN A NAME?

SISCOWET
Salvelinus namaycush siscowet

LEAN
Salvelinus namaycush

HUMPER
Salvelinus namaycush

Often the common names we know fish by are born out of history and culture. For example, the Native American name of lake trout, *namaycush*, translates roughly to "tyrant of the deep sea." The name is true, describing the lake trout as a predator fish found in deep offshore waters of the lakes.

The name of one of the three lake trout varieties found in Lake Superior, the "fat" or siscowet, translates from Ojibwa as "cooks itself." It is also an appropriate name because when siscowet—which can consist of up to 70 percent body fat—are added to a hot pan, the fat melts away, leaving very little meat. (The preferred way to eat siscowet is salted or pickled.) The other two lake trout, often called humpers and leans, also have apt common names.

UNIQUE PROPERTIES OF WATER

Water is unique in that its frozen, solid state—ice—is less dense and lighter than water in its liquid state, which is why ice forms and floats near the surface of lakes rather than sinking. This attribute is an extremely important element to life in the lakes and is the primary reason why the lakes are able to turn over or mix during the transitional seasons of spring and fall.

UPWELLINGS AND DOWNWELLINGS

Turnover and movement of nutrients and materials are not uniform across any given lake. Strong winds can play a role in the turnover process. At certain times of the year, wind and changes in water temperature can cause **upwellings**, in which strong winds push warm water at the surface laterally across or along the lake, forcing cold water from the deeper layers to move up toward the surface. Similarly, temperature changes and wind-generated water movements can cause a downwelling of water.

Certain patterns in wind speed, surface water movement, and up- and **downwellings** lead to the creation of streaks of gathered algae and **zooplankton**, or, as anglers call them, scum lines. Fish sometimes then move to these streaks for feeding, and anglers are able to use the presence of scum lines to target fish.

Circulation of water in the lakes and from one lake to another, in combination with wave action, creates littoral or longshore currents, carrying nutrients and materials along the shore and throughout the lakes.

This action changes with the intensity of weather patterns and the seasons. This variety and mixing is important for fish, because seasonal turnovers, upwellings, downwellings, littoral currents, and other water movements cause oxygen and nutrients to be mixed throughout the Great Lakes. These water movements also transport larval fish long distances, a process important for fostering recruitment of fish in habitats far from their hatching areas.

HOW DID THEY GET HERE?

As the glaciers retreated, all of the Great Lakes basin life-forms either evolved in the Great Lakes or moved in from one of three directions—from the Susquehanna River and Hudson River drainages of the Atlantic Coastal Plain, the Mississippi River drainage basin, or the Yukon basin of Alaska and Canada.

In more recent history, following European settlement, species have moved into or out of the lakes through man-made connecting channels such as the Erie Canal, the Welland Canal, and the Chicago Sanitary and Ship Canal.

New non-native and invasive species from around the world have also been **introduced** after traveling across the oceans in ship **ballast water**. Another path of introduction has been the unintentional transfer by humans from one area to another—for example, through dumping live fishing bait. Some species have even been purposefully introduced by humans to the Great Lakes basin, including some trout and salmon species like brown and rainbow trout and Chinook and coho salmon.

NATIVE

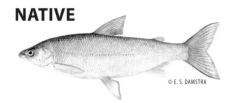

© E. S. DAMSTRA

© E. S. DAMSTRA

© E. S. DAMSTRA

LAKE WHITEFISH
Coregonus clupeaformis

Description: Usually 17–22 in., 1.5–4 lbs.; silvery with pale green-brown back; adipose fin.

Adult Diet: Benthivore, planktivore; feeding on *Diporeia*, some small fish, and fish eggs.

Habitat/Behavior: Benthic; spawn in November and December usually in shallows; found in schools; found in hypolimnion in summer where they range broadly, and move to shoals in spring. Important native commercial fish, sometimes caught by sport anglers.

LAKE TROUT
Salvelinus namaycush

Description: Often about 31 in. and 10 lbs., but can grow much larger; scattered light spots on dark body; forked tail.

Adult Diet: Forage fish such as chubs and ciscoes, sticklebacks, alewives, smelt, sculpins, and macroinvertebrates.

Habitat/Behavior: Mainly benthic, but may be found at various depths (pelagic and littoral); spawn on rocky reefs during November and December. A variety or strain called siscowet (or "fat trout") is found in deepwater areas of Lake Superior, and another variety, or strain, called "humpers," has a different, humped body shape.

BURBOT
Lota lota

Description: Between 15 and 22 in., 1–3 lbs.; mottled olive-green to shades of brown on back with a cream-colored belly; two dorsal fins—first is small, second is long. Elongated and cylindrical body looks like a cross between a cod and an eel.

Adult Diet: Feed during the night. Burbot in the Great Lakes typically feed on forage fish, primarily alewife, bloater, smelt, and sculpin.

Habitat/Behavior: Benthic; prefer medium to large streams and cold, deep lakes; winter spawner, moving into shallows at night and often spawning under the ice in lakes or streams. Top predator in deep waters of the Great Lakes.

© E. S. DAMSTRA

© E. S. DAMSTRA

© E. S. DAMSTRA

YELLOW PERCH
Perca flavescens

Description: Adults usually 6–10 in.; yellow belly and dark vertical bars on sides; one spiny-rayed and one soft-rayed dorsal fin.

Adult Diet: Forage fish, aquatic insects.

Habitat/Behavior: Moderately shallow waters tending toward benthic habitats of inshore (littoral) habitats; spawn from late April through early May or mid-June (depending on lake) near aquatic plants in shallow reeds or in coastal lakes. Feed from mid-depths to near the bottom in summer; the basis of much local consumption.

WALLEYE
Sander vitreus

Description: Usually 13–20 in.,1–3 lbs. but can grow much larger; dorsal fin with spiny-rayed and soft-rayed sections; large eyes and white tip on tail.

Adult Diet: Forage fish.

Habitat/Behavior: Moderately shallow waters tending toward benthic habitats of inshore (littoral) habitats; spawn in spring or early summer in rivers and lakes over coarse gravel or rocks. Found in turbid areas and use plants, boulders, sunken trees for cover; commonly caught in shallow bays, river mouths, and Lake Erie; popular native fish.

SMALLMOUTH BASS
Micropterus dolomieu

Description: 15–20 in., 1.5–5 pounds; golden brown through olive to green on back; sides lighter; cream to milk-white underside; split dorsal fin with short fin spines in front.

Adult Diet: Fish, frogs, and insects, although they show a preference for crayfish when available.

Habitat/Behavior: Nearshore. Prefer clear, gravel-bottom runs in flowing rivers; shallow rocky areas of lakes; spawn when water temperatures rise in the spring. Males stay to protect the eggs and fry, but many nests fail.

LAKE STURGEON
Acipenser fulvescens

Description: Typically between 3 to 6 feet, but can get much larger; usually 10 to 80 lbs. though long-lived specimens can reach up to 300 lbs.; olive-brown to gray on back and sides, with white belly; they do not have scales, but are covered with bony plates called scutes.

Adult Diet: Feed along lake bottoms, eating a variety of small animals including snails, crustaceans, aquatic insects, mussels, and small fish.

© E. S. DAMSTRA

Habitat/Behavior: Nearshore; live at water depths of 15 to 30 feet. Lake sturgeon live longer than any other fish species in the Great Lakes. Male lake sturgeon live an average of 55 years. Females live 80 to 150 years. They are slow to mature. It takes about 15 years for male lake sturgeon to reach reproductive maturity and 20 to 25 years for females.

NATIVE FORAGE

Forage fish are small fish that serve as food for larger fish. The forage fish profiled here are a representative sample of native species forage fish found throughout the Great Lakes. Most forage fish eat plankton, insect larvae, and some benthos, and larger species like the bloater (chub) have been known to eat other fish.

Any fish small enough to fit into a predator's mouth is potential forage. A forage fish's usefulness to predators depends on its size and where it can be found in a lake (nearshore, benthic, etc.). Many species of native forage fish, some unique to the Great Lakes, were once found all throughout the lakes. However, for larger species like ciscoes, early commercial fishing efforts depleted the populations.

NINESPINE STICKLEBACK
Pungitius pungitius

Description: 2–4 in.; small, thin fish; dorsal spines unconnected by fin tissues. Littoral, pelagic, and benthic; spawn in spring or summer. Some build nests of sticks or weeds. Eat aquatic insects and planktonic crustaceans.

DEEPWATER SCULPIN
Myoxocephalus thompsonii

Description: 7 in. or less; large head, stout body; large and fanlike pectoral fins; pelvic fins (usually with one spine) under pectoral fins.

Adult Diet: Sculpins eat mainly midge larvae, mysids, some crustaceans, and *Diporeia*.

Habitat/Behavior: Benthic; some spawn in the spring, others late in the summer or early fall. Deepwater sculpins live in deeper areas of the lakes, with a temperature below 50 degrees, and spawn during winter. Mottled and slimy sculpins tend to inhabit nearshore waters, nesting under rocks or debris and depositing eggs on the ceiling of the nest.

CISCO (LAKE HERRING)
Coregonus artedi

Bloater (chub) and **Lake Herring** (*Coregonus artedi*) are two prominent species within the ciscoes.

Description: 8–12 in., deep-bodied fish with adipose fin. Lake herring are pale, greenish on top; silver on sides. Bloater look very similar but have fewer gill rakers.

Adult Diet: Mainly zooplankton, including *Diporeia*. Rarely small fish.

Habitat/Behavior: Pelagic and benthic. Spawn in fall and winter. Migrate within the lakes in schools.

EMERALD SHINER
Notropis atherinoides

Description: 2–3 in.; silvery, iridescent body. Mainly pelagic; spawn in summer. Form schools offshore in summer, move inshore in fall and in spring; spend days in deep water and move to the surface at night. Feed mainly on plankton and algae, and eat some midge larvae.

INTRODUCED

PACIFIC SALMON

RAINBOW TROUT OR STEELHEAD
Oncorhynchus mykiss

Description: Usually 20–30 in. and 6–10 lbs.; light body with dark spots, side has pinkish band.

Adult Diet: Invertebrates, plankton, and forage fish.

Habitat/Behavior: Pelagic (open-water); spawn in rivers, streams (potamodromous); enter rivers in late October through early May; spawn from late December through the spring (mostly in the spring); do not die after spawning. Not native to the region—introduced into the Great Lakes from the Pacific Northwest.

CHINOOK SALMON
Oncorhynchus tshawytscha

Description: Pacific salmon species, non-native.

Chinook Salmon—Adults about 36 in., 18 lbs.; black mouth and inner gums, anal fin with 15–17 rays, black spots all over tail.

Coho Salmon—Can reach about 27 in., 6.5 lbs.; white or gray gums, anal fin with 13–15 rays, black spots on only upper half of tail.

Adult Diet: Alewife, smelt, and other forage fish.

COHO SALMON
Oncorhynchus kisutch

Habitat/Behavior: Pelagic (open water), moving throughout the Great Lakes; potamodromous (spawn in rivers, streams); spawn in fall when three to five years old; adults die after spawning. Significant natural reproduction occurs, but population numbers are sustained through hatchery reared and stocked fish; 6-month-old Chinook and 18-month-old coho migrate from rivers to Great Lakes. Not native to the region—introduced into the Great Lakes from the Pacific Northwest.

FOOD PYRAMID: WHAT DOES IT TAKE TO MAKE TEN POUNDS OF FISH?

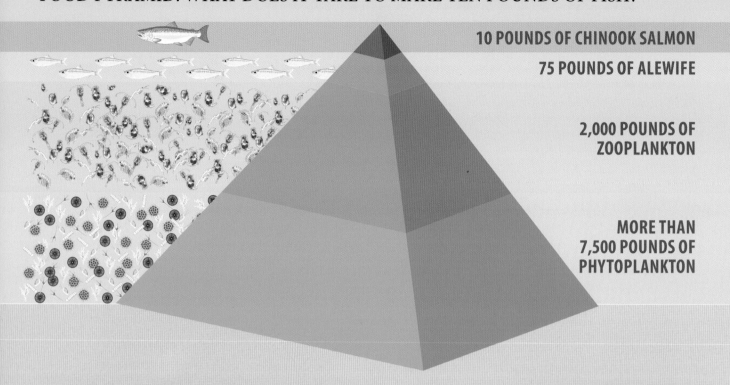

10 POUNDS OF CHINOOK SALMON

75 POUNDS OF ALEWIFE

2,000 POUNDS OF ZOOPLANKTON

MORE THAN 7,500 POUNDS OF PHYTOPLANKTON

The open-water pelagic food pyramid shown in this figure is a simplistic example based on Lake Michigan before the arrival of invasive zebra and quagga mussels. Chinook salmon feed almost exclusively on alewives. Alewives fed primarily on zooplankton before the arrival of mussels. Since the arrival of mussels, trophic relationships are more complex. Alewives now rely more on bottom-dwelling, or benthic, prey. They also eat more Mysis shrimp. These omnivorous shrimp often prey on other zooplankton, as does the invasive spiny water flea. This effectively adds a level to the food pyramid and increases the amount of phytoplankton needed to produce ten pounds of salmon.

DIVERSITY OF FISH IN THE GREAT LAKES

The Great Lakes region is home to an impressive variety of fish. At least 179 different **species** of fish are found in one or more of the Great Lakes, their tributaries, and the connecting waterways. A species consists of individuals that share similar genetics and that can successfully reproduce together. These species belong to 28 major fish families. A family is a taxonomic group, or rank, that includes similar species. For example, the native lake trout (*Salvelinus namaycush*) is a species of fish belonging to the Salmonidae family, which includes various species of salmon, trout, chars, whitefish, and grayling.

FISH SPECIES BY LAKE

❖ Lake Michigan has the greatest number of fish species, with 136 identified species.
❖ Lake Erie has the second highest number of fish species, with 129.
❖ Lake Superior has fewer fish species than the other lakes, with 83 species. However, this northernmost lake has three unique, native subspecies of lake trout—including the "lean," the "humper," and the fatty "siscowet."
❖ Lake Ontario has more fish from the (glacial era) Atlantic drainage than any of the other lakes.
❖ Lakes Superior, Ontario, and Erie, with an east-west orientation, have more species in their southern tributaries than in their northern streams and

rivers. This is probably because many fish moved into the region from the south, as glaciers melted and the climate of the region warmed.

Lake Superior is unique in its collection of fish, in part, because of its northern, upstream position in relation to the other lakes. Together Lakes Superior, Huron, and Michigan are commonly known as the upper Great Lakes. Because Lakes Huron and Michigan are at the same elevation and are connected through the Straits of Mackinac, they are generally considered one lake from a hydrological standpoint. Lakes Ontario and Erie have many fish in common because they are farther south than the other lakes and are closely connected through the Welland Canal.

DISTINGUISHING CHARACTERISTICS

Each family of fish in the Great Lakes region has unique physical traits, or adaptations, that set them apart from other fish. These characteristics and traits help fish survive in their environment. They can also be used to help identify fish species. With the exception of some primitive species, most fish have common characteristics that include gills, scales, fins, and bony skeletons. Head shape and mouth orientation, fin type and location, and average adult size are some of the characteristics that help differentiate fish. Color markings, such as vertical stripes or fin spots, may also help distinguish fish when used in combination with other factors, including geographic range.

FISH ID: ONE QUESTION AT A TIME

To correctly identify fish and classify newly discovered species, fisheries scientists use a dichotomous key based on distinguishing characteristics. A dichotomous key is a classification tool used to sort, organize, and identify a collection of objects or living organisms. A dichotomous key is made up of a series of questions with two choices. Each choice leads to another question. By making choices and progressing logically through the key, users follow a path that ends with the correct identification of the organism.

CLUES TO HABITAT AND SURVIVAL

The distinguishing characteristics, however, help do more than just identify fish species. They also provide clues about the specific habitats where a fish species typically lives and what it eats. For example, fish in the sturgeon and sucker families have ventral, or downward-oriented, mouths that enable them to find food along a lake or stream

bottom. Other traits such as coloration and markings, fin shape, and location can provide clues about whether a fish might live in flowing rivers, shallow and vegetated nearshore areas, or open pelagic offshore waters of the Great Lakes. For example, a northern pike's green and mottled coloration allows this ambush **predator** to camouflage itself among shallower nearshore rooted vegetation; whereas a silver Chinook salmon blends better with the shimmering open blue water of the Great Lakes pelagic zone, where it freely swims.

GREAT LAKES FOOD WEBS

Aquatic life and diversity in the Great Lakes depends upon the availability and abundance of food. A **food chain** consists of the linkages between predators and prey; it is a simplified way to show the relationship of organisms that feed on

each other. More realistically, many different food chains interact in the Great Lakes to form diverse, complex **food webs**, through which energy is passed from one group of organisms to others.

In describing food chains or food webs, it is helpful to describe or group organisms based on what they eat or at what level they gain food or energy. Each energy level is called a **trophic level**. As nutrients

THE PROBLEM WITH POLLUTANTS

Bioaccumulation refers to the buildup of a material in an organism's body throughout its lifetime. Different fish and wildlife species have varying levels of susceptibility to bioaccumulate substances such as pesticides or other chemicals in their bodies. Long-lived species such as bald eagles and lake sturgeon have a longer time to bioaccumulate potentially harmful substances. In addition, species with relatively high body-fat content like lake trout accumulate more fat-soluble **contaminants** such as PCBs (polychlorinated biphenyl) than do other, less fatty organisms.

Biomagnification is the process by which concentrations of persistent contaminants are increased along trophic levels of a food chain. For example, when animals such as zooplankton eat phytoplankton, they also consume the contaminants that have accumulated in the phytoplankton. At the next trophic level, when fish eat zooplankton, they absorb all the contaminants that the tiny animal received from its food and the water environment.

While some contaminants are filtered through the body and excreted, other contaminants such as PCBs and DDT that are persistent and fat-soluble remain in the body of the animal. These chemicals become increasingly concentrated or biomagnified in each animal along the food chain. As a result, consumers such as eagles and humans can have concentrations of contaminants that are over one million times greater than the water concentration. Therefore, even very low environmental concentrations of certain contaminants may reach health-affecting levels in top predators.

TEACHING GREAT LAKES SCIENCE CURRICULUM

Want to learn more about fish life cycles, food webs, invasive species, and defining characteristics of fish? Michigan Sea Grant offers free background information, lessons, games, and activities.

See: greatlakeslessons.com

PHYTOPLANKTON AND ZOOPLANKTON

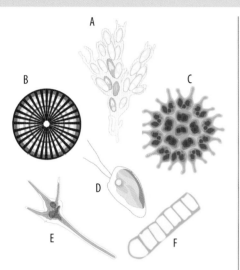

Fig. 1

Note: Not drawn to scale. Scales range from 10,000 to 20,000 times life size.

Phytoplankton Key

A—*Dinobryon spp.* (a chrysophyte)

B—*Stephanodiscus spp.* (a diatom)

C—*Pediastrum spp.* (a green alga)

D—*Rhodomonas spp.* (a cryptophyte)

E—*Ceratium spp.* (a dinoflagellate)

F—*Melosira spp.* (a diatom)

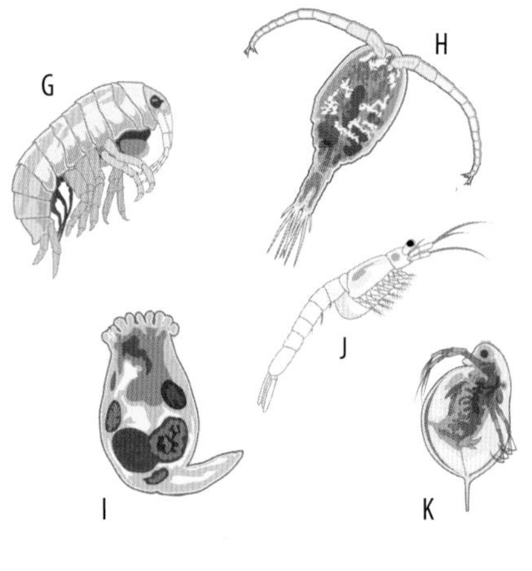

Fig. 2

ILLUSTRATIONS: MICHIGAN SEA GRANT

Note: Not drawn to scale. Scales range from 5 to 1,000 times life size.

Zooplankton Key

G—*Diporeia spp.* (a crustacean)

H—*Diaptomus spp.* (a copepod)

I—*Philodina spp.* (a rotifer)

J—*Mysis relicta* (a malacostran)

K—*Daphnia spp.* (a water flea)

PHYTOPLANKTON

Description: Microscopic to visible floating plants; found to depths where light penetrates water.

Examples: Diatoms, green algae, blue-green bacteria, protists.

ZOOPLANKTON

Description: Microscopic to visible, free-swimming animals; includes a variety of types.

Cladocerans: Water fleas such as *Daphnia*, *Bythotrephes longimanus*, and *Cercopagus pegnoi*; bodies have hard shells, branched swimming antennae; large eye.

Copepods: Oarsmen (cyclopoids and calanoids) cylinder-shaped bodies; long, segmented swimming antennae.

Malocastrans: Mysids such as opposum shrimp; 10 pairs of jointed legs; look like miniature crayfish; stalked eyes.

Rotifers: Feature a crown of cilia around the mouth, four segments including head, neck, trunk, and foot.

Adult Diet: Many are omnivorous, eating algae, detritus, other zooplankton like rotifers, protozoa, other crustaceans, and bacteria; some, including *Cyclops* and *Leptodora* (water flea), are predators that grasp their prey. Opossum shrimp, *daphnia* (water flea), and rotifers are filter feeders, straining food from the water.

Habitat/Behavior: Found throughout Great Lakes. Make vertical migrations daily that vary with light levels, season, and age and sex of the individual animal. Most migrate up as darkness sets in and return to deep at dawn, though some species reverse or twilight migration (at dusk and dawn).

Opossum shrimp (*Mysis relicta*) also make these migrations, but may be considered more benthic than other zooplankton, since they are more often found near the bottom during the day and are found in the hypolimnion during the summer. Opossum shrimp reproduce in fall, winter, and early spring, then carry their eggs and young in a brood pouch for up to three months; young leave the pouch when about 3–4 mm long. Opossum shrimp and most other zooplankton are important food for a variety of fish (especially smaller juvenile and forage fish) such as lake trout, lake whitefish, and ciscoes.

and food are converted through each trophic level, organisms use some of the energy for growth, reproduction, or movement, while some of the energy is lost. The following is an overview of the various energy levels that contribute to food webs.

TROPHIC LEVELS
PRODUCERS: PLANTS

Plants form the base—the first trophic level—of the Great Lakes food chains. Plants are called **producers** because they convert and store the sun's energy and available nutrients into living **biomass**, which is then available to other organisms in the food chain. In the Great Lakes, most of these producers are microscopic floating plants called phytoplankton. Examples of phytoplankton are **diatoms**—tiny, single-celled plants with hard shells of silica. They may cling to each other in groups, in loose filaments, or adhere to underwater objects. Other phytoplankton in the Great Lakes include green algae, blue-green algae (cyanobacteria), and dinoflagellates (small organisms with hair-like structures that allow them to move).

Peaks in phytoplankton growth usually occur twice a year, the first in spring (mostly diatoms) and the second in the fall (diatoms and blue-green and green algae). These bursts of phytoplankton growth are called **algal blooms** and follow spring and fall turnover, when the mixing of the water increases access to nutrients throughout the lakes.

Larger rooted plants, called **macrophytes**, are another prominent type of producer. Macrophytes grow in areas where light reaches the lake bottom and are primarily found in nearshore zones. Macrophytes include emergent, submergent, or floating plants such as cattails, milfoils, and water lilies.

Macrophytes and phytoplankton support different kinds of animal life.

PRIMARY CONSUMERS
ZOOPLANKTON

The next trophic levels are made up of tiny, sometimes microscopic, floating or mobile animals called zooplankton. These are primary consumers in the Great Lakes, the first level of organisms that typically feed on producers. These animals have a great variety of forms with unique life cycles. Protozoans are the most numerous types of zooplankton found in the Great Lakes and include microscopic, one-celled animals such as amoebae and paramecia. Other common types include rotifers, cladocerans (water fleas such as *Daphnia*) found mostly in the summer months, and copepods (such as cyclopoids and calanoids).

Zooplankton abundance varies throughout the spring, summer, and fall. Their numbers are influenced by food availability, which in turn is affected by such things as temperature, winds, seasonal mixing of water layers, upwellings, and productivity of the water.

MACROINVERTEBRATES

Another trophic grouping consists of **macroinvertebrates**—larger than zooplankton, these are animals lacking backbones. Different species live in deep and shallow areas of the Great Lakes.

DEEP WATER

Examples of small animals that dominate deepwater life include *Diporeia spp.*, an amphipod or "side swimmer" (sometimes mistakenly called a freshwater shrimp, and previously called opossum shrimp, *Mysis oculata relicta*). Oligochaetes (freshwater worms) and chironomids (larvae of midges) are also found in deep water.

SHALLOW WATER

The small invertebrate animals found in shallow waters of the Great Lakes are similar to those found in cold, inland lakes—leeches, clams, mussels, snails, crayfish, and nymphs of mayflies, dragonflies, and caddis flies. The average density of these small benthic animals, some of which are burrowing and others associated with vegetation, may reach hundreds of animals per square meter. Some areas of the Great Lakes may be even more productive, with tens of thousands of small animals per square meter.

MOVEMENT IN THE WATER COLUMN

Some of these invertebrates migrate dozens of meters up and down in the water column each day (many thousands of times their body length). Light levels, season, temperature, reproductive behaviors, and sometimes predators affect their movements. These organisms move nutrients and energy within the water column and between shallow and deep regions of the lakes.

SECONDARY CONSUMERS
PLANKTIVORES

Zooplankton and macroinvertebrates provide energy for fish at the next trophic levels in Great Lakes ecosystems. Some fish, such as alewives, various shiners, and ciscoes, feed mainly on zooplankton and are called **planktivorous** (plankton-eating) fish. These smaller fish feeding on invertebrates are considered secondary consumers in a simplified food chain.

Generally, even juveniles of large- or medium-sized Great Lakes fish, such as salmon, lake trout, and yellow perch, will feed on zooplankton and macroinvertebrates in their early life stages until they grow large enough to eat food like prey fish.

FISH-EAT-FISH WORLD

Prey fish are small planktivorous fish that serve as food or prey for larger fish. Those species are also called **forage fish** and include bloaters, ciscoes (including lake herring), sculpins, shiners, alewives, gizzard shad, and rainbow smelt. As juveniles, even large- or medium-sized Great Lakes fish may serve as food for larger predators.

TOP CONSUMERS
PREDATORS

Larger fish that eat other fish are called **piscivorous**, meaning predators of fish. In a simple food chain, these predators are tertiary or top consumers. Other top predators or consumers of Great Lakes fish include

❖ Amphibians (e.g., mudpuppies) and reptiles (e.g., turtles)
❖ Birds (e.g., bald eagles, herons, osprey, cormorants, mergansers, and loons)
❖ Mammals (e.g., mink, river otters, and humans)

However, the food chain does not end with these consumers.

DECOMPOSERS
DETRITIVORES

All organisms die, and whether they are large animals or microscopic plankton, decomposers such as bacteria and fungi begin their work. As the decomposers feed on dead material, also called detritus, organic materials are broken down and nutrients then again become available to the producers at the start of the food chain.

Some of these organisms are found in the sediment at the bottom of the lakes, even in deep regions. For example, *Diporeia spp.* and oligochaetes burrow into sediments and feed on detritus. Other small organisms, such as rotifers, feed in mid-water on the **detrital rain**, the

INVASIVE FORAGE FISH

ALEWIFE
Alosa pseudoharengus

Description: 6–8 in.; silvery, iridescent (shifting, rainbow-like color), single black spot behind head at eye level.

Adult Diet: Planktivore (plankton-eating); may also eat small fish and fish eggs.

Habitat/Behavior: Mainly pelagic, but also nearshore; spawn in shallows in late spring, early summer; strain plankton from water through structures called gill rakers (in gills); schools move nearshore to feed at night. Die-offs may occur in spring and summer. Not native to Great Lakes; invaded from Atlantic Ocean through the Erie Canal.

ROUND GOBY
Neogobius melanostomus

Description: Both round goby and tubenose goby species can be identified by a single fused pelvic (bottom) fin, forming a conical disk shaped like a "suction cup"—no native fish in the Great Lakes have this. Both species arrived in ballast water of international cargo vessels.

Round Goby—Usually 3–6 (up to 8) in.; characterized by large head, soft body, and no spiny fins; look similar to native sculpins; distinguished by a large black dorsal fin spot. Adults are yellowish gray with black and brown blotches over their bodies with some tinge of green on the dorsal fin; young are a solid gray.

RAINBOW SMELT
Osmerus mordax

Description: 7–8 in. and under 1 lb.; long silvery body, with rainbow-like iridescent color on sides; adipose fin.

Adult Diet: Planktivore (plankton-eating); may eat very small fish.

Habitat/Behavior: Mainly pelagic; potamodromous (spawn in streams, rivers, and gravel beaches); spawn in spring. Intentionally introduced to Michigan inland lakes as a forage fish for salmon. Unintentionally introduced to Great Lakes, likely by escaping or by movement in bait buckets.

INVASIVE PREDATOR

INVASIVE ZOOPLANKTON

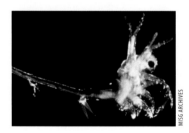

SEA LAMPREY
Petromyzon marinus

Description: Grows up to 34 in.; lacks jaws; has circular, sucking mouth with rasping tongue; no paired fins.

Adult Diet: Fluids and tissues of large fish, particularly salmon and trout, which have small scales.

Habitat/Behavior: Pelagic and benthic; spawns in rivers and streams in spring; larval lampreys (called ammocoetes) spend three to six years buried in sediments feeding on detritus and small organisms filtered from the water. Migrate to open waters of Great Lakes for adult, parasitic phase (approx. 18 months), growing from 6–8" to 24" as an adult. Each adult estimated to kill 40 pounds of fish during parasitic phase. Arrived in upper Great Lakes after the Welland Canal (bypassing Niagara Falls) was opened.

SPINY WATER FLEA
Bythotrephes longimanus

Description: Both water fleas are crustaceans and very similar in description; measuring spine or tail, both about 1 cm long; are considered zooplankton; long, spiny tail; large, single eye. Primary physical difference is that the fishhook flea is distinguished by a smaller body size (about the size of the spiny water flea) and a unique loop at the end of its tail—a characteristic difficult to determine without a microscope.

Adult Diet: Both are predatory planktivores or raptorial predators (meaning they grasp, pierce, and shred their prey), an important distinction because unlike most aquatic predators, they can eat things larger than their mouth. They eat zooplankton including *Daphnia*;

FISHHOOK FLEA
Cercopagis pengoi

and compete with fish (particularly juvenile fish) and invertebrates for zooplankton.

Habitat/Behavior: Pelagic zooplankton found in offshore areas; migrate to surface at night; reproduce rapidly during warm summer conditions; spines appear to serve as defense against predators; often found fouling fishing line and nets that have collected large numbers of them. Not native to Great Lakes, likely arrived in ballast water of international cargo vessels.

INVASIVE MUSSELS

ZEBRA MUSSEL
Dreissena polymorpha

QUAGGA MUSSEL
Dreissena bugensis

Description: Both mussels are thumbnail sized, usually about ¼ to 1 in.; light and dark banded shell coloration; quagga mussels may often have lighter-colored shells or finer stripes, but patterns of both species can vary. Shell shape is primary difference, and quagga mussels typically have more rounded shells then zebra mussels.

Adult Diet: Both filter-feed primarily on phytoplankton, as well as other small particles and organisms suspended in the water; compete with zooplankton for phytoplankton food sources.

Habitat/Behavior: Both mussels live in similar habitats; adult mussels are benthic and attach to hard surfaces; quagga mussels can also colonize softer substrates and a wider range of water depths; usually found in clusters; larvae are planktonic (free-floating, microscopic). Prolific spring and summer reproduction results in rapid growth and expansion of colonies. Arrived in Great Lakes in ballast water of international cargo vessels.

Quagga mussel, with open siphon.

dead algae and zooplankton that sink down from upper layers of water. These decomposers and detritivores play an important role in the Great Lakes. By recycling nutrients, they allow even deep areas (such as aphotic, benthic zones) of the Great Lakes to be productive and to support life.

WEBS OF LIFE

Great Lakes food webs are dynamic and complex. Many organisms in the Great Lakes feed on more than one type of food; in fact, some can readily switch food types if a regular food supply is depleted. Food web functions are influenced by habitat limitations such as food, water quality, shelter, and space. Pelagic food webs have their basis of productivity in floating algae, whereas littoral food webs are based on energy produced by macrophytes. Yet even in the **littoral** zone there is a tremendous amount of phytoplankton and algae production, and so macrophytes are not necessarily the sole plant producer. Likewise, benthic food webs are based on energy and nutrient flow from organisms that make use of the detritus floating down from above and settling into the sediments.

Each link in a Great Lakes food chain strongly influences other links. For example, zooplankton may play a role in limiting the standing crop of phytoplankton. Fish affect the size and species populations of zooplankton by visually searching out and eating larger plankton. In turn, the size and availability of zooplankton and forage fish consumed can influence the predators' growth rates.

HEALTHY LINKS AND DISRUPTIONS

Complexity of food webs may help to ensure survival and function of species and food chains. If one organism in a

chain becomes scarce, another may be able to fill its role. However, if too many links in the food web are lost or altered, the changes may eventually result in inability of food webs to function or effectively transfer nutrients and energy through these aquatic ecosystems. For humans, this may translate into losses of popular sport or food fish species—in either numbers or size or both. From an ecosystem perspective, broken webs will result in a decline in the health of fisheries and loss of biodiversity.

THREATS TO THE SYSTEM: NON-NATIVE SPECIES

Many non-native species have been introduced into the Great Lakes since the early 1800s, either accidentally or intentionally. Nonindigenous or non-native species are plants and animals living outside of the area where they evolved. A fraction of these species (about 10 percent) are considered invasive. What makes a species an invasive one rather than a non-native one? All non-native species, whether intentionally or unintentionally introduced, affect the food web. However, **invasive species** have a profound, negative, and potentially permanent impact on an ecosystem or human activity.

Invasive species have established populations, multiplied rapidly, and caused large, lasting impacts on the Great Lakes ecosystem. These impacts cause what ecologists call food web disruptions. Because they are nonindigenous, invasive species are often free from natural predators. They reproduce rapidly and compete with native species for food and habitat. They disrupt the food web by reducing food for native species or by preying directly upon native species. They are costly to manage and have led to a severe loss of biodiversity throughout the world. Because of this, invasive

ALTERED REALITY: WHEN INVASIVES MOVE IN

SILVER CARP

DAN O'KEEFE, MISG

ZEBRA MUSSEL

MISG

SPINY WATER FLEA

DAVE BRENNER, MISG

Aquatic invasive species have greatly altered Great Lakes food webs. New invaders—like the silver (*Hypophthalmichthys molitrix*) and bighead carp (*H. nobilis*)—could disrupt the Great Lakes even more dramatically. What are some of the ways invasive species have impacted the lakes? A few examples:

❖ When the alewife arrived in the Great Lakes in the early 1900s, the effects were felt both up and down the food chain. The alewife's presence reshaped the pelagic food web, which eventually prompted managers to stock Pacific salmon—now a popular non-native sport fish. The arrival of the alewife had negative consequences for native

species such as lake trout, perch, and walleye. Alewives have proved to be a poor food for lake trout, causing reproduction problems linked to vitamin deficiencies; and alewives have negatively impacted perch and walleye reproduction because they prey upon their young.

❖ Since zebra and, more recently, quagga mussels (dreissenids) have moved into the Great Lakes, the benthic life of the lakes has been changed. The deepwater life is now dominated by dreissenids, resulting in the loss of *Diporeia*, the nutrient-rich zooplankton that most fish depend upon at some life stage. The invasive mussels are capable of filtering one or more liters of water

each day. They also trap nutrients in their biomass, preventing nutrients from moving from nearshore and benthic zones to offshore pelagic zones, which has upset food webs of Lake Michigan and Lake Huron.

❖ The spiny water flea, *Bythotrephes*, is not what one usually thinks of when considering aquatic invasive species. The water flea is a zooplankton that preys on other zooplankton. That means they put additional pressure on zooplankton populations by both competing with them for survival requirements and by preying on them. The water flea's spiny "tail" also serves as a defense mechanism, discouraging smaller fish from feeding on it.

species are often called "biological pollutants." Unlike chemical or physical pollution, however, they are considered impossible to remove once established.

In the Great Lakes, sea lampreys, alewives, zebra and quagga mussels, round goby, and the spiny water flea are among the many invasive species that have altered ecosystem functions. They have each contributed to reductions in native species and impacted sport and commercial fishing. Invasive plants, such as purple loosestrife (*Lythrum salicaria*), the common reed (*Phragmites australis*), and Eurasian water milfoil (*Myriophyllum spicatum*), have established themselves in many Great Lakes wetlands as well as inland lakes.

They successfully out-compete native species, resulting in a loss of native plants—and the wildlife that depends upon those native plants.

BIODIVERSITY

Preserving and encouraging biodiversity helps to ensure that when one species dwindles or disappears, other organisms can continue to support the food web. When multiple species in the system are suppressed and the food web is not rebounding, it is sometimes referred to as "collapsed."

HABITATS AND FISH PRODUCTION

Due to constraints of energy transfer in a functioning food web, the lakes can support only a finite amount of life. This **carrying capacity** and the overall productivity of an area within a lake are determined by a variety of factors acting together.

Fisheries scientists study the size, health, habitat use, and movements of Great Lakes fish populations to understand such things as how many fish of that particular species are surviving, rates of growth, reproduction capacity, and even how many individual fish might be available for harvest. A group of individual organisms of the same species living in a particular

Continued on page 40

FISH LIFE CYCLES

Life cycles of fish vary among species. For example, lampreys are unique in how they develop. They hatch from eggs into small, wormlike larvae, which burrow into stream bottoms for an average of three to six years before they transform into the parasitic adult, entirely skipping the **fry** and juvenile stages of other fish species.

However, more generally, Great Lakes fish species progress through similar stages as they mature from eggs to adults. The following diagram is an example of life cycle development for lake whitefish.

1 EGG

Most fertilized eggs do not survive to maturity even under the best conditions. Threats include changes in water temperature and oxygen levels, wave action, flooding or sedimentation, predators, and disease. Eggs that survive develop into fish. Lake whitefish eggs are deposited over a hard, sandy, or stony bottom in fall where they spend the winter before hatching in spring.

2 SAC FRY

Sac fry live off a yolk sac attached to their bodies. When the yolk sac is gone, the young fish begin to seek out food. Lake whitefish sac fry remain in the area where they were spawned as they grow and develop the strength to swim.

3 LARVA

Larvae (or fry) are ready to start eating on their own. Larvae undergo several more developmental stages, which vary by species, as they mature into adults. Most larval fish must feed on zooplankton soon after their yolk sac is depleted. Many fish fail to find food and starve to death at this stage. Like other species, larval lake whitefish look nothing like adult whitefish. Once they begin to resemble adults of their species, larval fish become juveniles.

6 SPAWNING

Female fish release eggs into the water (either into the water column or into a nest) and male fish fertilize eggs by releasing milt. Not all eggs are fertilized. Some fish spawn each year after reaching maturity (e.g., walleye), others may go several years between spawning (e.g., sturgeon), and some species spawn only once and then die (e.g., salmon). Lake whitefish spawn each year in the fall.

4 JUVENILE

The time fish spend developing from fry into reproductively mature adults varies among species. Most fish do not survive to become adults. Threats to survival include changes in water temperature and oxygen levels, competition for habitat, and predators. Juvenile lake whitefish move into deeper water by early summer and transition from feeding on zooplankton to eating bottom-dwelling invertebrates.

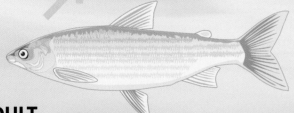

5 ADULT

When fish can reproduce, they are considered adults. The time it takes to reach maturity varies among species and individual fish. Fish with shorter life spans mature faster. For example, female round gobies mature in approximately one year and live for two to three years. Lake sturgeon can live up to 80-150 years, but females don't reach maturity until they are approximately 20-25 years old. Lake whitefish often mature between age 3 and 7.

NOT TO SCALE. ILLUSTRATION: MICHIGAN SEA GRANT.

HOW IT ALL COMES TOGETHER

Whatever their course of development, the success (survival) of fish depends on the match between the organism and environment. Adaptations of the species and the genetics of individual fish determine what environmental features are important to that fish. In addition, genetics determine the range of tolerance of a particular species. For example, lake trout are genetically adapted to cold, clear, highly oxygenated waters; they grow best in waters around 50.9°F (10.5°C); and temperature extremes can be deadly for lake trout and other species. Adaptations and genetics of particular fish species—combined with the actual characteristics of the fish's environment—work together to affect that fish's survival, growth, and reproduction.

The result of all of the collective factors discussed throughout this section is **fish production**. In fisheries management, that is referred to as the amount of new biomass produced by a given species in a particular area over a period of time.

Scientists use many different research techniques and technologies to monitor Great Lakes fish populations. They also employ various management strategies—ranging from **stocking** to regulation of harvest—to enhance populations, maximize production of fish for human uses, and ensure that they are not overexploited. In respect to human values in Great Lakes fisheries, this knowledge allows managers be more effective in managing productive and sustainable sport and commercial fisheries. Fish production can be measured in various ways, such as total pounds caught and catch rates, growth rates of fish, or a stable system able to produce a diversity of species.

THEN AND NOW

The Great Lakes changed radically in response to early aquatic invasive species such as sea lamprey, alewife, and rainbow smelt. In the 1990s, a second wave of ballast-borne invaders took hold and spread throughout the lakes. Dreissenid mussels (both zebra and quagga), spiny water fleas, and round gobies altered ecosystems in fundamental ways. Dreissenid mussels filter nutrients from the water, reducing the amount of food available for open-water species. Environmental regulations such as the Clean Water Act of 1972 also played a role in reducing excess phosphorus, a nutrient needed for primary production at the bottom of the food chain. Meanwhile, high numbers of salmon and trout at the top of the food chain led to heavy predation on forage fish in some areas of the Great Lakes.

The relative importance of "bottom-up" and "top-down" effects such as these has been a matter of long debate among ecologists. In the Great Lakes, the real-world impact of this debate is felt by anglers and commercial fishers who wonder how the changing lake will affect their livelihood. Long-term monitoring of environmental conditions and fish populations has provided some valuable insight regarding bottom-up and top-down regulation, in addition to giving us a snapshot of conditions in the lakes before dreissenid mussels were widespread (1985–1990) and after (2005–2010). Unless otherwise noted, the trends discussed below refer to the 1998–2010 time period, during which dreissenid mussels were rapidly expanding.

LAKE ERIE

The fertile waters of western Lake Erie stand out because water clarity remained low during the mussel population explosion while nutrient concentrations remained high. Salmon and trout do not thrive in the western basin, but walleye are one of several popular fish species that tolerate warm Lake Erie water. On a lake-wide basis, walleye abundance increased following the arrival of mussels. Unfortunately, high nutrient loads and the filtering activity of mussels also resulted in harmful algal blooms. The central and eastern basins are not as nutrient-rich as the western basin. Nutrient inputs increased in the eastern basin, and phytoplankton increased in the central basin, but nutrient concentrations remained steady in all basins after the arrival of mussels.

LAKE MICHIGAN

Radical changes have occurred in Lake Michigan, which has seen a significant increase in water clarity and declines in forage fish biomass. Bottom-up effects are evident at the base of the food web, where declines in phosphorus are linked to declines in plankton. However, forage fish biomass was in decline as trout and salmon biomass was increasing during 1998–2008. This disconnect between declining productivity at the base of the

food web and relatively high biomass of predatory fish eventually led to declines in trout and salmon harvest in 2013–2016. Bottom-up control of phytoplankton and zooplankton was evident in Lake Michigan during the expansion of exotic mussels, but the decline of prey fish was more related to top-down control by salmon and trout than to problems in the lower food web.

LAKE ONTARIO

Water clarity increased and zooplankton biomass decreased during the dreissenid mussel population expansion, while phosphorus levels remained relatively stable in Lake Ontario. However, strong declines in nutrient availability and forage fish biomass occurred before the mussel invasion. Forage fish in Lake Ontario have been on the decline since the 1980s, and trout and salmon biomass declined each year from 1998 to 2007. This is an example of a bottom-up effect, since dwindling prey has influenced predators, but declines in stocking may also play a role. Neither bottom-up nor top-down effects are evident at other levels of the food chain, in contrast to Lake Michigan and Lake Huron.

LAKE HURON

A dramatic collapse of salmon fishing occurred in Lake Huron around 2004. Populations of alewife and sculpin declined

by 98 percent or more as dreissenid mussels expanded, plankton declined, and water clarity increased. As in Lake Michigan, forage fish biomass declined starting in the late 1990s. Overall trout and salmon biomass remained relatively steady in Lake Huron during this time period, but Chinook salmon biomass declined dramatically. Following the crash of Chinook salmon and alewife, natural reproduction of native species increased and anglers began catching more lake trout and walleye. Lake Huron provides an example of strong bottom-up control at every level of the pelagic food chain, although changes to the predatory fish community were also influenced by changes in natural reproduction and stocking decisions.

LAKE SUPERIOR

Unlike most waters of the Great Lakes, Lake Superior was not subjected to the dreissenid mussel population explosion. Fewer historical data are available for Lake Superior, but phytoplankton and prey fish biomass both declined in the 2000s. Bloater, cisco, and rainbow smelt declined, while lean lake trout remained stable in nearshore waters. However, the fatty lake trout (or siscowet) is the more abundant deepwater predator, and population trends for siscowet have not been studied extensively.

Lake	Trout and Salmon (pounds/acre)	Zooplankton (pounds/acre)	Water Clarity (feet)	April Total Phosphorus (ppb)
Lake Erie *(Western basin)* 1985-1990	NA	5	6.7	17
2005-2010	NA	18	4.7	38
Lake Ontario 1985-1990	9.3 Lake Trout / Chinook Salmon	25	29.1	8
2005-2010	2.6 Lake Trout / Chinook Salmon	16	47.1	6
Lake Michigan 1985-1990	4.6 All Trout / Salmon Species	27	32.8	5
2005-2010	4.3 All Trout / Salmon Species	16	41.7	3
Lake Huron 1985-1990	1.0 Lake Trout / Chinook Salmon	12	28.9	4
2005-2010	0.6 Lake Trout / Chinook Salmon	8	45.4	2
Lake Superior 1985-1990	NA	NA	NA	NA
2005-2010	NA	11	50.9	2

Source: Bunnell, D.B., Barbiero, R.P., Ludsin, S.A., Madenjian, C.P., Warren, G., Dolan, D., Brenden, T., Briland, R., Gorman, O.T., He, J.X., Johengen, T.H., Lantry, B.F., Nalepa, T.F., Riley, S.C., Riseng, C.M., Treska, T.J., Tsehaye, I., Warner, D.M., Walsh, M.G., and Weidel, B.C. 2014. Changing ecosystem dynamics in the Laurentian Great Lakes: bottom-up and top-down regulation. BioScience, 64:26–39. doi:10.1093/biosci/bit001

FISH PRODUCTION AND RESOURCE ALLOCATION

Survival, growth and reproduction rates of fish influence fish production — the amount of biomass in a given area during a given time. What contributes to survival, growth and reproduction? Environment and genetics. This graphic explores how a fish population is created, what factors influence production within a population and how it is allocated.

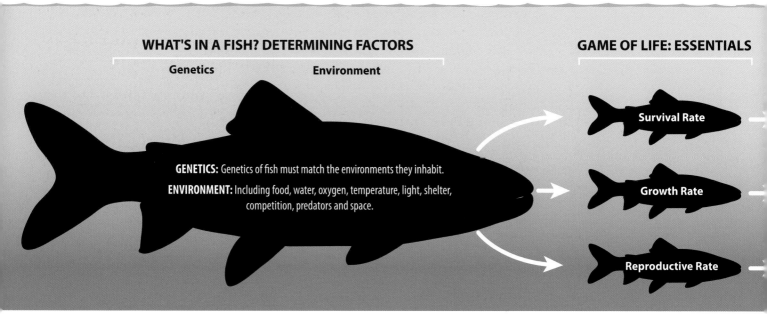

WHAT'S IN A FISH? DETERMINING FACTORS

Genetics · Environment

GENETICS: Genetics of fish must match the environments they inhabit.
ENVIRONMENT: Including food, water, oxygen, temperature, light, shelter, competition, predators and space.

GAME OF LIFE: ESSENTIALS

Survival Rate

Growth Rate

Reproductive Rate

---

area is called a population. Also important are ecosystem interactions between populations of different species. As defined earlier, an ecosystem is a community of organisms interacting with one another and the physical environment.

REQUIREMENTS FOR LIFE

Like all living organisms, fish need to survive long enough and grow large enough to reproduce. Different species of fish require specific habitats to meet their needs. Critical habitat requirements for life:

❖ **Water:** Fish not only live in water, but they get oxygen from water. They breathe by taking water into their mouths and forcing it out through gill passages.
❖ **Food:** Whether they feed on micro-organisms, small fish, or larger prey, fish must be able to find enough to eat at various life stages.
❖ **Shelter:** Fish need a place to reproduce and to hide from predators. Some fish find shelter among submerged aquatic plants and shoreline vegetation,

while others hide among rocks or soft sediments or blend into clear, open waters.
❖ **Space:** Often known as a territory or "home range," space requirements vary by species. Fish need space to find sufficient food and water for survival, shelter areas to avoid predators, spawning areas, tolerated proximity to others (e.g., schooling fish versus more solitary fish), and in some cases, migratory corridors connecting these areas.

Fish are adapted to living in a variety of habitats, including rivers and streams, inland lakes, coastal wetlands, and the nearshore or offshore waters of the Great Lakes. These habitats can vary greatly in water quality, turbidity, speed of water flow, amount of vegetation, water temperature, and water composition. As mentioned earlier, fish are particularly sensitive to water temperature and oxygen content, which play a major role in determining which species can survive in a given water body or area of that water body.

NEEDS THROUGHOUT LIFE

Specific needs and aquatic habitat vary by species, and may also change through a given fish species' life cycle. Nearly all Great Lakes fish can be found in shallow water during part of their life cycles. Many species use the shallow waters of lakes or rivers as spawning habitat in either the spring or the fall. Spring spawners include steelhead, lake sturgeon, various suckers, channel catfish, bullheads, yellow perch, walleye, northern pike, and smallmouth bass. Fall-spawning fish include lake trout, lake whitefish, lake herring, and Chinook and coho salmon.

Fish species require certain types of habitat for spawning and for early development of their fry, or newly hatched young. Some, such as northern pike, prefer wetlands with aquatic vegetation; others, such as lake whitefish, prefer shallow reefs because they provide rich areas of food, rocky structure (shelter) to retain eggs, and safety from predators once the eggs hatch. While we know some basic needs of Great Lakes fish, much remains to be learned about their early life stages.

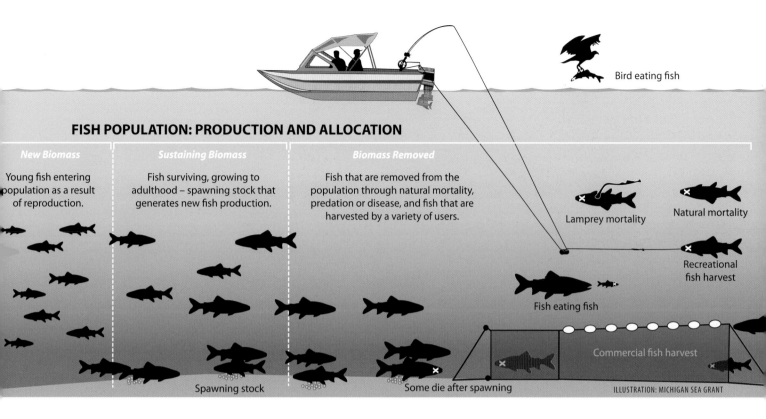

FISH POPULATION: PRODUCTION AND ALLOCATION

New Biomass
Young fish entering population as a result of reproduction.

Sustaining Biomass
Fish surviving, growing to adulthood – spawning stock that generates new fish production.

Biomass Removed
Fish that are removed from the population through natural mortality, predation or disease, and fish that are harvested by a variety of users.

Bird eating fish

Lamprey mortality

Natural mortality

Recreational fish harvest

Fish eating fish

Commercial fish harvest

Spawning stock

Some die after spawning

ILLUSTRATION: MICHIGAN SEA GRANT

MANAGEMENT

Now that we have covered the basic principles of Great Lakes ecology, the next step is to examine how management decisions are made.

Fisheries science is the systematic scientific study of fish, aquatic resources, and their uses and users. This science involves understanding the structure, dynamics, and interactions of habitat, aquatic organisms, and humans. **Fisheries management** is an area within fisheries science that involves decision-making focused on how people interact with fish and aquatic ecosystems. That often requires managers to translate data and information about people, aquatic populations, and habitats into usable information that helps define strategies. The information is then used to form goals for particular aquatic populations or ecosystems.

LESSONS LEARNED

Lessons in fisheries production and management have come from learning

from the challenges. Great Lakes fish populations have declined in numbers over the past century due to a combination of factors such as overfishing, poor environmental quality, and pressure from invasive species. For example:

❖ Atlantic salmon in Lake Ontario probably declined because of habitat loss from early logging and dam building and because of overfishing.

❖ Lake sturgeon, which grow and mature slowly, were also affected by changed habitat, fishing, and other pressures throughout the Great Lakes.

❖ Lake trout declined due to factors such as sea lamprey predation, habitat degradation, nutrient deficiency, overfishing, and waning prey.

As discussed earlier, noting these changes in populations is important because when populations of one particular fish species change significantly, it has an impact throughout the food web.

THE COMPLEXITIES OF STOCKING

In some cases, fisheries managers may choose to raise and stock fish for the purpose of rehabilitating their populations or to supplement or enhance certain fisheries. Managers have also intentionally introduced new species to the Great Lakes food web, both to assist in limiting numbers of other organisms and to provide fishing opportunities. For example, coho and Chinook salmon were introduced to reduce alewife populations and to provide sportfishing opportunities.

PREY FISH

Prey fish populations are regularly monitored, but managers generally agree it is not feasible to stock enough prey fish to fully support the entire Great Lakes predator populations. Stocking prey fish has, however, been explored in specific scenarios. For example, regulatory agencies are experimenting with rearing and

ARCTIC GRAYLING
Thymallus arcticus

© EMILY S. DAMSTRA

ARCTIC GRAYLING: GONE FOREVER?

The Arctic grayling (*Thymallus arcticus*) is a freshwater, cold-water fish in the same family (Salmonidae) as salmon, trout, and whitefish. It grows to about 10–12 inches when mature. Grayling are very sensitive to water temperature and require cool water throughout the year. The most distinctive characteristics of grayling are its large, sail-like dorsal fin and iridescent scales. The grayling was one of Michigan's most popular native fish and is now found only in the west (e.g., Montana, Alaska), in certain areas of Canada, and Siberia.

Arctic grayling populations in Michigan's Lower Peninsula rivers—once abundant—declined precipitously beginning in the 1880s and were virtually gone shortly after the turn of the twentieth century. Logging activities, degradation of rivers and streams across the region, competition from introduced non-native species like brook and rainbow trout, and overfishing are all thought to have contributed to their demise.

MANAGEMENT CHALLENGE

The earliest attempts to manage the grayling took place in 1877 when adults were transferred from the Manistee River to one lake and three streams in Calhoun, Jackson, Kalamazoo, and Van Buren Counties. Additional adult Arctic grayling were transferred to streams outside their known native range in 1880 and 1925. None of these plants were successful. Stocking records kept by the State of Michigan indicate that between 1900 and 1933 more than 3.3 million Montana-strain Arctic grayling fry were stocked in Michigan rivers and lakes. Later sampling showed no signs of the grayling.

Fast-forward a few decades. Between 1987 and 1991, the State of Michigan stocked 145,000 yearling Arctic grayling in 13 inland lakes and seven streams in northern Michigan. Eggs came from wild Arctic grayling populations in Wyoming and the Northwest Territories, Canada. Most grayling stocked in rivers disappeared within six months.

WHY NO SUCCESS?

The grayling did initially survive well in lakes where other fish species were either absent or sparse. The Michigan DNR reported that most of the stocked grayling eventually succumbed to predators, competition for food, low pH levels in water, hooking mortality (getting caught and released but not surviving), poaching, and infections.

Good survival to age five occurred in only one lake, which was closed to fishing, patrolled to detect poachers, and held only a few brook trout competitors. However, in the end, the population was not sustained.

In more recent times, the Little River Band of Ottawa Indians received a grant from the U.S. Fish and Wildlife Service in 2011 to explore the likelihood of reintroducing the grayling to Michigan waters once again. The Michigan Department of Natural Resources continues to explore options for reintroducing this native species.

Arctic Grayling Catch from Bear Creek, Manistee County, about 1896.

BENTLEY HISTORICAL LIBRARY

stocking native ciscoes (lake herring variety), exploring the prospects of re-establishing breeding populations of these important native prey fish in areas of the lakes. Rehabilitating these prey fish populations and stocking them in locations where they were previously abundant could enhance the biodiversity of prey fish available for predator species such as walleye, lake trout, or salmon.

NATIVE SPECIES STOCKING

Fishery managers focus more on stocking predator species. Today, researchers and managers collaborate in lake trout stocking efforts, both to supplement fisheries valued by stakeholders and to reinstate naturally reproducing, self-sustaining populations of this native species. The lake sturgeon is another example of a native species being stocked in order to restore the population. Sturgeon are also a great example of the complex considerations managers must take into account when supporting a particular species through stocking. Managers not only assess which species they should stock, but they also have to consider what genetic strains or variety of that species they stock. Population genetics are increasingly important aspects to consider in fisheries hatchery and stocking programs.

Stocking fish in the Great Lakes is just one of many tools that can be employed for fisheries population management. It can complement other population management strategies, such as conservation and **restoration** of critical habitats, protecting spawning stocks of adult wild fish (benefiting from natural reproduction), and managing with a goal of balancing predator-prey relationships. These techniques are used to achieve a self-sustaining system that also meets stakeholder needs.

BOB RASHID

Bill Waubanascum and Eugene Webster, Jr. both from Wisconsin, take a break from dancing during the Menominee Tribe annual return of the sturgeon feast and powwow. Collaborative fisheries management has helped ensure that endangered fish populations like that of the lake sturgeon — an important fish to many cultures through the region — continues to grow.

OVERSEEING THE GREAT LAKES FISHERIES

Great Lakes fish are known as **common property resources** held in trust for everyone. Government agencies are responsible for caring for these public trust resources on the public's behalf, keeping both human and ecological needs in mind. Responsibility for conservation and management activities of these resources lies with the eight Great Lakes states, the province of Ontario, federal agencies of the United States and Canada, as well as the tribes and First Nations. State, provincial, and tribal agencies are also responsible for allocating fishery resources among user groups and ensuring a healthy population in future years. Since the Great Lakes extend beyond international borders, state and tribal agencies on the U.S. side collaboratively manage fishery resources with the Ontario provincial government, the Canadian federal government, and Ontario stakeholders.

STATE AND PROVINCIAL LEVEL

On the U.S. side of the lakes, the lead responsibility for conservation and

regulatory management of the Great Lakes rests with the state management agencies. That includes managing access to the fishery for commercial and sport fisheries through license sales and setting rules for fish harvest, including length and timing of seasons, catch limits, and even fishing gear. State agencies also evaluate status and health of fish populations, implement fish stocking and management plans, conduct educational programs, and protect or manage habitats, such as wetlands protection programs or habitat restoration projects. These state agency activities are usually conducted through authorities provided by legislative and executive branches of state governments and with citizen oversight through appointed commissions, industries, and citizen advisory committees. Similarly, in Canada, authority and primary responsibility for managing Great Lakes fisheries lies with Ontario's provincial agencies, as delegated through the federal Fisheries Act.

TRIBE LEVEL

Tribal agencies play a key fishery management role. Multiple individual tribes have organized and delegated authority to larger management agencies, including the Great Lakes Indian Fish and Wildlife Commission and the Chippewa Ottawa Resource Authority. These tribal resource management organizations, which are membership organizations consisting of many individual tribes, take part or lead efforts in fisheries research, education, resource planning and management, habitat improvement, law enforcement, and stocking activities.

NATIONAL LEVEL

At the national level, resource management and environmental agencies collaborate with states, tribes, and each other to accomplish fisheries science and management goals. The Environmental Protection Agency, the U.S. Fish and Wildlife Service, the U.S. Geological Survey's Great Lakes Science Center, Environment and Climate Change Canada, and Fisheries and Oceans Canada are all active in research and monitoring, conservation, or restoration of habitats and native species, and decision-making about the Great Lakes.

Several branches of the National Oceanic and Atmospheric Administration (NOAA) are also involved, including the NOAA Great Lakes Environmental Research Laboratory and the Sea Grant programs in each of the Great Lakes states. Agencies such as U.S. Fish and Wildlife Service typically have specific authorities and roles related to Great Lakes fisheries that are assigned by Congress through federal legislation or may result from signed treaties with other sovereign nations, such as with tribes or Canada. That legislation includes: the Federal Endangered Species Act, the Lacey Act (relating to interstate commerce of species, including harmful species like Asian carp), and the Great Lakes Fish and Wildlife Restoration Act (providing for native species restoration programs).

HOW COLLABORATIVE MANAGEMENT WORKS

Because of the complexity, both in the biological and in the human systems in the Great Lakes region, the potential for conflict is great—as is the opportunity to cooperate to solve complicated fisheries issues.

To apply the most current scientific information to decision-making, Great Lakes scientists, fisheries managers, and representatives of many organizations come together through several binational commissions—the Great Lakes Fishery Commission, the International Joint Commission, and the Great Lakes Commission.

❖ **The Great Lakes Fishery Commission (GLFC)**, established in 1955 by the Convention on Great Lakes Fisheries, facilitates coordination and cooperation of fisheries research and management efforts among state, provincial, tribal, and federal resource management agencies of the Great Lakes. The commission has a specific and significant role in coordinating basin-wide control efforts of the invasive sea lamprey. Collaborating under a Joint Strategic Plan for Management of Great Lakes Fisheries, agency partners to the GLFC operate various advisory and technical committees, including lake committees, which support research and develop fish community objectives for each of the Great Lakes.

❖ The Joint Strategic Plan for Management of Great Lakes Fisheries is the primary mechanism by which all fishery management agencies on the Great Lakes collaborate across borders.

❖ Canada and the United States also cooperate under the **International Joint Commission (IJC)**, created under the Boundary Waters Treaty of 1909 to manage levels and flows of boundary waters and waters crossing the U.S.-

Agencies, universities, and other organizations often seek opportunities to engage citizens — youth and adults alike — in learning about fisheries science, management and issues in the Great Lakes.

MISG

Canadian boundary. The **treaty** also forbade activities on one side of the border that polluted water on the other side, which led to investigations resulting in a further agreement between Canada and the United States: the Great Lakes Water Quality Agreement of 1972 and 1978. The IJC has an impact on Great Lakes fisheries through its responsibility to manage Lake Superior and Lake Ontario levels and report on the U.S. and Canadian implementation of the Water Quality Agreement.

❖ The **Great Lakes Commission** was established in 1955 through the Great Lakes Basin Compact. The commission has an information integration, policy coordination, and advocacy role in the conservation and management of Great Lakes waters and related natural resources.

PROFESSIONAL ORGANIZATIONS

Researchers and management professionals communicate and share information through many professional societies such as the American Fisheries Society, the Society of Environmental Toxicology and Chemistry, and the International Association for Great Lakes Research. Sea Grant programs throughout the Great Lakes states also provide a network for managers, research scientists, and stakeholders to share information about the Great Lakes fishery and its management.

These cooperative organizations recognize the vast and shared nature of Great Lakes waters and fisheries resources. They also reflect successes in establishing agreements and partnerships among the states and between the two countries in coordinating information about, research on, and management of these resources. Fisheries management today engages a wide multitude of the region's fisheries stakeholders. Many stakeholder organizations are partners with fisheries managers in making decisions about Great Lakes fisheries.

FISHERY-DEPENDENT OPERATIONS

State- and provincial-licensed commercial fishermen have established professional organizations reflecting their industry interests, as have charter-fishing business operators. Tribal fishers coordinate through their respective intertribal research and management authorities. Commercial and tribal fishers and charter operators have a business stake in fisheries management, and they help collect data and keep records about fish resources to assist resource management agencies.

OHIO SEA GRANT

Smallmouth bass provide an important nearshore fishery in many of the Great Lakes.

SPORT ANGLERS

Sport anglers also provide information and assist Great Lakes fisheries managers. Concerns about declining fish populations and citizen interest in Great Lakes fisheries led to the formation of a variety of fishing and conservation organizations. Examples of national organizations include Trout Unlimited and B.A.S.S. (Bass Anglers Sportsman Society). Special interest regional, provincial and state groups also focus on the fisheries, including the Great Lakes Sport Fishing Council, the Ontario Federation of Anglers and Hunters, Michigan United Conservation Clubs, and many others throughout the region. These

BROWN TROUT
Salmo trutta

© EMILY S. DAMSTRA

organizations cooperate with fisheries agencies in resource management activities such as artificial reef and habitat improvement projects, hatchery and pen-rearing projects, and raising funds to sponsor fisheries research and conservation. Some also assist management agencies by volunteering their time for fisheries research, serving on advisory committees, collecting data, or responding to surveys.

MANAGEMENT FUNDING: WHERE DOES IT COME FROM?

Funding for fisheries management comes from several sources. About one-third of the funds come from sportfishing licenses, while about half is from government general funds from states, Ontario, and U.S. and Canadian federal governments. Another portion of funding comes from federal excise tax on fishing equipment and taxes on motorboat gasoline. In the United States these excise taxes are collected under the Federal Aid in Sport Fish Restoration Program, through what is commonly called the Wallop-Breaux Trust Fund and what was previously known as the Dingell-Johnson Act. More than $80 million (just over one-fifth of the U.S. total) of Wallop-Breaux revenues were returned to Great Lakes states in 2010 for their fisheries management programs. Altogether, tens of millions of dollars are spent on Great Lakes fisheries management each year. Billions of dollars are also spent each year on managing the entire Great Lakes basin for issues such as water quality and invasive species that directly and indirectly benefit fisheries. Most recently, the Great Lakes Restoration Initiative is a significant federal program, launched in 2010, supporting efforts to restore the health of the Great Lakes by investing in water quality, habitat restoration, fisheries, and ecosystem conservation efforts.

Tribal fishing on the Great Lakes.

MANAGEMENT CASE STUDY: TREATY FISHING

Fishing rights held in treaties are comparable to modern property rights, where an owner sells the land but retains certain rights such as an easement. Each treaty has its own language with respect to a tribe's relationships with state and federal governments, the public, and the fisheries resources. No two are alike, and, in the United States, many court cases have been heard on state and federal levels to interpret these treaties.

Today, the tribes manage and share information regarding the fishery among themselves through authorities such as the Great Lakes Indian Fish and Wildlife Commission and the Chippewa Ottawa Resource Authority, much the same way as the United States organizes fisheries management work through the Fish and Wildlife Service and state agencies.

Where treaty rights are affirmed, the tribes regulate licensing, biological management, and law enforcement over the tribal fishery. For example, tribal biologists in individual bands and at intertribal levels take responsibility for managing the fishers and the fishery resource itself. Tribal management authorities set regulations that establish license/permit requirements, fishing seasons, and harvest limits. Biologists also conduct Great Lakes fisheries research, such as annual fish stock assessments and surveys, monitor tribal

harvests, and map fish spawning habitat. Tribal fish hatcheries raise fish like walleye, lake trout, and coaster brook trout for stocking in the Great Lakes.

As equal partners, the tribal management authorities also cooperate with state, federal, and international fisheries management efforts, including participation on the lake committees and technical committees organized through the Joint Strategic Plan. However, given all of the other pressures on the fisheries, state and federal agencies remain responsible for biological management of the fisheries to ensure they are not depleted. Therefore, coordinated management of the Great Lakes is imperative.

1836 TREATY

Many Great Lakes tribes' rights to conduct fishing activities are derived from the terms of the 1836 treaty between the U.S. government and the Ottawa and Chippewa Indians. In the treaty the tribes gave up land in what became northern Wisconsin, Michigan's Upper Peninsula, and the upper Lower Peninsula, but retained the right to hunt and fish in the treaty-ceded territory, including the waters of southern Lake Superior and the northern portions of Lakes Michigan and Huron. These rights were reaffirmed in court cases during the 1970s and locked in by the 1985 Consent Order negotiated by the state of Michigan, the tribes, and the U.S. federal government.

Management of the Great Lakes is complex and there are many different stakeholders to consider. For example, here sport anglers share fishing waters near the Grand Haven pier.

That Consent Order, however, expired in 2000. After years of negotiations, the 20-year-long Consent Decree was signed in 2000. The decree is designed to eliminate tribal/state zones and to build a mutually beneficial agreement based on collaborative, science-based management of the fishery. The agreement focuses on allocation, management, and regulation of state and tribal fisheries in the waters covered by the 1836 treaty. Those participating in the agreement, for example, have committed to the **rehabilitation** of lake trout in Lakes Michigan and Huron and to work cooperatively to resolve issues.

NEW AGREEMENTS, LEARNING AND BUILDING FROM THE PAST

The year 2000 Consent Decree was the product of significant changes that occurred through the 15 years of the agreement between 1985 and 2000. The Little Traverse Bay Band and Little River Band, for example, are two tribes that gained federal recognition. Also, the fishery had changed, with fish populations fluctuating throughout the different fishing areas. Over time, the tribes have developed an effective system of regulation, conservation, and enforcement, becoming involved in every aspect of the fishery and working in tandem with the state and federal governments of the Great Lakes.

In 2020, this agreement is set to expire, and, guided by the federal court process, the parties to this agreement—tribal and state, commercial and recreational fisherman—will once again need to work together to negotiate a new agreement looking to the future. And once again, many ecological changes have also occurred since the latest agreement, including recovering lake trout populations, food web changes caused by invasive species, and resulting challenges these food web shifts have caused for recreationally important Chinook salmon and commercially valuable lake whitefish populations. This new agreement will consider many new biological changes that have occurred since the year 2000, including continually changing ecosystems and fisheries that look very different today, evolving science and management efforts, and changing fishing trends and social values regarding this shared fishery.

SUMMARY

ECOLOGY AND MANAGEMENT OF THE GREAT LAKES

Throughout this section, quite a bit of ground (or water) was covered—from why we study ecology to the principles and challenges of natural resource management. To summarize:

❖ Ecology helps us understand how natural systems work and allows us to better predict their responses to change.

❖ The Great Lakes support an abundance and diversity of life. Each lake's unique fish community is closely tied to its living (biotic) and nonliving (abiotic) lake components—collectively called the ecosystem.

❖ The Great Lakes provide a variety of species with different habitats—where fish can find all their life requirements: food, water, shelter, and space.

❖ Sunlight and nutrients are essential drivers of life in the Great Lakes, and the availability of both determines the level of life a particular area, river, or lake can support.

❖ Trophic zones, food chains, and food webs, the impact of non-native species, and fish life cycles and life requirements combine to provide a picture of the ecological life of the lakes.

❖ Learning about the Great Lakes web of life helps to increase our understanding about the history of the fishery, current fisheries issues, environmental quality issues, and possible challenges that may arise in the future.

❖ Understanding the biological basis for these fisheries is also important when decisions are made about allocating fisheries resources among various resource-user groups.

❖ Today, fisheries scientists and managers, as well as many other professionals and citizens, are involved in making fisheries management decisions.

The Great Lakes are a unique and important freshwater system. Grasping how the systems interact and making informed decisions about the management of this resource are critical.

TODAY'S GREAT LAKES FISHERIES

With such an abundance of resources in the Great Lakes, it is not surprising that fishing—commercial, recreational, and tribal—has been so instrumental in shaping the culture, economy, quality of life, and people in the region throughout history. Though it may change over time, that influence continues to shape the Great Lakes region today.

People continue to use Great Lakes **fishery** resources in many different ways. While sport and commercial fisheries are the major fisheries in the Great Lakes, subsistence and tribal fishing, as well as **aquaculture**, are also part of the landscape of the Great Lakes fishery. The Great Lakes offer a wide diversity of fish species and varying aquatic habitats where these fish are found and caught. The status of Great Lakes fisheries is also a reflection of the people of the region and how we interact with, manage, harvest, and use the fish resources found throughout the lakes.

The fisheries differ in significant ways, including

❖ Species sought
❖ Fishing techniques and gear used
❖ Management regulations
❖ Fishing culture and values
❖ Purpose

Yet the fisheries also share some important characteristics. For example, sportfishing is viewed primarily as recreation, while commercial fishing is viewed as a business venture. However, there is overlap. Sportfishing has an economic or "business" component. For example, many communities depend on tourism and the revenue generated in their areas through sportfishing and tournaments, in addition to commercial fishing businesses. Charter fishing operators offer sportfishing, but also run businesses and build and maintain markets for their services.

The commercial fishery is similar to the sport fishery in that it contributes to the culture, history, and sense of place in some areas of the Great Lakes. It can draw tourism to areas with strong cultural identities, for example old fishing villages like Fishtown in Leland, Michigan, or Rogers Street in Two Rivers,

Wisconsin. The most striking similarity between the fisheries is that they all depend upon a healthy Great Lakes ecosystem that supports a diversity of high-quality, healthy fish.

SPORT FISHING

RECREATIONAL ANGLING EFFORTS AND TRENDS

Fishing the Great Lakes means different things to different people. The type of recreational fishing trips pursued by individuals often depends on angler preference and the resources available to them. Some anglers invest in large boats and expensive tackle to target salmon in Lake Michigan or walleye in Lake Erie. Other anglers participate in the Great Lakes recreational fishery by casting from a local pier for yellow perch or smallmouth bass. Researchers and managers work to understand the

THE VALUABLE GREAT LAKES FISHERY

Great Lakes fish provide a variety of values:

ECOLOGICAL VALUE: Fisheries are a critical component of a healthy, functioning Great Lakes ecosystem. Fish support healthy wildlife populations, fill ecological niches that help maintain predator-prey relationships, and keep the Great Lakes ecosystem in balance.

ECONOMIC VALUE: Various studies and estimates place the total economic impact of the sport and commercial fisheries on the Great Lakes regional economy in excess of $1.5 billion per year—some indicating this fishery to be valued as high as $4 to $7 billion annually.

EDUCATIONAL VALUE: Fisheries provide educational opportunities that encourage people to learn about ecosystems and their processes. For example, the lakes provide hands-on

MARY BOHLING, MBSG

opportunities for people in the Great Lakes region to learn about aquatic systems and food webs.

FOOD AND NUTRITIONAL VALUE: The variety of fish found in the Great Lakes provides people with many different food options. They are high in omega-3 fatty acids and are an excellent source of protein with less fat and fewer calories than other meats.

FUTURE VALUE: A sustainable Great Lakes fishery helps ensure the long-term protection of Great Lakes natural resources, allowing future generations to connect with the lakes and the environment.

HISTORICAL AND CULTURAL VALUE: Many commercial fishing families, including state-, province-, and tribe-licensed fishing operators, maintain a way of life similar to their ancestors. Others learn about the history of Great Lakes fisheries by visiting historic fishing villages and Great Lakes museums. The history and culture provide depth to the Great Lakes identity and are linked irrevocably to other values like education, economy, and stewardship.

SOCIAL VALUE: Many people enjoy fishing and related activities, participate in fishing organizations, and attend events such as fishing festivals or tournaments. The Great Lakes are at the heart of the region's sense of place—an increasingly important aspect of keeping communities healthy and vibrant.

---

diversity of preferences and interests of Great Lakes anglers. This understanding of angler values and attitudes is necessary to help predict the future demand for fisheries resources and to allocate the fisheries resources available today.

Surveys conducted every five years by the U.S. and Canadian governments—though not perfect—are good indicators of participation by anglers in Great Lakes fisheries. A recent U.S. Fish and Wildlife surveys show that approximately 1.7 million anglers spent nearly 20 million days fishing U.S. waters of the Great Lakes in 2011. In Canadian waters of the Great Lakes, nearly 440,000 anglers fished more than 4.5 million days in 2010. According to combined license sales records for Great Lakes states,

nearly 8 million people in total purchased fishing licenses. Comparing these two data surveys, one can estimate that approximately 21 percent of licensed anglers in these states, more than one in five, are directly participating in Great Lakes fishing activities.

The surveys show that recreational fishing is most popular on Lake Erie and Lake Michigan. Combined data from both the U.S. and Canadian surveys indicate that 38 percent of all Great Lakes anglers concentrate their efforts on Lake Erie, while 25 percent concentrate their efforts on Lake Michigan.

Lakes Huron and Ontario have much smaller fractions of the total number of Great Lakes anglers—16 and 9 percent

respectively. Despite being the largest lake, Lake Superior also receives very little angling pressure—9 percent. The remaining portion of anglers target Lake St. Clair, the St. Lawrence River, and tributaries to the Great Lakes.

SPORT FISH TARGETS

The Great Lakes are home to many sport fish species. The diversity of fish species spans the spectrum: from warmer-water species of the shallower bays and nearshore areas such as bluegill, bass, yellow perch, walleye, pike, and muskellunge to cold-water species such as lake trout or salmon found in deeper, open waters.

FISHING METHODS

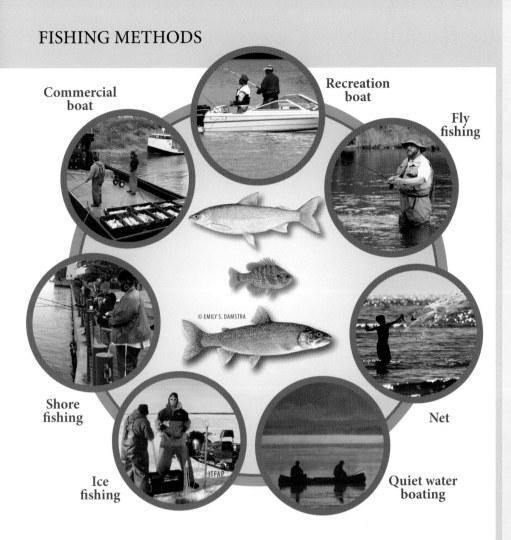

Commercial boat · Recreation boat · Fly fishing · Net · Quiet water boating · Ice fishing · Shore fishing

© EMILY S. DAMSTRA

The methods anglers use to take Great Lakes sport fish vary widely by

❖ Geographic location
❖ Particular species targeted
❖ Access (e.g., fishing from shore or pier, wading, boat fishing, ice fishing

Variability in aquatic habitats gives Great Lakes anglers opportunities to pursue an array of fish species. To increase their chances of success, Great Lakes anglers pay close attention to the seasonal patterns, life requirements, and preferred habitats of the species they target.

POPULAR CATCHES
WALLEYE AND PERCH

When we consider accessibility, it is not surprising that the most popular species sought by U.S. and Canadian anglers in the Great Lakes are yellow perch and walleye. Both can be easily caught from the shore, piers, and small boats along the coastline—and they are good table fare. Areas of the Great Lakes that are typically dominated by yellow perch and walleye (e.g., western Lake Erie, Saginaw Bay in Lake Huron) also have high densities of people along the coastlines. The combination of these factors results in significant numbers of anglers targeting these species.

BASS, PAN FISH, AND SMELT

Other highly valued sport fish include largemouth bass, smallmouth bass, and panfish such as sunfish, crappie, and rock bass. Their abundance and vicinity to shore make them a popular choice for anglers of all ages. Seasonal runs also expose shore-bound anglers to different species of fish. Smelt are caught in the shallow water with dip nets during spring spawning runs, for instance.

TROUT AND SALMON

Cold-water species such as lake trout and Pacific salmon (e.g., Chinook salmon, coho salmon, steelhead) are also highly sought after by anglers. Because considerable investment in equipment—large boats, electronics, tackle—is

ANGLER TRENDS: UPS AND DOWNS

Numbers of sport anglers in U.S. and Canadian waters have significantly declined since surveys were first administered in the early 1990s. The number of Great Lakes anglers has dropped by around 35 percent in U.S. waters (down from 2.6 million anglers in 1991) and 56 percent in Canadian waters (down from 1 million anglers in 1990). However, more recent surveys from both countries have reported stabilizing trends in fishing participation during the past decade—angler numbers have remained stable in Canada since 2005 and even slightly increased in the United States since 2006.

One fear is that fewer people participating in outdoor activities will result in less interest in natural resource conservation. However, many anglers and angling groups have recognized the importance of introducing the next generation to fishing and have made concerted efforts to get young people interested in fishing and natural resources. Giving people a reason to love the Great Lakes is an important step toward building a citizenry that has a stake in protecting the lakes in the future. Although current angler numbers remain greatly reduced from the early 1990s, these stabilizing and even increasing trends offer hope for Great Lakes fishing futures.

GREAT LAKES SPORT FISHING PARTICIPATION

U.S. GREAT LAKES ANGLERS BY STATE

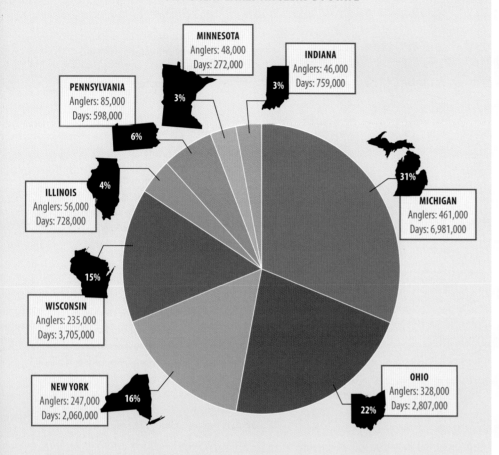

MINNESOTA
Anglers: 48,000
Days: 272,000

INDIANA
Anglers: 46,000
Days: 759,000

PENNSYLVANIA
Anglers: 85,000
Days: 598,000

ILLINOIS
Anglers: 56,000
Days: 728,000

MICHIGAN
Anglers: 461,000
Days: 6,981,000

WISCONSIN
Anglers: 235,000
Days: 3,705,000

NEW YORK
Anglers: 247,000
Days: 2,060,000

OHIO
Anglers: 328,000
Days: 2,807,000

The chart shows the number of anglers from each state that fish the Great Lakes, the number of days they spent fishing the Great Lakes, and the proportion of Great Lakes anglers from each state.

Source: U.S. Dept. of Interior, U.S. Fish and Wildlife Service and U.S. Dept. of Commerce, 2006, National Survey of Fishing, Hunting and Wildlife-Associated Recreation.

U.S. WATERS OF THE GREAT LAKES

Lake	Anglers	Days Spent Angling
Erie	639,000	8,451,000
Michigan	413,000	2,585,000
Ontario	143,000	2,214,000
Tributaries	159,000	1,254,000
Huron	262,000	4,410,000
Superior	147,000	1,527,000

Source: U.S. Fish and Wildlife Service, 2011.

CANADIAN WATERS OF THE GREAT LAKES

Lake	Anglers	Days Spent Angling
Huron	136,683	1,305,150
Ontario/ St. Lawrence	156,291	1,746,821
Erie	89,792	843,770
St. Clair	34,649	484,133
Superior	22,361	148,328

Source: Ontario Ministery of Natural Resources, Canada, 2010.

FISH, ANGLERS, AND DAYS SPENT TARGETING SPECIFIC SPECIES

U.S. WATERS OF THE GREAT LAKES

Species	Anglers	Days Spent Angling
Walleye	584,000	5,612,000
Yellow Perch	497,000	5,805,000
Salmon	379,000	5,297,000
Lake Trout	215,000	3,573,000
Bass	559,000	4,830,000
Steelhead (Rainbow Trout)	198,000	3,092,000
Pike, Muskellunge	224,000	2,271,000
Other species	179,000	1,722,000
Other Trout	97,000	700,000

Source: U.S. Fish and Wildlife Service, 2011.

CANADIAN WATERS OF THE GREAT LAKES

Species	Fish Caught
Yellow Perch	8,377,163
Bass	4,062,310
Sunfish, Crappie, Rock Bass	3,632,756
Walleye	1,554,883
Steelhead (Rainbow Trout)	1,017,875
Pike, Muskellunge	796,839
Chinook, Coho Salmon	566,909
Lake Trout, Splake	218,030
Other fish	1,554,689

Source: Ontario Ministery of Natural Resources, Canada, 2010.

THROUGH THE ICE

In the Great Lakes region, the winters can be long and cold. For many anglers, though, the annual freeze represents opportunity. While data on ice-fishing participation and its economic contribution are not comprehensive, the numerous shantytowns, season-specific tournaments, and community of anglers that crop up during the winter months seem to indicate a vibrant industry.

While ice fishing shares some similarities to open-water fishing—like

MATTHEW R. STANGIS

using bottom contours, weed lines, and other fish-attracting features to target fish—it also has its own unique characteristics. Ice fishing offers

STACY A. NIEDZWIECKI

❖ Access to areas that are usually weedy or off limits to anglers without boats during the summer.

❖ A chance to catch different species, with some deepwater species—including lake trout, whitefish, and burbot—moving into shallower waters to spawn during the colder weather months.

❖ The use of different equipment and techniques. Ice anglers can use tip-ups (set lines that pop up a flag when fish bite), hook and line, spears, and different bait and lures to catch fish.

❖ An opportunity to get outside during the cold months of the year.

required to fish offshore waters of the Great Lakes, a substantial charter-fishing industry has been established to meet the demand of anglers pursuing these fish species. The thrill of catching a fish in excess of 20 pounds has drawn anglers from near and far, bolstering tourism in many port cities.

Seasonal spawning migrations also give anglers opportunities to catch trophy salmon in Great Lakes tributaries without investing in expensive boating equipment. Steelhead, for example, are targeted during the spring and fall as they move to and from the lakes to rivers and streams. For many anglers, this is an affordable and attractive alternative compared to fishing offshore waters. As a result, the numbers of salmon and lake-run trout harvested in rivers and streams are often similar to the numbers harvested in offshore waters.

UNIQUE OPPORTUNITIES

There are many areas within the Great Lakes that have become extremely popular because of the unique fishing opportunities that exist, for example, the relatively shallow and accessible Lake St. Clair and the Detroit River. The muskellunge, or muskie, is often referred to as the "fish of 10,000 casts," and the high catch rates in Lake St. Clair and the Detroit River have made them famous locations in the world of muskie fishing. For anglers who are able to pattern the muskie, it is not uncommon to hook 10 or more fish in a single day.

Another area that has fantastic fishing opportunities for a wide range of species is the St. Marys River, which connects Lake Superior to Lake Huron. All species of salmon found in the Great Lakes, including Atlantic and pink

salmon, make impressive runs in the river. Fighting these powerful fish in the swift currents of the St. Marys has made the river legendary among fly-fishing fanatics. Other regions are also known for their access to great fishing along the Great Lakes coasts, including more urban regions like the Greater Chicago area and Milwaukee.

UNDERRATED SPECIES

Growing numbers of anglers find sport in catching less popular species, commonly referred to as rough fish. Bowfin, gar, common carp, freshwater drum (a.k.a. sheephead), bigmouth buffalo, and other varieties of suckers are all examples of species that provide an appealing challenge to anglers. With the right motivation, knowledge, and equipment, catching just about any fish can be fun and engaging.

UNIQUE TO THE GREAT LAKES

Great Lakes salmon and trout tournaments substantially differ from the bass tournaments that account for the majority of North American tournaments. Great Lakes salmon and trout anglers use different vessels and fishing gear, compete as teams instead of individuals, and typically keep their catch. In bass tournaments, catch-and-release has become the standard, and this has generated intense scrutiny of handling procedures and other factors in postrelease mortality.

Great Lakes tournaments, particularly Lake Michigan tournaments, often target short-lived Pacific salmon

that are maintained, in part, by stocking programs. This creates less of a concern regarding the mortality associated with tournaments, and at events, contestants are encouraged to donate their catch to a food bank or local charity with the assistance of tournament organizers. Proceeds from Great Lakes tournaments are often used to fund community projects or local charities, and many are coupled with youth events and entertainment that contribute to a festive atmosphere.

PHOTOS: DAN O'KEEFE, MISG

ECONOMIC AND CULTURAL IMPACT

The sportfishing industry has brought new life to many Great Lakes coastal towns. Some communities have developed their shorelines with sport anglers in mind. Bait and tackle shops and other support industries are commonplace. Some develop and build fishing gear, such as lures that are marketed and used worldwide. Fishing gear, such as the downrigger, was originally developed in this region to meet the needs of Great Lakes anglers and is now used in many different areas. Sportfishing contributes to the economy and regional identity of many communities in the Great Lakes region in many ways.

DOLLARS AND SENSE

Accounting for every dollar spent on fishing-related activities in the Great Lakes is an impossible task, making it extremely difficult to determine the total economic contribution of sportfishing to the Great Lakes region. Economists

have generated estimates of absolute value ranging from $1.5 billion to greater than $7 billion (U.S. dollars). Despite the disparity between these estimates, it is important to recognize that the sportfishing economy is extremely important to communities around the Great Lakes.

Both U.S. and Canadian surveys suggest that Great Lakes anglers, on average, spend more than $1,100 each year on trip and equipment expenditures for Great Lakes fishing. A large proportion of this figure can be attributed to the costs associated with owning and maintaining a boat. According to the 2011 U.S. survey, approximately 40 percent of Great Lakes anglers spend an average of $432 annually for boating (e.g., launching, mooring, storage, insurance, pump-out fees, fuel, etc.). Anglers also spend considerable amounts on transportation, food, and lodging—spending an average of $375 each year on transportation and accommodations for Great Lakes fishing trips.

The mentioned costs are necessary to get the anglers on the water, yet are not directly related to catching fish. On average, Great Lakes anglers spend an additional $134 on average for fishing equipment, such as rods, reels, and tackle each year.

LURE-ING VISITORS: TOURISM AND CONTESTS

The Great Lakes region has taken on a sportfishing identity, and tourism has been touted as an economic development opportunity. Many coastal communities have organized popular fishing festivals and sportfishing tournaments to attract visitors and to celebrate their Great Lakes fisheries resource heritage. Even during a time of declining participation in Great Lakes fishing, interest in tournament fishing remains high.

Tournaments, of course, attract anglers who compete in the events, but they can also appeal to nonanglers who enjoy the atmosphere. Tournament anglers and those who travel with them spend an average of $1,463 per team, in addition to entry fees. A recent study on fishing tournaments by Michigan Sea Grant and Michigan State University's Center for Economic Analysis found that team spending at the 16 events in Michigan, Indiana, and Wisconsin of the 2009 Lake Michigan Tournament Trail generated $852,113 and 21,386 employment hours in ports that hosted tournaments.

For many in coastal communities, the fisheries not only offer recreational opportunities and economic benefits, but also help define one's sense of place and personal connections with the Great Lakes.

CHARTER FISHING

Given the costs associated with owning a boat and specialized equipment, some anglers opt to hire guides or "charter" a captain to experience Great Lakes fishing. Approximately 10 percent of Great Lakes anglers employ the services of charters each year, with trips for salmon and walleye being most popular.

The cost of a guided fishing trip is often in the range of $400 to $600 for a group of four to six anglers. The charter industry is comprised of many skilled sport anglers who have created businesses serving as fishing guides. One study estimated 1,746 Great Lakes charter businesses provided over 93,000 charter-fishing trips for paying customers in 2002. The information indicates an overall decline in the number of professional charter captains from a previous 1994 study; however, remaining captains were making more trips.

The charter industry, while not as large as in the past, continues to provide productive economic returns to the Great Lakes region. A study on charter fishing released in 2011 by Michigan Sea Grant and Michigan State University's Center for Economic Analysis found that charter fishing generated an average of 465,417 employment hours per year and brought in an average of $19.8 million each year over the course of the last 20 years. In 2009, each fishing party spent an average of $1,263. Overall, coastal communities

benefited from charter fishing—with gross sales of at least $14.9 million and 343,845 labor hours. Charter fishing also drew out-of-state tourists, who booked 2,995 excursions throughout the year and generated at least $2.1 million in labor income for Michigan workers.

GREAT LAKES, GREAT TIMES

More than 4 million recreational boating vessels are registered in the region, around 911,000 boaters enjoying the Great Lakes. These Great Lakes boaters spend an estimated $3.8 billion annually on boating trip, boats and equipment. Many also take advantage of the region's Great Lakes–related natural resources, including more than 10.7 million anglers, 4.9 million hunters, and 22.9 million bird-watchers in this region each year.

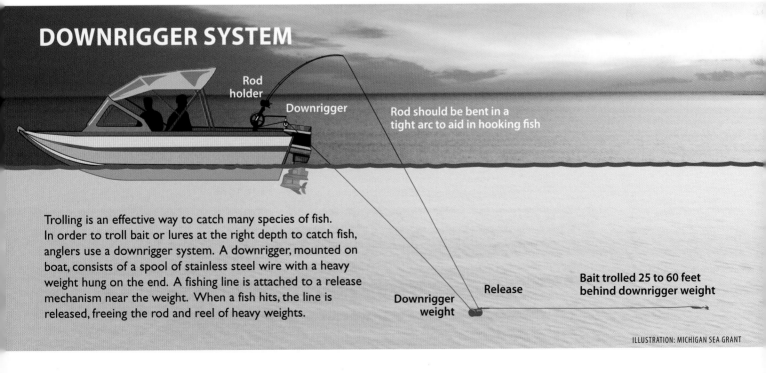

DOWNRIGGER SYSTEM

Rod holder

Downrigger

Rod should be bent in a tight arc to aid in hooking fish

Trolling is an effective way to catch many species of fish. In order to troll bait or lures at the right depth to catch fish, anglers use a downrigger system. A downrigger, mounted on boat, consists of a spool of stainless steel wire with a heavy weight hung on the end. A fishing line is attached to a release mechanism near the weight. When a fish hits, the line is released, freeing the rod and reel of heavy weights.

Downrigger weight

Release

Bait trolled 25 to 60 feet behind downrigger weight

ILLUSTRATION: MICHIGAN SEA GRANT

GREAT LAKES COMMERCIAL HARVEST (2015)

TOTAL COMMERCIAL HARVEST BY LAKE

LAKE	U.S. Total lbs.	U.S. Value	Canada Total lbs.	Canada Value (US$)*	Grand Total lbs.	Grand Total Value*
Erie	5,669,670	$5,645,447	23,255,006	$23,742,604	28,924,676	$29,388,051
Huron	2,021,941	$3,568,980	2,187,056	$2,756,940	4,208,997	$6,325,920
Michigan	3,738,142	$6,202,768	--	--	3,738,142	$6,202,768
Superior	3,216,623	$3,634,622	646,105	$474,446	3,862,728	$4,109,068
Ontario	47,395	$111,115	366,060	$388,239	413,455	$499,354
TOTALS	**14,693,771**	**$19,162,932**	**26,454,227**	**$27,362,229**	**41,147,998**	**$46,525,161**

Source: U.S. Geological Survey, Great Lakes Fishery Commission, Ontario Commercial Fisheries Association, Ontario Ministry of Natural Resources. Catch data from 2015. *U.S. currency values

TOTAL POUNDS HARVESTED BY LAKE

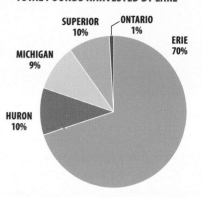

SUPERIOR 10% · ONTARIO 1% · ERIE 70% · MICHIGAN 9% · HURON 10%

TOTAL COMMERCIAL HARVEST OF TOP SPECIES

SPECIES	U.S. Total lbs.	U.S. Value	Canada Total lbs.	Canada Value (US$)*	Grand Total lbs.	Grand Total Value*
Yellow Perch	1,426,806	$3,915,458	4,626,329	$10,743,945	6,053,135	$14,659,403
Lake Whitefish	6,230,618	$10,864,596	1,814,870	$2,230,236	8,045,488	$13,094,832
Walleye	42,095	$114,533	4,873,625	$9,562,437	4,915,720	$9,676,970
White Bass	982,285	$695,318	3,844,636	$2,004,798	4,826,921	$2,700,116
Rainbow Smelt	34,959	$34,043	8,057,042	$1,447,750	8,092,001	$1,481,793
White Perch	689,197	$326,111	1,931,473	$742,887	2,620,670	$1,068,998
Cisco (Lake Herring)	1,201,380	$773,841	396,489	$236,592	1,597,869	$1,010,433
Lake Trout	1,017,743	$782,054	406,116	$167,418	1,423,859	$949,472
Chubs (Bloater)	178,102	$475,309	3,685	$6,909	181,787	$482,218
Freshwater Drum	1,061,105	$245,540	241,506	$33,852	1,302,611	$279,392
Channel Catfish	612,563	$243,517	50,064	$13,027	662,627	$256,544
Buffalo	327,458	$178,310	--	$0	327,458	$178,310

Table includes 98% of total Great Lakes harvest by value (96% of total harvest in pounds). Other species commercially harvested in lesser amounts and values include: bigmouth buffalo, common carp, quillback, bullhead, panfish, gizzard shad, goldfish, suckers, northern pike, alewife, burbot, Pacific salmon, and round whitefish. Source: USGS, GLFC, OCFA, OMNR, Upper Great Lakes Management Unit for Lake Huron. Catch data from 2015. *U.S. currency values.

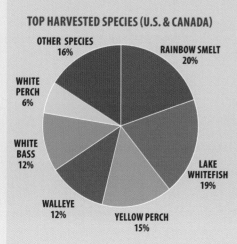

TOP HARVESTED SPECIES (U.S. & CANADA)

OTHER SPECIES 16% · RAINBOW SMELT 20% · WHITE PERCH 6% · WHITE BASS 12% · WALLEYE 12% · YELLOW PERCH 15% · LAKE WHITEFISH 19%

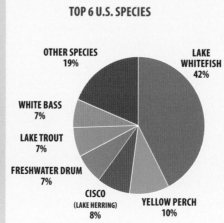

TOP 6 U.S. SPECIES

OTHER SPECIES 19% · WHITE BASS 7% · LAKE TROUT 7% · FRESHWATER DRUM 7% · CISCO (LAKE HERRING) 8% · YELLOW PERCH 10% · LAKE WHITEFISH 42%

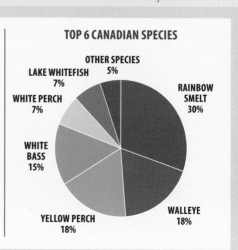

TOP 6 CANADIAN SPECIES

OTHER SPECIES 5% · LAKE WHITEFISH 7% · WHITE PERCH 7% · WHITE BASS 15% · YELLOW PERCH 18% · WALLEYE 18% · RAINBOW SMELT 30%

By pounds harvested. Catch data from 2015.

WALLEYE
Sander vitreus

© EMILY S. DAMSTRA

CHANGING INDUSTRY

From 1990 to 2009, trips booked by out-of-state customers decreased by 34 percent and trips booked by customers from the Detroit and Flint metro areas decreased by 75 percent. Yet trips booked by customers from other regions of Michigan increased by 15 percent.

The number of charter excursions taken annually on each lake has fluctuated through the years. Lake Huron experienced a 49 percent decline in trips from 2002 to 2009 as the Chinook salmon fishery collapsed. This loss of effort represents a loss of $1.46 million in economic output and 51,429 labor hours in 2009 alone, with most of the decline in central and southern ports. However, over the same period, economic impacts to Saginaw Bay ports increased by $355,197 in output as walleye fishing improved.

A bright spot is that trip satisfaction was high across the state and was most influenced by the hospitality of the captain and mate and the comfort of the vessel, in addition to the number of fish caught.

While the Michigan example may not be completely transferable to other Great Lakes states and Canada, the overall trends observed in Michigan may be indicative of changes in the charter-fishing industry throughout the region.

SPORT FISHING MANAGEMENT

As stated throughout this section, the recreational sport fisheries are highly valuable to communities and economies in the Great Lakes region. As a result, fisheries managers are charged with a task of balancing public values and use of today's fishery, while also ensuring resource stewardship and sustainability for future generations.

Without management, the Great Lakes sport fishery would look quite different than it does today. The recovery of the fishery from its low point in the 1960s to the fishery that now exists is remarkable. Managers and economists agree that the following have supported the recovery of the recreational fishery:

❖ Size limits
❖ Creel limits
❖ Seasons
❖ Gear restrictions
❖ Control of invasive sea lampreys

The diversity of sport fish populations within the Great Lakes provides a multitude of opportunities for anglers and helps reduce angler pressure on individual species. Successful management of the sport fishery can increase both angler participation and economic value from these fisheries, while retaining ecological health by reducing fishing pressure or overharvest of fish populations. As a bonus, successful and transparent management can increase stewardship awareness among those who fish.

Effective sport fish management takes into account not just the fishery side of the equation, but the human side as well. Fisheries managers must understand ecological and biological conditions of sport fish populations, such as fish abundance or age structure of the population, as well as the health and condition of the habitats required to sustain these fish. Yet it is equally important to understand the number and demographics of anglers using the fishery, angler participation (e.g., numbers of anglers and days fishing), and harvest trends (e.g., species targeted and catch rates). Considering multiple factors allows fishery managers to see the complete scope of work set before them, leading to better management.

COMMERCIAL FISHING

Commercial fishing, when managed properly, can provide an important and sustainable Great Lakes food source—and can help support a lake-based economy. Many people who do not fish may still enjoy a meal of Great Lakes fish. Commercial fisheries help provide food fish, like walleye, for these markets, and they capitalize on other fishery resources.

For example, they seek out other fish species that the average sport, charter, or tournament anglers do not usually target, such as whitefish or carp.

COMMERCIAL FISH SPECIES AND ECONOMIC VALUE TO REGION

Commercial fishing in the Great Lakes today continues to provide productive returns from the fishery resources. In 2015:

❖ The estimated total catch by state- and treaty-licensed commercial fishermen in U.S. waters of the Great Lakes was nearly 14.7 million pounds.

❖ The landed (dockside) value of this harvest was estimated at nearly $19.2 million.

❖ Canadian commercial operators harvested nearly 26.5 million pounds with a **landed value** of approximately $27.4 million.

❖ The processed (retail) value of these commercial harvests is significantly

higher than the landed (wholesale) value. For example, in Canada, the **processed value** of the commercial harvest is estimated to be at least five times more than the landed value, as processed fish are filleted, deboned, and packaged for sale.

The most profitable species landed in U.S. and Canadian waters in 2015 were yellow perch, lake whitefish, and walleye.

❖ The landed value of these three species in U.S. and Canadian waters was estimated at nearly $14.9 million and over $22.5 million, respectively.

❖ These three species also constitute more than 46 percent of the region's total catch by weight, with more than 19 million pounds of fish harvested in 2015.

❖ White bass, rainbow smelt, white perch, cisco (lake herring), lake trout, and bloater (chubs) are among the other primary catches in the region.

The following provides an overview of the commercial fishery on each lake according to 2015 records. All dollar references are U.S. currency in 2015 dollars.

LAKE SUPERIOR

Lake whitefish was the most harvested and most profitable fish from Lake Superior waters in 2015. It comprised around 47 percent of the total Lake Superior commercial harvest (1.8 million pounds) and returned a dockside value of over $2.4 million. Ciscoes were the second most harvested species in Lake Superior due to demand for cisco roe (caviar) in European markets. Commercial operators were paid more than $982,000 for their harvest of over 1.5 million pounds of cisco from both U.S. and Canadian waters. Lake trout (lean and siscowet) were also harvested from Lake Superior. Although much less than whitefish and cisco harvests, over 348,000 pounds of lake trout were caught with a dockside value of nearly $230,000.

LAKE MICHIGAN

Lake Michigan produces 38 percent of total lake whitefish harvested across the Great Lakes. In 2015, commercial operators harvested nearly 3.1 million pounds of lake whitefish with a dockside return of approximately $5.4 million. Lake trout and bloater (chubs) were also important contributors to the total commercial harvest in Lake Michigan. Over 443,000 pounds of lake trout and 94,000 pounds of chubs were harvested in Lake Michigan, which amounted to a dockside value of $332,000 and $288,000, respectively. Yellow perch also rated among the list of top species with a minimal 55,000 pounds worth $138,000 harvested from Lake Michigan.

LAKE HURON

Similar to Michigan, Lake Huron is known for its lake whitefish production, with nearly 2.9 million pounds harvested (more than one-third of the total Great Lakes

WILD CAUGHT AND CLOSE TO HOME

The Great Lakes whitefish has quietly sustained people in the Great Lakes for thousands of years. Recognizing the potential to promote a great native species, Michigan Sea Grant facilitated a marketing program aimed at bolstering the local fishing economy and creating a sustainable market for the fish. Since the initial effort, a cooperative of whitefish fishermen has formed, the price per pound of Great Lakes whitefish has gone up, and awareness and demand for the native species has increased. The effort culminated in the 2010 cookbook, *Wild Caught and Close to Home: Selecting and Preparing Great Lakes Whitefish*, produced by Michigan Sea Grant.

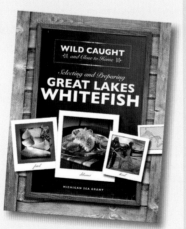

Other efforts to promote eating Great Lakes seafood include Michigan Sea Grant's Catch and Cook program, where select restaurants prepare anglers' catches, an annual Michigan Seafood Summit, and *Freshwater Feasts*, a blog all about cooking and eating Great Lakes seafood.

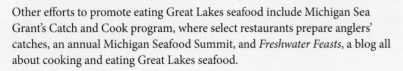

THE LIFE OF A COMMERCIAL FISHERMAN

Rarely glamorous and often challenging, the life of the commercial fisherman is similar to that of the family farmer. The work is hard and sometimes dangerous and the income uncertain and variable. The commercial fishing operation is frequently a family venture, with information, techniques, and equipment passed on through generations.

In many cases, family members take part in all aspects of the business,

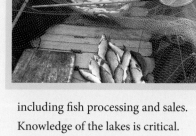

J. GUNDERSON

including fish processing and sales. Knowledge of the lakes is critical. Commercial operators often have detailed understanding of depth, current, substrate, landmarks and navigation, fish movements and subpopulations, and weather patterns. They are also skilled mechanics and craftsmen, which allows them to do a majority of their own boat and net repairs.

While various technological advancements have aided the commercial fisher in recent years, it is still a time-consuming and difficult occupation. Despite the challenging lifestyle, many speak of how fishing and the lakes are "in their blood."

whitefish harvest) in 2015. Nearly 1.5 million pounds of lake whitefish caught in U.S. waters of Lake Huron had a dockside value of nearly $3 million, while more than 1.4 million pounds caught in Canadian waters had a dockside value of $1.8 million. Although lake whitefish dominates the total harvest, Lake Huron commercial operators get the best price for their catches of walleye and yellow perch. Over 294,000 pounds of yellow perch and nearly 182,000 pounds of walleye—mostly caught in Canadian waters—received a dockside return of over $628,000 and $381,000, respectively. Over 630,000 pounds of lake trout are also harvested from Lake Huron, valued at nearly $388,000.

LAKE ERIE

Although Lake Erie is smallest of the Great Lakes, it boasts the greatest commercial harvest. In fact, there are more fish harvested from Lake Erie than in all of the other Great Lakes combined. With the majority of the catch coming from Canadian waters, Lake Erie commercial fishermen harvested over 28.9 million pounds of fish in 2015—

over 70 percent of the total Great Lakes commercial harvest that year. Yellow perch and walleye are the most lucrative species, as Canadian commercial operators received $10.1 million for their catch of yellow perch (5.6 million pounds) and $9.2 million for their catch of walleye (4.7 million pounds). Over 8 million pounds of smelt were harvested using trawls in Canadian waters of Lake Erie, yet the dockside value of this species was only around 18 cents per pound. Other species of importance to Canadian commercial operators on Lake Erie included white bass, white perch, freshwater drum, catfish, and lake whitefish.

American commercial operators are not allowed to harvest walleye in U.S. waters of Lake Erie because of their significance to sportfishing. There is, however, a substantial trap net fishery for yellow perch, which has resulted in significant perch landings. Nearly 1.3 million pounds of yellow perch caught in U.S. waters of Lake Erie brought a dockside return of nearly $3.6 million in 2015. Other species of importance to U.S.

commercial operators include freshwater drum, white bass, white perch, channel catfish, buffalo, and carp.

LAKE ONTARIO

The commercial fishery in Lake Ontario is the smallest in the Great Lakes, with only slightly more than 499,000 pounds of fish harvested in 2015. The harvest of over 46,000 pounds of yellow perch constituted more than 98 percent of the reported U.S. commercial catch on the lake. In Canadian waters of Lake Ontario, 131,000 pounds of lake whitefish and 52,000 pounds of yellow perch were the predominant species caught. These two species account for 50 percent of the total Canadian harvest, and sunfish, walleye, brown bullhead, northern pike, and freshwater drum are among other species caught.

TOOLS OF THE TRADE: NETS

The contribution of the state-, province-, and tribe-licensed commercial fisheries in the Great Lakes region today is substantial. Many people in the basin

GILL NET

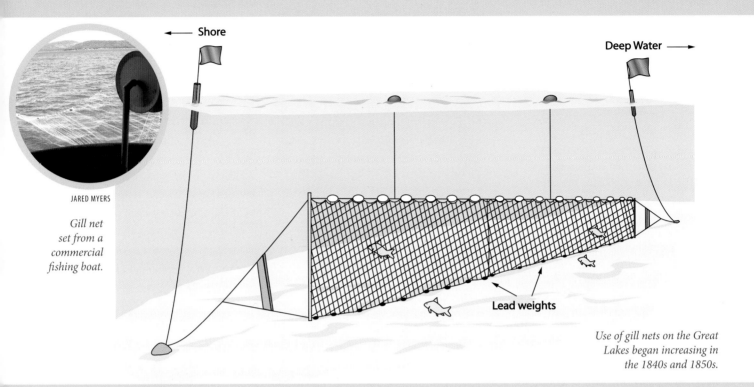

Shore ←

Deep Water →

JARED MYERS

Gill net set from a commercial fishing boat.

Lead weights

Use of gill nets on the Great Lakes began increasing in the 1840s and 1850s.

TRAP NET

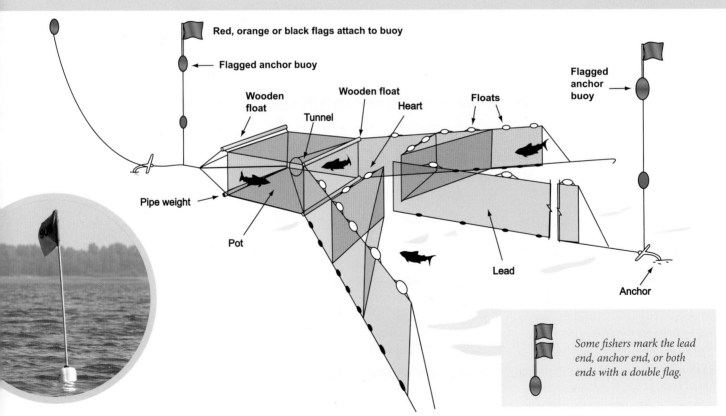

Red, orange or black flags attach to buoy

Flagged anchor buoy

Wooden float

Wooden float

Tunnel

Heart

Floats

Flagged anchor buoy

Pipe weight

Pot

Lead

Anchor

A trap net flag.

Some fishers mark the lead end, anchor end, or both ends with a double flag.

ILLUSTRATIONS: MICHIGAN SEA GRANT

Commercial fishers retrieve whitefish from a trap net. Trap nets are increasingly used in parts of Lakes Michigan, Huron, and Superior.

depend on commercial fishing for their livelihood. Most commercial fishing in the region is done with trap nets, pound nets, or gill nets, although trawls are used in certain places.

GILL NETS

Monofilament gill nets are an example of extremely efficient gear used throughout the Great Lakes. They are size-selective, meaning panels of the gill net are designed to allow fish to swim partially through square mesh before the girth of the fish causes it to become entangled. Smaller fish swim through the nets without getting caught. Bottom-set gill nets are used to capture demersal or benthic species, while canned (suspended) gill nets are used to target fish in the pelagic zone.

Enclosed vessels, called gill net tugs, allow commercial operators to lift their nets during all but the very worst weather. Gill netting gained a negative reputation in some parts of the Great Lakes due to the low survival of unintended captures, a phenomenon known as bycatch. However, most commercial operators work diligently to limit the harvest of unmarketable sizes

and nontarget species by changing the **mesh size** and location of their nets.

It is common for jurisdictions to limit the total footage of gill net that can be set under a single license, often based on expected catch per foot of net set by fishers. As a result, many commercial operators use a combination of gill nets and trap nets within a single year.

TRAP NETS

Trap nets are designed to funnel fish into a box net—or trap—where they can still swim freely prior to being retrieved. The advantage of trap nets allows undesirable fish, due to size or species, to be released without harm once the net is retrieved. Entrapment gear, including both hoop and trap nets, have the advantage that fish survive well for live sale markets. Trap nets can be extremely large with the leads reaching greater than 1,000 feet long and 50 feet high. The cumbersome nets require specialized boats with large, open platforms so operators can work the net.

OTHER NETS, OTHER SPECIES

Although gill nets and trap nets are the predominant capture methods used in the Great Lakes, they are not the only ones used for commercial harvest. For example, trawls—nets pulled behind boats—are used to harvest rainbow smelt in Canadian waters of Lake Erie and in certain regions of Lake Michigan. Hoop nets are deployed primarily in Lake Ontario for harvest of bullhead and sunfish. Even small pound nets, similar to the modern trap net, are still used in the Duluth-Superior harbor on Lake Superior for harvesting rainbow smelt during their spring run.

COMMERCIAL FISHERY MANAGEMENT

Overfishing is occurring in many parts of the world, and as a result, there is a growing awareness of and demand for sustainably caught fish. Commercially caught fish from the Great Lakes are touted as an excellent alternative to

FISHTOWN HONORS PAST, PRESENT, AND FUTURE OF COMMERCIAL FISHING

Fishtown in Leland, Michigan, is one of the few remaining commercial fishing complexes on the Great Lakes. The historic fishing village allows visitors to learn about Great Lakes commercial fishing and maritime traditions and experiences.

They can see commercial fishing vessels like *Janice Sue* (launched in 1958) and *Joy* (launched in 1981) as well as shanties, smokehouses, and docks that support the fishing industry. The *Janice Sue* and *Joy*, which are now owned by the Fishtown Preservation Society (FPS), still fish the waters off Leland, and

there is still a retail and wholesale fish operation in Fishtown, selling Great Lakes fish caught by state- and tribal-licensed commercial fishermen.

"Fishtown Preservation continues a tradition set by generations of commercial fishermen who cared for Fishtown as an everyday part of their lives," says Amanda Holmes, executive director of FPS. "Now this care is in the hands of FPS and the broader community, including a new generation of fishermen and descendants of many of Fishtown's commercial fishing families."

TREATIES

Treaties reflect agreements between sovereign nations. Often these treaties included references to usage rights and outlined access to Great Lakes fisheries resources.

Great Lakes treaties include

❖ Those between First Nations and Canada.

❖ Those between tribal Native Americans and the United States, including the Treaty of 1842, covering western Lake Superior waters of Michigan's Upper Peninsula, Minnesota and Wisconsin, and the Treaty of 1836, covering eastern Lake Superior, and northern Lake Michigan and Lake Huron waters of Michigan.

Under the terms of the 1836 treaty between the U.S. government and

Ottawa and Chippewa Indians, five individual Great Lakes tribes derive rights to conduct fishing activities. As interpreted by federal courts, the treaty retains the right to fish in the Great Lakes waters of the treaty-ceded territory. These rights were reaffirmed in court cases during the 1970s and locked in by the 1985 Consent Order, which expired in the year 2000. After

years of negotiations, the 20-year-long 2000 Consent Decree was signed. This agreement expires in 2020, opening the door for new discussions and agreements about fish harvest and allocation among the state and tribes.

A key to the newer Consent Decree was to eliminate tribal/state zones and to build a mutually beneficial agreement based on joint, science-based management of the fishery and shared allocations of fish harvested from the lakes. The agreement focuses on allocation, management, and regulation of state and tribal fisheries in the waters covered by the 1836 treaty. For example, those participating in the agreement have committed to the rehabilitation of lake trout in Lake Michigan and Lake Huron and to work cooperatively to resolve issues.

---

overharvested seafood. Additionally, consumers increasingly demand and place higher economic value on healthy and local food sources, as is demonstrated through the popularity of local farm markets. Creative commercial fishing operations also find ways to maximize value of their harvest through marketing the unique attributes of Great Lakes caught fish. Ecologically healthy fisheries equate to economically healthy commercial businesses. When managed properly, Great Lakes commercial fisheries can provide consumers with a local, healthy, and sustainable food source.

Sustainable harvest and economically viable commercial operations continue in the Great Lakes today because of improved science and management. Many important fish stocks collapsed in

the Great Lakes during the 19th century, largely because of overfishing, invasive species, and environmental degradation. Fisheries managers have since recognized the importance of closely monitoring harvest rates so they can ensure sufficient numbers of fish remain in the lakes. Managers place great emphasis on shared and multiple uses of the Great Lakes fishery, balancing the harvests from both the sport and recreational fisheries.

A management trend in the U.S. waters of the Great Lakes has been to regulate certain variables. Strategies used to control the pressure on fish stocks include

❖ Limiting the number of commercial licenses available.

❖ Restrictions on where and when fishing can occur.

❖ Type, size, and number of nets used for capture.

The goal is to reduce harvest pressure on the fishery while maintaining ecologically healthy and economically sustainable catch rates for the remaining commercial operations.

TRIBAL AND SUBSISTENCE FISHERY

As presented in the "History" section of this book, fishing and the use of gill nets for food and trade were important to the Great Lakes tribes before and after European settlement. Great Lakes Indians developed a life patterned around lakeside fishing villages with small gardens to supplement their diets. Fish was an important primary food source, and some used the leftovers for other things such as fertilizing crops or using fish bladders to tan animal hides.

The Great Lakes fishery is still central to some tribes throughout the region. However, today's tribal fishery is used and regulated in different ways.

TREATY RIGHTS: LIMITS AND GEAR

Great Lakes fishing treaties reach back hundreds of years. However, modern regulations—for much of the Great Lakes that means the 2000 Consent Decree—focus on an allocation of fish species. For example, some Great Lakes tribes focus their commercial fishing efforts on whitefish, while others target traditional sport species. Harvest of species such as lake trout that are of both sport and commercial interest are split 50-50 between state anglers and tribal fishers.

The 2000 agreement addresses the issues of gear and social conflict by designating specific areas, seasons, equipment, and allocations of fish in ways that maximize benefits for tribal, commercial, and sport anglers sharing the Great Lakes fishery resources. Many tribal commercial fishing operations converted from using gill nets to using trap nets or impoundment gear. Trap nets allow the tribes to maintain or expand their commercial fishing for whitefish, while reducing incidental harvest pressure on lake trout and other sport fish. Under the decree, the state also manages the sport harvest of fish such as lake trout, primarily through size limits.

Tribal, state, and federal biologists have worked collaboratively to create lake trout and whitefish population models. Based on these biological models, the Technical Fisheries Committee established by the 2000 Consent Decree works to
* Predict population changes due to controllable factors such as fishing.

* Determine biologically safe harvest levels.
* Set gear and harvest limits accordingly.

Many believe this joint management and harvest is critical for conserving fishery resources, particularly for achieving lake trout rehabilitation in the Great Lakes. The goal of the 2000 agreement is that, through joint management and resource conservation, fishing opportunities for all user groups will be enhanced.

SUBSISTENCE

The Great Lakes also support a subsistence fishery. Subsistence fishing is classified as fishing for personal or family consumption or use. It is often related to customary and traditional use of fish, but primarily refers to those who need to fish for food or ceremonial purposes. Subsistence fishers may include immigrants or Native Americans. In Canada, the term applies to First Nations fisheries focused on food and ceremonial purposes.

Many people throughout the Great Lakes region—who fish with or without sport licenses—also rely on fish as a primary food source. For example, there is a population of fishers in urban areas such as Milwaukee, Chicago, and Detroit for whom fish is a primary food.

Furthermore, anglers throughout the region, particularly the northern reaches of the Great Lakes, report that they rely on fishing as a means of procuring food for themselves and their families. Subsistence fishers may use hook and line, nets, or spears to harvest fish.

HATCHERIES AND AQUACULTURE

Aquaculture provides the Great Lakes region with economic benefits and another source of fish for the food market. Aquaculture production in the Great Lakes basin is diverse and varies from food fish to baitfish, aquarium fish for the pet trade, to fish for stocking, and even plants for food, wetland mitigation, and water gardening. Aquaculture, primarily run through state or federal agencies, provides fish for stocking in public waters of the states and provinces, whereas private fish producers may grow, or culture, fish to stock in private recreational waters or for sale to other fish growers and for fee-fishing operations (e.g., trout farms).

As reported by the U.S. Department of Agriculture's 2012 Aquaculture Census, there are nearly 340 aquaculture operations across eight Great Lakes states. In the United States, 66

WHAT IS AQUACULTURE?

The broad term "aquaculture" refers to breeding, rearing, and harvesting of plants and animals in all types of water environments, including ponds, rivers, lakes, and the ocean. Aquaculture can take place in the natural environment or in a man-made environment.

In the Great Lakes, aquaculture is primarily the cultivation of aquatic plants, invertebrates, fish, and amphibians for commercial use. The industry has grown in recent years and some fisheries experts believe there is potential for expanded growth in the Great Lakes region.

This sturgeon research and rearing facility on the Black River near Cheboygan, Mich., is an example of aquaculture that supports native fisheries restoration efforts.

aquaculture operations reported sales specifically related to baitfish; products of these aquaculture businesses are valued by many Great Lakes anglers.

Fish growers in the region raise many types of fish, including trout, salmon, bass, catfish, sunfish, tilapia, and yellow perch. In many states, aquaculture is legally considered a type of agriculture. Aquaculture operations in the Great Lakes basin are not necessarily tied directly to the Great Lakes. However, there are prominent examples of aquaculture operations using Great Lakes waters that are directly related to fisheries management and food fish raised in cage culture operations.

Here we talk about two kinds of managed aquaculture: government-run and private industry.

GOVERNMENT-RUN HATCHERIES

Hatcheries play an important role in Great Lakes fisheries management. The goal of government-run hatchery programs is to release—or stock—fish into the environment with the intent of rehabilitating or augmenting fish populations. In 2016, approximately 30 federal, state, tribal, and provincial agency-run hatcheries contributed nearly 32 million fish stocked into Great Lakes waters.

Some native species, such as lake trout or lake sturgeon, may be reared and stocked for the purpose of restoration and rehabilitation of native species populations. Native species restoration programs often stock fish with the purpose of growing fish to reproductive age so that populations might someday achieve self-sustaining natural reproduction. Other species, such as salmon or steelhead, might be stocked with the purpose of enhancing populations of fish highly sought by anglers.

Historically, stocking programs have played a pivotal role in the success of rehabilitating Great Lakes fisheries and providing valued fishing opportunities for sport anglers and commercial operators. However, in some areas of the Great Lakes, naturally reproduced fish have been more abundant than stocked fish, especially during recent years.

Agency hatcheries face increasing concerns about preventing the spread of diseases through hatchery operations. They are concerned also with the genetics of fish raised and stocked in aquaculture. Wild fish often have diverse biological stocks—sometimes regionally specific stocks—and are found in different locations throughout the Great Lakes basin. Given the expenses and challenges associated with hatcheries, it is important for resource managers to balance the costs and benefits of hatchery operations for different species in each of the Great Lakes.

PRIVATE AQUACULTURE

The private sector of Great Lakes aquaculture includes both cage culture operations and a baitfish industry. The only cage culture operations in Great Lakes—where fish are grown in cages in an open body of water—are found in Georgian Bay and the North Channel, in the Canadian waters of Lake Huron, where more than 9.5 million pounds of rainbow trout were produced in 2016.

Baitfish culture and harvest is an important commercial sector that occurs throughout the Great Lakes waters of both the United States and Canada. In some ways, baitfish operations reflect elements of commercial fishing, where fish such as spottail shiners, emerald shiners, and other minnows are harvested from Great Lakes waters, held alive in ponds or tanks, and then sold as bait. The baitfish industry is extremely important for sportfishing throughout the Great Lakes, providing a reliable source of baitfish for sport anglers.

Private-sector aquaculture industries have also been under increased scrutiny due to risks associated with moving and transplanting fish. Risks include unintentional release of non-native species or unintended introduction of diseases and **parasites**. For example, two species of Asian carp (i.e., silver and bighead) were initially brought to the southern United States in the 1970s to improve water quality in aquaculture ponds and water treatment systems and to boost harvests from catfish ponds. However, the carp have subsequently reached other water systems, in particular the Mississippi River basin, after heavy flooding in the 1990s; they have caused problems throughout the country and they are considered a potential threat to the Great Lakes, with some evidence that Asian carp have been found in waters close to the Great Lakes.

There are controls in place, however. Since 1999, Michigan and Minnesota Sea Grant fisheries experts have cooperatively developed Aquatic Invasive Species-Hazard Analysis and Critical Control Point (AIS-HACCP) plans with these industries to identify and control potential hazards related to aquaculture and bait producers. The AIS-HACCP program focuses on reducing the risk of spreading non-native species or disease through the aquaculture industry.

SUMMARY

TODAY'S FISHERIES

The most prominent fisheries in the Great Lakes vary in many ways, including purpose, scope, and gear used. Yet they also overlap because the same species are often harvested for different uses. Perhaps the most notable similarity is that each fishery is dependent upon a healthy Great Lakes ecosystem.

Great Lakes fisheries—tribal, commercial, and recreational—are critical to the region's economy and culture. The following elements are at the heart of maintaining the Great Lakes fisheries today and in the future:

❖ Resource managers balance the use of today's diverse fishery, using science-based information.

❖ Expert scientists can apply complex technological tools to help solve increasingly complex issues.

❖ Sustained funding is needed to address habitat restoration, monitoring, research, and education.

❖ Outreach that focuses on fisheries stakeholders, legislators, and the general public interest is required to ensure resource stewardship and sustainability for future generations.

❖ Resource managers protect and restore the diversity of habitats and fish species that the Great Lakes provide.

❖ Accessible and affordable fisheries education tools are needed to address the ecology, biology, management, and economic value of the Great Lakes fisheries

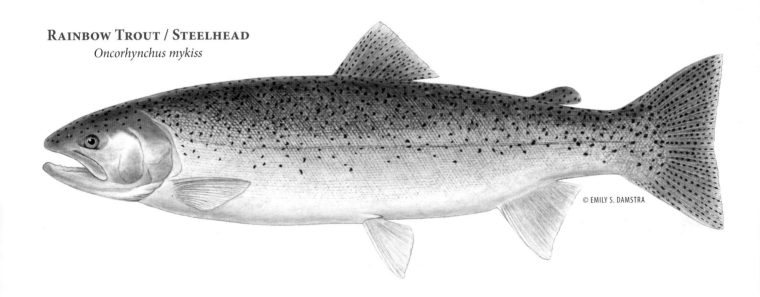

RAINBOW TROUT / STEELHEAD
Oncorhynchus mykiss

© EMILY S. DAMSTRA

HISTORY

of the

GREAT LAKES

FISHERIES

Waves of change have always moved through the lakes. Social, technological, and environmental changes have spread, sometimes simultaneously, through the entire basin. Taken together, those changes make today's Great Lakes fisheries quite different than they were hundreds of years ago. In the last century, and particularly in recent decades, the pace of change has accelerated. To understand what the fisheries are today and what they may be in the future, it is important to review their complex and evolving history.

The history of the Great Lakes can be broken into different eras of settlement and human development. This "History" section briefly touches on the formation of the Great Lakes and then, further explores more recent times, when humans began to significantly influence the health and character of the Great Lakes region during the last 200 years.

TIMES OF PLENTY: AN ABUNDANCE OF FISH

ERA: 12,000 YEARS AGO TO ABOUT AD 1800

People arrived in the region by way of land bridge from Asia or from South America. They hunted large mammals, such as the mastodon, about 12,000 to 11,000 years ago. Fishing became more common for people living in the Great Lakes region from 6000 to 3000 BC (Middle Archaic Period). Archaeologists believe fishhooks were invented during this time.

EARLY FISHING METHODS

Native Great Lakes peoples were fishing as early as 3000 BC (Late Archaic Period). These groups developed techniques for spearing fish like lake sturgeon, northern pike, and suckers, and angling for fish from a canoe or through the ice. Spears were made of copper, bone, and antler. Fishing hooks and gorges—straight tools similar to hooks— were made of copper or bone. Small dam structures called weirs were sometimes used to help concentrate fish to make harvesting easier. This early gear was used to catch mainly those fish that were abundant during the spring spawning season in the nearshore, shallow areas of the Great Lakes and tributaries.

By about 1000 BC, the abundance of fish was a major influence on the people in the region. Groups in the upper (northern) Great Lakes region subsisted mainly by fishing and hunting and supplemented their diet with plants like wild rice. The seasonal movements of fish into the shallow areas of the upper Great Lakes guided the people's subsistence and settlement patterns because they chose to settle proximate to food and water resources. In the lower (southern) Great Lakes region, corn arrived around 300 BC, agriculture emerged, and people then supplemented their agricultural diet with fish and game.

HARPOONS AND SEINE NETS

Two technological changes in fishing gear occurred among the people of the upper Great Lakes during the Woodland Period (1000 BC to AD 1600) and prior to the arrival of the Europeans. Harpoons with detachable heads connected to a line allowed for more efficient capture and retrieval of larger fish, such as lake sturgeon, than was possible with simpler spears.

14,000 to 9,000 years ago

The glaciers of the last ice age retreat from what is now the Great Lakes basin.

About 1000 BC to 1600 AD (Woodland Period)

Native peoples add seine nets and harpoons to fishing gear.

About 8000 to 1000 BC (Archaic Period)

Prehistoric peoples hunt, fish, and gather food. Fishing tools include spears, hooks, gorges, and weirs.

WEST SHORE FISHING MUSEUM

HISTORICAL FACTORS INFLUENCING TODAY'S GREAT LAKES FISHERIES

ENVIRONMENTAL CHANGES

Modification of Drainage Basins
- Landscape, physical, chemical, and biological changes

Invasive Species
- Varied sources of introduction
- Prevention and management strategies

Physical and Chemical Modifications
- Cultural eutrophication
- Contaminants

Atmospheric and Global Changes
- Atmospheric deposition of contaminants
- Movement of contaminants in ecosystems
- Climate change

SOCIAL CHANGES

Settlement
- Cultures mixing (Native, European)
- Immigration
- Population pressures
- Urbanization

Changes in Values Over Time
- Subsistence
- Developing markets in United States and Canada
- Rise of recreation and tourism
- Global markets, economics
- Changing tastes
- Environmentalism, sustainability

Sociopolitical Changes
- Treaties
- Policy changes: state, federal, tribal
- Cross-jurisdictional (interstate) and international cooperation

TECHNOLOGICAL CHANGES

Land Use Patterns
- Logging, dams, canals
- Conversion of land from prairie and forest to agricultural, industrial, and residential uses
- Sprawl

Harvest and Other Technologies
- Nets, floats
- Boats, engines
- Radios, navigational equipment
- Fish finders
- Transport and refrigeration

Management Science Technologies
- Hatcheries
- Genetics
- Population and ecosystem modeling
- Computers
- Restrictions
- Disease detection, monitoring, and management

Woodland Period people made seine nets of wild hemp or nettles, with cords of basswood bark or leather, edged at the bottom with small, notched stones (net sinkers). These seines were used to corral fish like northern pike, freshwater drum, bass, and suckers to the shore for harvesting. These technological changes facilitated some social changes. The fishing techniques required cooperation. Often, family groups would gather at Great Lakes shorelines to work together during fishing seasons.

Native peoples began developing and using gill nets around the year AD 800. This allowed the harvest of offshore fall spawners such as lake trout and lake whitefish. Fall fishing meant that a large catch could be preserved by smoking or freezing for use throughout the winter.

WORLDS COLLIDE: NATIVE PEOPLE AND THE EXPLORERS

When Europeans first began exploring the "New World," an estimated 60,000–117,000 native people lived in the region. By comparison, about 37 million people currently live in the basin. Fish were generally abundant relative to the number of people. The tribal groups in the region at that time included the Anishinabeg (i.e., Ottawa, Potawatomi, and Ojibwa or Chippewa), the Iroquois and Huron, and the Menominee, Winnebago, Illinois, and Miami, among others. By this time, fishing had grown to be vitally important in the lives of the people of the upper Great Lakes region. Villages were organized around the nearshore fishery. The people of the lower Great Lakes and the St. Lawrence River

About 1000 AD

Viking explorer Leif Ericsson visits what is now northeast Canada.

About 800 AD

Native peoples develop gill nets, allowing the harvest of offshore, fall spawners such as lake trout and whitefish.

1600s

- An estimated 60,000 to 117,000 native people live in the region.
- Europeans begin to explore the Great Lakes.
- Fish are abundant relative to the number of people.

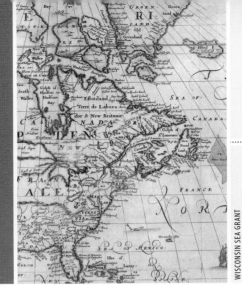

WISCONSIN SEA GRANT

1604

French settlers establish colonies in Canada.

1670

The Hudson's Bay Company is established.

also relied on fisheries resources such as sturgeon, whitefish, and American eel for part of their diets.

EUROPEANS ARRIVE

French explorers and early missionaries began arriving in the upper Great Lakes in the 1660s. Europeans learned about the long-established North American fishing techniques and wrote about the unique dip-net fishing done from canoes in the St. Marys River between Lakes Superior and Huron. Europeans also saw the extent of the Native American fishery, observing them harvest fish both nearshore and in open water during the different seasons, and through the ice in winter.

For the first hundred years after it was "discovered," the French primarily controlled the Great Lakes region, although the British were also trading with native people. The lakes became the key routes for travel, trade, warfare, communication, and diplomacy. Two worlds met, and Europeans and native peoples exchanged more than furs. Items of trade included nets and other gear that made hunting and fishing easier. The Treaty of Paris concluded the French and Indian War in 1763. As a result, the Great Lakes region was transferred from French to British control, though many French settlers remained in the area. In 1783, another Treaty of Paris drew an end to the American Revolutionary War, and the boundaries of the new republic were agreed upon—down the middle of the lakes.

FISH AND FUR

By the late 1700s, the focus of fishing in the Great Lakes began to shift. Instead of relying upon fish as a primary source of food (subsistence), fishing was being used as a means of supporting other industries that were growing in the region. For example, the demand for fur in Europe bolstered the Great Lakes fur trade. This, in turn, necessitated early commercial fishing to feed the traders and settlers.

The Northwest Fur Company dominated the western end of Lake Superior, particularly the Chequamegon (Wisconsin) area in the 1780s to 1790s. The company fished the north side of Isle Royale to feed people at its trading stations in western Lake Superior. In the 1790s, a hook-and-line commercial fishery developed on Lake Erie (near Presque Isle, Pennsylvania). Little is known about these early commercial fishing enterprises.

The tribes, the British, and the settlers were still active in the fur trade, particularly in the western end of the upper Great Lakes. The frontier was in transition for several decades; both the newly formed U.S. and British governments encouraged settlers to move to the Great Lakes region.

NATIVE SETTLERS

Native peoples inhabited North America tens of thousands of years before the arrival of settlers from Europe and the Far East. By the 16th century, the native peoples of North America had evolved into distinctive cultures. Notable tribes around the Great Lakes included the Chippewa, Fox, Huron, Iroquois, Ottawa, Potawatomi, and Lakota (Sioux).

In the United States and Canada, approximately 120 bands of native people have occupied the Great Lakes basin over the course of history. In Canada, tribes are called First Nations. In the Ontario region alone, more than 75 bands of First Nations are reported. A band is based on kinship and family affiliation. A nuclear family is part of a clan (cousins); a clan is part of a band (aunts, uncles, extended cousins); and a collection of bands make up a tribe. Tribes are traditionally highly organized, politically independent groups.

1673

Fort Frontenac, on the present site of Kingston, Ontario, becomes the first fort on the lower lakes.

1679

The *Griffon*, captained by the French explorer La Salle, sets sail on the Great Lakes.

1700s

- Early French and British fur trappers and traders begin to establish posts throughout the region.
- Fish and fishing gear are traded.

1754

The French and Indian War begins.

1763

French and Indian War ends. Treaty of Paris transfers control of the region from France to Great Britain.

PAUL SCHULER

CESSION AND SURRENDER

Prior to the arrival of Europeans, native tribes oversaw access to the region's land and water. After the U.S. Revolutionary War, treaties with Native Americans led to land "cessions" in the United States and to land "surrender" in Canada. As European settlement of this region proceeded, both native peoples and Europeans needed the land and resources. Sometimes the lands were obtained through warfare or other aggressive means. Typically, however, the resources were procured through negotiation or purchased through treaties. As land cessions and surrenders occurred, communities of European origin began to grow, and populations of settlers increased greatly.

Before the 1800s, Great Lakes fish populations were thought to be unlimited and inexhaustible. However, all of the changes brought by the new settlers set the stage for dramatic and rapid changes in the next era.

POPULATION EXPLOSION, EXPLOITATION, AND DEGRADATION

ERA: ABOUT 1800 TO 1870S

The Great Lakes region became a popular destination in the 1800s. Tremendous numbers of settlers began arriving, and the fast-paced population growth would have serious implications for environmental quality and fish populations even after the migration to the region slowed.

COMMERCIAL FISHING TAKES OFF

The first large commercial fishery on Lake Huron was established around Fort Michilimackinac by 1800 and was an important element of the continuing fur trade. After the War of 1812, the British agreed to withdraw to Canadian territory, and the upper Great Lakes were fully open to American fur traders. After

the war, some of the first widespread commercial fisheries in the Great Lakes were established on Lake Erie, near the Maumee River and the Detroit River. Both areas were abundant with fish, were accessible from Toledo and Detroit, and were centrally located on shipping routes.

Commercial fishing was well established on the Canadian side of the lakes by the 1820s and 1830s. The commercial fisheries served their surrounding areas and eventually supplied fish to eastern cities growing larger with immigrants. In 1826, the first shipments of salted whitefish and lake trout left Detroit for markets back east.

KAVANAUGH FAMILY

The Jenny Weaver, a commercial fishing schooner of W.P. Kavanaugh Fishery, based in Bay City, Mich., 1880s.

CESSION AND SURRENDER

Cession and *surrender* are terms for the process by which the governments acquired native peoples' lands to grant or sell to settlers.

A treaty is a tool and process used by one government to give its word to another government; the intention in a treaty is to protect a particular intergovernmental agreement over a long period.

1775

The American
Revolution begins.

1776

The Continental
Congress adopts
the Declaration
of Independence.

1780s

❖ The Northwest Fur
Company dominates
the western end of
Lake Superior.

❖ The fisheries and
other resources of
the Great Lakes
region are thought
to be inexhaustible.

DETROIT HISTORICAL SOCIETY

FUR IN DECLINE

Mackinac Island, once the center of
fur trading in the lakes, diminished in
prominence, and the American Fur
Company moved its headquarters to
western Lake Superior after 1834. The
company built two schooners, which no
longer required a rowing crew, to carry
furs to be sold in Sault Ste. Marie. The
boatmen no longer needed for rowing
found employment as fishermen. Fishing
stations were established throughout the
western basin of Lake Superior. The men
fished with handmade twine nets from
wooden boats propelled by oars or sail.

Others were employed at the fishing
stations to clean, salt, and pack the fish
and to make the barrels in which fish
were shipped to growing markets in the
Ohio River Valley. The Hudson's Bay
Company, likewise, employed men at
fishing stations. Thus began large-scale,
organized commercial fishing in the
Great Lakes. However, after the financial
panic of 1837, a depression put an end to
the fishing business of the American Fur
Company. By this time, the demand for
furs in Europe had dropped dramatically.
The company divided, and fishing
continued on a smaller scale for a while.

NEGOTIATING TREATIES

Throughout this period, treaties were
established between the native peoples
and the new governments in the region.

WILD RICE

Known as *manoomin*, which translates to "the good berry" in Ojibwe, wild rice is
significant to the Ojibwe people. According to oral tradition, long ago the Ojibwe
were instructed to find the place where "the food grows on the water" during
their long migration. This ultimately led them to the shores of Lake Superior
and the northern inland lakes of Michigan, Wisconsin, and Minnesota, where
abundant fields of manoomin were found.

Seen as a special gift from the Creator, manoomin became a staple in the Ojibwe
diet. When preserved correctly, wild rice can be stored for long periods, making
it available when other foods are not. Wild rice is not just part of the traditional
diet, it has also developed cultural and spiritual prominence and remains an
important element in many feasts and ceremonies.

PHOTOS: GREAT LAKES INDIAN FISH & WILDLIFE COMMISSION

The U.S. government led another effort to gain land through cession in the early 1800s to help the government through economic hard times. Although the Native Americans lost their land base through the negotiation of these treaties, they retained fishing and hunting rights in the region. Specifically, the agreements allowed Native Americans to retain their rights to fish in the waters of the Great Lakes ceded under the treaties. Thus, tribes were established as sovereign nations, managing their own governance systems and natural resources.

The Treaty of 1836, or the Ottawa-Chippewa Treaty, ceded one of the largest tracts of land in the Great Lakes region to the United States. The area eventually became Michigan. Under the Treaty of 1842, the Red Cliff, Bad River, and Keweenaw bands of Ojibwa secured their treaty-fishing rights in Lake Superior. Several treaties still govern tribal fishing in the U.S. portion of the Great Lakes region and its waters. Canada protects tribal fishing rights on the Great Lakes today under the Canadian Constitution Act of 1982. By the end of this era, most of the Native American land in the region had been ceded and reservations were being established.

CONNECTED WATERWAYS

Boats and navigation in the Great Lakes began to change in the early 1800s.

Steamboats first arrived in Lake Erie in 1818, and shortly thereafter, they were found throughout the region. Navigational improvements followed. In 1825, the Erie Canal opened, directly connecting Lakes Ontario and Erie with the Atlantic Ocean via the Hudson River and the port of New York. The Welland Ship Canal was constructed between Lakes Ontario and Erie in 1829 to provide a route around Niagara Falls. On the Canadian side, the Rideau Canal system was completed in 1832, connecting Kingston with Ottawa, Ontario.

Iron ore was discovered in the Upper Peninsula of Michigan in 1844, and waves of immigrants arrived to work in the iron and copper mines of the upper Great Lakes. Rapid technological changes allowed engineers to make modifications to waterways, which in turn provided easier transportation routes for the arriving immigrants and for shipping the metals to manufacturing centers in Chicago, Milwaukee, Detroit, Toledo, Cleveland, Buffalo, and Rochester. Communities throughout the Great Lakes region began to grow substantially.

The St. Marys Falls Ship Canal (popularly known as the Soo Locks) connecting Lake Superior and Lake Huron was enlarged in 1855 to accommodate large shipping vessels. The Chicago Sanitary and Ship Canal was opened in 1900, improving drinking water for the city

and connecting the Great Lakes with the Mississippi River watershed. These new commercial transportation connections benefited immigrants, industries, businesses, and communities. However, these connections play major roles in the history and management of Great Lakes fisheries in years to come.

INCREASED EFFICIENCIES OF THE 1800s

NETS

Before 1850, simple fishing techniques on Lake Erie included seines (for sauger, walleye, and smallmouth bass), brush weirs, spears, dip nets, and trotlines (lines with multiple fishhooks). Almost all of the effort was concentrated in nearshore areas and focused on lake whitefish, yellow perch, and walleye and cisco species like bloater and lake herring. In Lake Ontario, major spawning runs of Atlantic salmon were targeted.

BOATS

Wooden boats allowed travel farther from shore. Pound nets (similar to trap nets, but staked into the bottom using large poles) were used throughout the Great Lakes, and the use of gill nets was increasing by the 1840s and 1850s. Handmade cotton twine nets were replaced in the 1840s with cheaper machine-made nets. Linen nets were first used in the 1850s. These upgrades allowed fishing in

1808

John Jacob Astor forms the American Fur Company and trading increases.

1818

Steamboats first arrive in Lake Erie, and shortly thereafter they are found throughout the region.

1812

First widespread commercial fisheries are established after the War of 1812 to serve workers in the region and eastern cities with salted fish.

1820s

As fur trading declines, fur companies establish fishing stations. Commercial fisheries are better organized throughout the region.

---

deeper, offshore waters and led to larger catches. By the 1870s, seines were almost completely replaced by gill nets and pound nets. Steam-powered fishing tugs were introduced by the mid-1870s, allowing fishermen to travel even greater distances to catch fish and to work in foul weather.

RAIL

In 1851, the Erie Railroad became the first line connected to the Great Lakes, further altering the transportation of fish. In 1855, the Northern Railway connected Collingwood on the southwest portion of Georgian Bay on Lake Huron with a large market in the developing Toronto area. With the advent of rail, faster shipping of iced and frozen fish to eastern markets became possible. Improvements also meant that fishermen could store frozen fish until markets and prices were favorable for selling.

BIOLOGICAL AND CHEMICAL POLLUTION

Habitat degradation due to increasing human populations and activities and the arrival of invasive species were two major environmental changes that began to influence Great Lakes fisheries in the 1800s. The Lake Ontario basin was the first in the region to be altered by canals and dams. Changes that occurred there during the 1800s were progressively echoed in the other lakes from 1900 to the present.

The most profound early environmental changes in the lakes occurred during the logging era. Heavy logging increased soil erosion into streams, causing turbidity (muddy, cloudy water) and a loss of fishery habitat.

LOGGING

Logging had a profound impact on the Great Lakes and was one of the first large-scale environmental changes. Logging activity peaked first in New York in the mid-1800s, and then moved further west to Michigan in the 1860s to 1870s. These logging and settlement activities caused the first type of environmental change: loss of fish habitats due to extreme modifications of waterways that drain to the Great Lakes.

By the mid-1800s, water-powered mills of all sorts, including sawmills, were common on streams in the region. Many

Great Lakes tributaries were dammed, preventing fish from passing upstream to spawn and concentrating them in downstream areas where they were more susceptible to overfishing without the ability to reproduce, among other challenges.

POLLUTION

Heavy logging increased soil erosion into streams, causing turbidity (muddy, cloudy water), covering spawning areas, and warming the waters. All of those activities further degraded fish spawning habitat. Wetlands— crucial to fish spawning and juvenile

1825

Erie Canal opens, connecting Lake Ontario with the Atlantic Ocean. It is the first significant canal that allows direct water access past natural barriers of Niagara Falls.

1829

Welland Canal opens, allowing ships to travel around Niagara Falls. Three more canal projects eventually deepen and widen the passage, allowing oceangoing ships and (non-native species) to reach the upper lakes.

1826

The first shipments of salted whitefish and lake trout leave Detroit for markets back east.

1832

Rideau Canal system is completed in Ontario, connecting Kingston with Ottawa.

development—were drained and modified. Logging waste and sawdust were disposed of throughout coastal areas and in streams. Human and animal waste from settlements and cities also entered the waterways. Pollution in the Great Lakes coincided with European settlement and is not just a present-day issue.

With development and increased human activity came the second type of environmental change—biological pollution. In the 1800s, non-native species began to arrive in the Great Lakes. The sea lamprey was noted in Lake Ontario by the 1830s. The alewife, a cold-water fish from the Atlantic

Ocean, traveled through the Erie Canal and became established in Lake Ontario by 1873. The effects of the invasive alewife would be widely felt throughout the Great Lakes food web within a few decades.

FISH POPULATIONS DECLINE

Major changes in Great Lakes fish populations began in the early 1800s in Lake Ontario. The earliest intensive fishery in the region was for Atlantic salmon, the most valued and heavily exploited native fish from the late 1700s to the mid-1800s. Milldams concentrated these fish and made them more vulnerable to harvest. Other changes

in the **tributary** streams decreased the amount of accessible spawning habitat. By the 1830s and 1840s, this loss caused the first major fisheries-related alarm in the Great Lakes. Atlantic salmon temporarily recovered in the 1860s, after establishing harvesting restrictions and stocking efforts. Despite attempts, however, the turn of the century brought the last record of native Atlantic salmon in Lake Ontario.

INTENSIVE FISHING

During the early 1800s, intensive fishing for other Great Lakes fish also occurred. Lake whitefish was the most fished species at the time in the upper Great Lakes. Lake trout were second in all the lakes; harvest of lake trout became even more important when lake whitefish numbers were low and as Atlantic salmon decreased in Lake Ontario. Other important fish included cisco (lake herring) in Lake Erie, Saginaw Bay, and Green Bay; lake sturgeon throughout the lakes, and deepwater ciscoes in Lakes Huron, Michigan, and Superior. By 1860, the catch of lake whitefish in Green Bay had declined by 50 percent. By the 1860s, laws in the region began to restrict fishing by establishing catch limits and closed seasons. As early as 1861, Ohio declared its first closed season for some fish. Significant changes in the Great Lakes fisheries had already begun.

BENTLEY HISTORICAL LIBRARY

The lock at Sault Ste. Marie, Mich., August 11, 1896.

1835
Sea lampreys are discovered in Lake Ontario.

1840s
Pound nets are used throughout the Great Lakes. Use of gill nets increases.

1836
- ❖ The Treaty of 1836 cedes one of the largest tracts of land in the Great Lakes region from Native Americans to the United States.
- ❖ Intensive overfishing of Atlantic salmon in Lake Ontario leads to the first major alarm on the Great Lakes.

OVERFISHING, REGULATIONS, AND STOCKING

ERA: 1870s TO EARLY 1900s

After the Civil War, the Great Lakes region experienced more settlement. Railroad construction expanded, and large shoreline cities like Chicago grew even larger. More Native American reservations were established as lands in the region were ceded to the U.S. government and surrendered to the British government in the British Canadian colonies. During this era, some sportfishing began. For example in 1885, daily sportfishing excursions were offered on Lake Erie. When Great Britain entered World War I in 1914, fishing in Canada was declared an essential service.

The technological advancements during this period continued to increase the efficiency of the commercial harvest. The Great Lakes were still considered inexhaustible by some; however, the levels of harvest would prove to be unsustainable at best, and devastating at worst. The decline in harvest ultimately created a need for fisheries science.

STEAM TO GAS

The first Canadian steam-fishing tug above the Niagara River began to work in Lake Huron in 1870. Around the same time, steam engines were improved and work on internal combustion engines began. Gasoline engines began catching on around the turn of the century, and Ole Evinrude of Minnesota developed the first commercially successful outboard motor in 1909. Diesel engines with fuel injection were available by 1910, and the first diesel vessels on the Great Lakes were built in 1920. Throughout this era, however, the steam tug remained the most common power vessel on the Great Lakes.

As engine technologies changed, the technologies used to haul larger and larger nets from the water did too. In 1895, the Connable Steam Net Lifter was patented, and its use around the turn of the century allowed more gill nets to be set and hauled. Gasoline net lifters were also developed.

FISHING NETS IMPROVE

Fishing techniques also changed around the turn of the century. During the 1890s, a new type of gear called the trap net was used in the Great Lakes in Saginaw Bay and the St. Marys River. This net was a more efficient, easier-to-move variation on the pound net. It was popular in U.S. waters, but it was not legal in Canadian waters until 1950 (although it was used earlier in Georgian Bay).

Pound net fishermen and gill net fishermen disagreed over which nets should be used, and some fishermen

THE ARRIVAL OF SCIENCE

The roots of fisheries science were established during the mid-1800s. In 1848, Professor Louis Agassiz and 15 students and researchers began one of the earliest scientific expeditions on the Great Lakes, studying the north shore of Lake Superior. These scientists compiled some of the earliest technical descriptions of Great Lakes fish. Other scientists were beginning to study lake level fluctuations and water chemistry. Agassiz's spirit of science lives on today. The *R/V Agassiz*—a research vessel used by Michigan Technological University—is named after him and continues to support research on the Great Lakes.

1844

Iron ore is discovered in upper Michigan. More settlers arrive. Several states acquire statehood in the early to mid-1800s.

1851

Railroads move into the Great Lakes region. Within 25 years, refrigerated railroad cars carry frozen fish to the east.

1848

Professor Louis Agassiz and 15 others conduct one of the earliest scientific expeditions on the Great Lakes, from Sault Ste. Marie to the north shore of Lake Superior.

Mid-1850s

Water-powered mills, including sawmills, are common on streams in the region.

worried that the efficient trap nets would result in overfishing. While this controversy was beginning to simmer, even more efficient variations on the gill net were appearing. About 1900, fishermen began "canning" their gill nets. Canning, or vertically floating, gill nets rather than anchoring them to the bottom allowed nets to be moved to various water depths with changes in seasons and temperature.

The result? Catches increased. In 1905, U.S. fishermen on Lake Erie invented a variation of the gill net called the bull net. Until then, gill nets used to catch ciscoes were only about 5 feet tall; however, bull nets were up to 22 feet tall. Around 1900, less expensive cotton nets were introduced. During this era, nets became cheaper, larger, easier to move and to haul out of the water, and more efficient. At the same time, the mesh sizes of fishing nets were shrinking, taking younger and younger fish as the larger, older size classes were "fished out." The overall environment had degraded because of all the human-initiated changes, putting additional stress on Great Lakes fish populations.

ENVIRONMENTAL QUALITY

The two themes of environmental change—modification of watersheds and tributaries (i.e., drainage systems) and invasive species—continued between 1870 and the early 1900s. Human population growth, forest cutting, land clearing, development, wetland drainage, harbor dredging, pollution from lumbering activities, and sewer outflows continued throughout the Lake Michigan basin after 1850 and into the early 1900s.

In this era, an important environmental change was just starting to take its toll on water quality and fisheries. Eutrophication (a term coined in the 20th century) is the process by which waters increase in nutrients. While eutrophication occurs naturally as lakes age over geological time, cultural eutrophication is a process of rapid changes due to human influences in the watershed. This process was already affecting areas of Lake Erie and Lake Ontario during the late 1800s and at the turn of the century.

LOGGING

During this era, logging activities and the rapid settlement of portions of the Great Lakes basin, particularly in connecting waterways (e.g., Lake St. Clair) and the lower Great Lakes (e.g., Erie and Ontario) continued to negatively impact the fisheries. These activities caused more and more soil erosion, and increased the water temperatures and runoff of nutrients from land to water. This led to more

A bustling fishing port in Thunder Bay, Ontario, circa 1909. Governments in the Great Lakes began to adopt regulations on fishing, such as setting catch limits and creating seasons, around the middle of the 19th century.

1861

❖ The American Civil War begins.

❖ Ohio declares its first closed season for some fish.

1855

St. Marys Falls Ship Canal (known as the Soo Locks) connecting Lake Superior and Lake Huron is enlarged to accommodate large vessels.

1860s

❖ Logging and settlement activities cause the first type of environmental change.

❖ Because fish populations decline, fishing laws establish catch limits and seasons.

❖ Catch of lake whitefish in Green Bay on Lake Michigan declines by 50 percent.

cultural eutrophication. Shallow bays such as Green Bay on Lake Michigan and Saginaw Bay on Lake Huron were also susceptible to these activities. Cold-water fish species adapted to the oligotrophic conditions of the upper lakes experienced population declines linked to cultural eutrophication.

Many serious fires raged throughout the region in the decades immediately following the peak of logging. In 1871, a fire burned the northwestern edge of Lake Michigan, from just north of the city of Green Bay, Wisconsin, to just south of Escanaba, Michigan. Other fires during this era burned along the coasts of Lake Huron. With fires came soil erosion, increased turbidity, and water pollution. Areas like Green Bay began to experience the severe environmental quality problems that Lake Erie and Lake Ontario had experienced earlier.

FISH HARVESTS DECLINE

Individual species were uniquely affected by all of these changes.

LAKE STURGEON

After the loss of the Atlantic salmon in Lake Ontario, the next major decline of native fish species in the Great Lakes was the lake sturgeon. At first, the species was not commercially important and was intentionally destroyed because it damaged fishing nets. Later, many uses

---

IS IT LAKE HERRING? CISCO? BOTH?

A fish of many names! Now called cisco, this fish has been more commonly referred to as lake herring throughout history. In addition to lake herring, it has been known by a number of other names, such as herring, tullibee, blueback, and northern cisco.

The moniker *lake herring* is misleading because it is not actually a member of the herring family (*Clupeidae*), which includes alewife and gizzard shad.

The cisco, *Coregonus artedi*, actually belongs to the Salmonidae family—the same family as salmons, trouts, chars, grayling, and lake whitefish. Within this family, several species of whitefish, ciscoes, and chubs are grouped together as a subfamily (Coregoninae), among which are several closely related species sometimes collectively and simply referred to as ciscoes or herrings. Several distinct species or forms of ciscoes currently and historically inhabit the Great Lakes, including

❖ Longjaw cisco (*Coregonus alpenae*, extinct)

❖ Bloater (*Coregonus hoyi*)

❖ Deepwater cisco (*Coregonus johannae*, extinct)

❖ Kiyi (*Coregonus kiyi*)

❖ Blackfin cisco (*Coregonus nigripinnis*, extirpated from Great Lakes)

❖ Shortjaw cisco (*Coregonus zenithicus*)

❖ Cisco, formerly lake herring (*Coregonus artedi*)

A new monograph provides information on taxonomy, geographical distribution, ecology, and status of ciscoes. *Ciscoes (Coregonus, subgenus Leucichthys) of the Great Lakes and Lake Nipigon* can be found online at www.glfc.org.

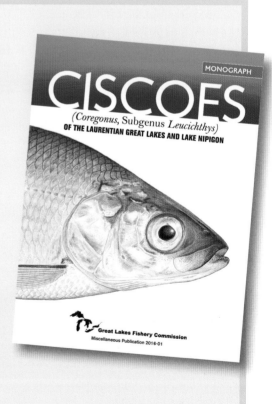

MONOGRAPH

CISCOES
(*Coregonus*, Subgenus *Leucichthys*)
OF THE LAURENTIAN GREAT LAKES AND LAKE NIPIGON

Great Lakes Fishery Commission
Miscellaneous Publication 2016-01

1870s

- More than 32.2 million lbs. (14.6 million kg) of Great Lakes fish are handled at major fish markets.

- Steel is first used in shipbuilding, although wood is still used for most fishing vessels.

- Lake Michigan's commercial fishery industry employs more than 2,000 people and 600 vessels.

BENTLEY HISTORICAL LIBRARY

for sturgeon were found and products were derived from it. Sturgeon eggs (caviar) became popular, and oil from the fish was used for a variety of purposes. Its air bladder was used to manufacture isinglass (a gelatin used to make beer and wine), and carcasses were used as fertilizer, food, and fuel.

Between 1890 and 1910, lake sturgeon declined in all the lakes. In 1879, the sturgeon catch for Lake Michigan was 3.8 million pounds (1.7 million kg) and some decline had likely already occurred. By 1911, the catch was only 14,000 pounds (6,350 kg), and after that, the fish was nearly nonexistent in commercial catches. Lake Erie's sturgeon catch was about 5 million pounds (2.3 million kg) in 1885, but dropped to only 100,000 pounds (45,360 kg) in 1916 and never recovered. Lake Huron's sturgeon population experienced a similar decline, but reached low levels later in the 1930s. Lake Ontario's sturgeon catch dropped from 581,000 pounds (263,500 kg) in the 1890s to only 10,000 pounds (4,500 kg) by the 1920s.

Much of the sturgeon population decline was due first to overfishing and the loss of spawning habitats in nearshore areas and rivers. The biological characteristics of the sturgeon made it extremely difficult for the fish to recover: it grows slowly, matures late, spawns infrequently, and is relatively easy to capture.

Sturgeon are now found in certain local areas of the Great Lakes such as Lake Huron's North Channel, the Menominee River, parts of Lake Superior, and the St. Clair River. It is listed as an endangered fish in six of eight Great Lakes states. Fishing for sturgeon is prohibited in Great Lakes waters of Ontario, where lake sturgeon are listed as threatened under Ontario's Endangered Species Act. Commercial and recreational fisheries have generally been closed; however, limited hook-and-line and spear fisheries still exist in some U.S. waters.

COREGONINES: CISCO AND LAKE WHITEFISH

One group of fish, the **coregonines**, experienced heavy fishing pressure during the 1800s. The coregonines are members of the family Salmonidae, forming the subfamily that includes lake whitefish and cisco species including lake herring. Each of the Great Lakes saw fluctuations in the coregonine harvests.

- **Lake Ontario:** By 1879, great increases and decreases had occurred in lake whitefish catches (as well as cisco species including lake herring). By the 1920s, however, lake whitefish had recovered in Lake Ontario.
- **Lake Erie:** 1880, pound netters in Lake Erie complained of decreased lake whitefish harvests. In the

western basin of Lake Erie, smaller lake whitefish were being harvested and smaller and smaller net mesh sizes were used to catch cisco varieties.

- **Lake Superior:** From 1885 to 1911, Lake Superior saw declines in lake whitefish numbers and effort switched to another species. This period began the "glory years" for lake trout.
- **Lake Michigan:** From 1894 to 1927, lake whitefish populations in Lake Michigan were fairly stable with a harvest of 1–2 million pounds (453,000–907,000 kg) per year. In the 1920s, lake whitefish catches increased in Lake Michigan.

LAKE TROUT

Lake trout were resistant to intensive fishing for a longer period. From the late 1800s to the early 1900s, lake trout supported a seemingly stable fishing effort. The lake trout is a large predator that occupies a variety of areas in the Great Lakes, from shore to shore and from top of the water column to bottom. Because lake trout feed on many different species of forage fish—including ciscoes and sculpins—and because the forage base as a whole remained stable throughout much of this era, trout populations remained secure in the upper Great Lakes. However, when faced with enough ecosystem changes paired with fishing pressures, even lake trout eventually declined.

1870s

❖ J. S. Milner surveys the Great Lakes, documenting serious declines in fisheries.

❖ Cheaper, machine-made linen nets replace handmade cotton twine nets, allowing fishing in deeper waters with larger yields.

1873

The alewife, a cold-water fish from the Atlantic Ocean, travels through the Erie Canal and becomes established in Lake Ontario.

1870

The American Fish Culturists' Association—later the American Fisheries Society—is formed

1872

United States and Canada commercially harvest 39.3 million lbs. (17.8 million kg) of Great Lakes fish.

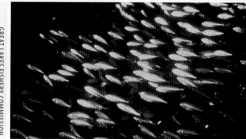

GREAT LAKES FISHERY COMMISSION

In the lower Great Lakes, lake trout populations began to experience the combined effects of intense fishing pressure and eutrophication. In Lake Erie, lake trout populations began to decline earlier than in the other lakes. Since Lake Erie is at the southern end of the range of the cold-water lake trout, they likely were never abundant and had been relatively rare in the shallower western and central basins. Nevertheless, by the end of the 1800s, lake trout had declined, and were seldom caught in Lake Erie after the 1930s.

The lake trout story in Lake Ontario was more complex. Lake trout there experienced the combined effects of overfishing, cultural eutrophication, and the impacts of invasive species in a relatively short span of time. In the 1870s, after the loss of the Atlantic salmon, the alewives increased in Lake Ontario. Alewives may have competed with and forced the decline of other plankton-eating fish such as ciscoes and yellow perch. In the 1880s, sea lamprey populations increased in Lake Ontario, in part because the increased water temperature in streams (a result of environmental changes) were better suited for sea lamprey reproduction. Sea lampreys parasitically feed on lake trout and other fish, causing populations of these species to decline in Lake Ontario.

STUDYING THE FISHERY

In this era, fisheries research was just beginning. The major philosophy at the time was that fish were declining because they were having trouble reproducing. Thus, if more hatchery-reared fish were added—that is if the reproductive process and the early survival of fish were helped along—more fish would ultimately be available to harvest. Concern about fish populations, however, prompted some researchers to investigate underlying factors that affect fish production, such as water quality and food availability. It was then that fisheries management became more systematic and organized. For example:

❖ In 1870, the American Fish Culturists' Association, a professional organization, was formed and eventually evolved into the American Fisheries Society.

❖ In 1871, J. S. Milner began a survey for the U.S. Commission of Fish and Fisheries. He toured the shores and islands of Lake Michigan, collecting information on the life histories of fish important to the commercial fishing industry. Unfortunately, much of his fish collection, stored at the Chicago Academy of Science, was lost in the Great Chicago Fire of 1871. In 1872, he extended his survey to Lakes Superior, Huron, Erie, and St. Clair. His reports addressed what were likely the first scientific efforts to study lake whitefish

EARLY INVASIVE AND NON-NATIVE SPECIES

The arrival and impacts of non-native species in the Great Lakes were first noted during the late 1800s. Sea lampreys were noticed in Lake Ontario in the 1830s, and by the 1880s, they had a negative impact on fish populations there. Either sea lampreys had arrived through the Erie Canal or they had been native to the Lake Ontario basin, arriving through the St. Lawrence River. By 1921, sea lampreys entered Lake Erie through the canal system. During the next two decades, they spread to all of the other lakes.

Another marine invader, the alewife, first appeared in Lake Ontario in 1873.

Some non-native species were intentionally introduced into the Great Lakes during the heyday of hatchery propagation, including steelhead, Chinook salmon, brown trout, and carp.

In 1912, the non-native rainbow smelt was intentionally introduced into Crystal Lake near Lake Michigan.

1879

The sturgeon catch for Lake Michigan is 3.8 million lbs. (1.7 million kg), and some decline had probably already occurred.

Late 1870s to early 1880s

Great fluctuations occur in lake whitefish catches from Lake Ontario, as well as fluctuations in ciscoes.

1880

❖ In Lake Erie, pound netters complain of decreased lake whitefish harvests.

❖ Hatchery rearing and stocking of rainbow trout, brown trout, and other fish begins.

❖ Fish declines prompt researchers in the United States and Canada to investigate water quality.

migrations by tagging fish. Milner's studies gave evidence of serious declines in Great Lakes fisheries, and he recommended protective legislation and hatchery propagation of fish.

❖ Concerns in the Great Lakes prompted a successful international agreement. In 1909, the Boundary Waters Treaty between the United States and Canada established the International Joint Commission. The purpose of the commission was to help prevent and resolve disputes about the use and quality of water in the Great Lakes and to advise the two countries about water resources.

GROWING FISH

Hatchery rearing of fish was a major focus of fisheries management in the Great Lakes during this era. While some hatchery work had been tried in North America in the 1850s and 1860s, these efforts did not evolve into large-scale efforts until later. In 1874, in Michigan, the newly created Board of Fish Commissioners established a fish hatchery on the Detroit River.

Several other states also established hatcheries. During the 1880s and 1890s, the U.S. government began operating hatcheries in Northville and Alpena, Michigan; in Sandusky and Put-In-Bay,

Ohio; in Duluth, Minnesota; and in Cape Vincent, New York. Little is known about the success of these early programs. What is certain was the reaction to stocking. By the turn of the century, people were disgruntled that the stocking efforts were not noticeably increasing fish abundance.

RISE AND FALL: A SUMMARY OF THE TIMES

This era had brought tremendous changes to the life of the Great Lakes. Early in this period was the heyday of commercial fishing on many of the lakes. In 1871, more than 32.2 million pounds (14.6 million kg) of Great Lakes fish were handled at major fish markets and more were consumed locally.

Lake Michigan alone had a commercial industry employing an excess of 2,000 people and 600 vessels. By 1889, more than 10,000 people fished the lakes. In 1899, Lake Ontario experienced a peak in its catch. Around 1900, the catch from Lake Erie surpassed or equaled the production of all other lakes combined. The combined effects of social, technological, and environmental changes, however, were beginning to exert considerable influence on fish populations.

Overfishing with improved technologies seriously affected populations of Atlantic salmon and lake whitefish, among others. Invasive species had already been

Fish hatchery containers from the Wolf Lake Fish Hatchery near Kalamazoo, Mich. The hatchery was established in 1927 and still produces a wide range of fish species for both inland and Great Lakes waters.

1889

Commercial harvest peaks at 146.3 million lbs. (66.4 million kg), tripling the total Great Lakes harvest in less than 20 years

1890s

❖ Lake sturgeon decline in all of the lakes.

❖ Fishermen catch fewer lake trout, lake sturgeon, lake whitefish, blue pike, and chubs.

❖ Trap nets are first used in the Great Lakes.

❖ Arctic grayling and Atlantic salmon disappear from the Great Lakes.

detected in the lower lakes and would quickly influence the entire Great Lakes fishery. By the end of this era, agencies responded to the decline of some fish by establishing fishing regulations. Fisheries laws developed at this time included gear restrictions, closed seasons, and catch limits. For example, by the late 1800s, laws regulated the mesh size of gill nets used in the Great Lakes. In 1906–1907, Ohio and Michigan began to license commercial fishermen. Fisheries law enforcement started in the region; however, similar to today, officers were few compared to the vastness of the lakes they were responsible for covering. Differences in state and provincial fishing laws also made enforcement difficult.

NEW INVADERS, NEW CHALLENGES

ERA: 1920s TO 1950s

During the 1920s and into the 1930s, a new way of looking at the Great Lakes emerged. The tourism business boomed. Visitors flocked to shoreline resorts, even to remote areas such as Isle Royale, and the wealthy developed their own lakefront retreats. Visitors of all types dined on Great Lakes fish. Charter fishing became more common during the 1920s, when commercial fishermen took recreational anglers fishing for lake trout. Commercial and subsistence tribal fisheries continued.

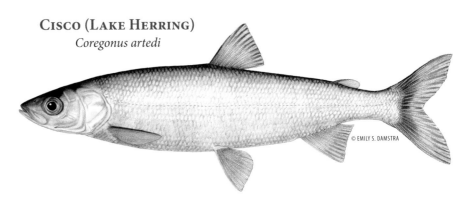

CISCO (LAKE HERRING)
Coregonus artedi

© EMILY S. DAMSTRA

SETTING THE STAGE

In 1924, U.S. citizenship was granted to Native Americans. In 1930, a court case in Michigan declared that Native Americans had no special fishing or hunting rights under state regulations. At this point, Native Americans did not challenge this court decision, and they had to buy state commercial fishing licenses.

In 1929, the U.S. stock market crashed, and many fish wholesalers went out of business. In 1939, Canada entered World War II, and by the end of 1941, the United States was also at war. Fishing was again declared an essential service, and commercial fishermen were exempt from the draft. By 1945, the war was over, and the world had changed. Global markets were opening, and sportfishing began to rise again.

INDUSTRIALIZED FISHING

During the 1920s and 1930s, the fishing fleet in the Great Lakes began converting to diesel engines. These were less bulky and used less fuel and labor to operate. The older steam fishing tugs had required a crew of seven—a captain, an engineer, and five workers/fishermen. Diesel boats, however, did not need an engineer and needed only half as many laborers. Also at this time, the first steel-hulled Great Lakes fishing boats began to replace wooden-hulled boats.

DEEP TRAP NETS

In the 1920s, the bull net was still in use; peak bull net use and increasing gill net use in Canadian waters of Lake Erie occurred in the mid-1920s. During that time, a new version of the trap net appeared on Lake Huron. Called a deep trap net, it was set at greater depths and on a variety of bottom types. It could be

1900s

The United States and Canada enter two world wars, during which fishing is declared an "essential service."

❖ The fisheries peak in the early part of the century and then rapidly decline.

❖ Environmental activism is born and laws are created to protect the health of the Great Lakes.

1900

The Chicago Sanitary and Ship Canal is completed, connecting the Great Lakes with the Mississippi River watershed.

1909

The Boundary Waters Treaty between the United States and Canada establishes the International Joint Commission to help prevent and resolve disputes relating to the use and quality of boundary waters.

1905

❖ Motorized net lifters are used to haul increasingly larger nets from the water.

❖ Governments in the region begin to adopt regulations on fishing, limits, and quotas on catches, restricting access to certain species at certain times and setting constraints on gear.

THUNDER BAY RESEARCH COLLECTION, ALPENA COUNTY PUBLIC LIBRARY

A fisher takes his catch out of a net.

handled more easily than previous pound nets and was used to catch lake whitefish in their deep summer habitats. It was introduced on Lake Huron in 1928; throughout the next two years, fishermen scrambled to convert to the new gear. Catches of lake whitefish doubled. Then lake whitefish began disappearing from the northern fishing grounds of Lake Huron.

Gill and pound netters protested the new gear. Governments began investigating this issue in 1931. By 1934 the conflict among the various fishermen had escalated, and southern fishermen drove out the encroaching northern deep trap netters trying to fish their southern waters. The deep trap net was

banned in U.S. waters by the mid-1930s (it had never been used in Canada); eventually, its use was governed by size and depth restrictions. This conflict is one that had previously occurred in the Great Lakes and would repeat itself again: disagreement among fisheries user groups on how to best allocate the resource upon which they all depended.

NYLON NETS

An important change in net technology began when nylon was invented in 1935. Nylon was lighter, did not absorb water, and decayed more slowly than cotton and linen nets. Nylon nets could be left in the water longer, were easier to handle, and were nearly invisible to the fish. By the 1950s, nearly all of the gill nets in the Great Lakes were replaced with nylon, and within 10 years, the pound and trap nets were also replaced. In addition, around World War II, the old-style wooden floats, or "corks," which fishermen had carved from cedar, were replaced with plastic or aluminum floats that allowed fishing in deeper water.

FISHERIES RESEARCH AND UNDERSTANDING YIELDS

More efficient catches led to greater concern about the sustainability of Great Lakes fisheries. As a result, fisheries science made important advances. The collapse of the cisco (lake herring) fishery

in Lake Erie by 1925 prompted large-scale studies on Great Lakes ecology. One study sponsored by Ohio examined the effects of pollution in Lake Erie.

A 1927 study by the U.S. Bureau of Commercial Fisheries was the beginning of federal fisheries research on the Great Lakes. This study examined the **limnology** (the chemistry, plankton, and benthos) of Lake Erie. The U.S. government, the states of Michigan and Wisconsin, and four net manufacturers conducted a third study on Lake Michigan. The study examined gill net size and effects on harvest of chubs while avoiding unintentional catches of small lake trout.

In the 1940s, a better understanding of the factors influencing fish production led fisheries managers to use a philosophy of **maximum sustainable yield (MSY)**. The approach requires understanding fish reproductive and growth requirements in relation to the productive capacity (biomass) that the fish habitat will support. Managers can use this knowledge to create quotas or regulations that result in a harvest of surplus production—essentially "skimming off the top," taking only fish numbers not critical in sustaining stable populations. In theory, the maximum harvest or MSY can be maintained without causing declines in fish populations or health.

1911

Lake sturgeon catch on Lake Michigan declines to 14,000 lbs. (6,350 kg).

1914

Fishing in Canada is declared an essential service as Great Britain enters World War I.

GREAT LAKES FISHERY COMMISSION

❖ U.S. fisherman on Lake Erie invent a variation of the gill net called the bull net that is up to 22 feet tall and is even more effective at catching fish.

1917

The United States joins World War I.

OTHER FORCES

Cultural eutrophication became a major force of environmental change during this era. Water quality continued to decline throughout the Great Lakes. The effects of these changes were compounded by invasive species. This is the second major type of environmental change that would happen during this time—invasive alewife, sea lamprey, and smelt had a negative and lasting impact on native fish populations. The decline in native fish populations of the previous era continued into the 1920s and beyond.

COLLAPSE: CISCO

Among the most dramatic declines ever experienced in the Great Lakes was the collapse of the cisco fishery that began in the 1920s. The collapse included several species of cisco, including *C. artedi*, or lake herring. In Lake Erie, for example, the harvest of *C. artedi* dropped from a high rate of around 32 million pounds (14.5 million kg) per year to a low of 5.7 million pounds (2.6 million kg) per year.

Once lake trout populations began to decline, numbers of ciscoes increased somewhat in the 1930s and 1940s. However, with the unavailability of lake trout, fishermen switched to catching ciscoes, exploiting them in sequential order from the largest to the smallest species. Cisco catches were high— for a short time. In the 1940s, cisco

populations in Lake Ontario and Lake Huron collapsed due to a combination of overfishing, environmental degradation particularly of spawning habitat, and possible competition from non-native rainbow smelt and alewife. The cisco catch in Lake Superior and Lake Michigan remained constant through the 1950s, but collapsed in the following decades.

As they had done when other favored fish collapsed, fishermen responded to decline in ciscoes by switching their efforts to other species. Perch catches in Lake Huron and Lake Erie increased in the late 1920s and early 1930s. Eventually, smelt became so well established in the lakes that fishermen began to utilize them, and a smelt fishery using trawl nets emerged.

INVERSE RELATIONSHIPS

Sea lampreys and alewives caused some of the most significant ecological changes in the Great Lakes. Once the invasive sea lamprey became established in one of the Great Lakes, the first declines occurred in the larger, deep-water species such as lake trout, burbot, and the largest of the deepwater ciscoes. Sea lampreys occasionally targeted the other species, such as coregonines like lake whitefish as well as walleye, bass, channel catfish, and bullheads. As sea lampreys became more established, their prey declined.

OTHER TECHNOLOGICAL ADVANCES

Other advances were made in a short period during these decades. For example, in the 1930s, refrigerated trucks transported fish to markets.

Radar, depth-finders, and radios came into use in the late 1930s to 1940s. Fishermen employed this new technology to help them find fish.

Because the numbers of large predator fish (mainly lake trout) were declining, alewife populations increased, especially in Lake Huron and Lake Michigan. Lake Superior and its tributaries were likely too cold for alewives to be established. Alewives eat mainly large plankton, just as native ciscoes (lake herring) do. As the invasive alewife population increased, the cisco's (lake herring) and other fish species' populations decreased. The alewife, which travels in dense schools, may have out-competed the young of native species or simply preyed on their eggs and fry. Eventually, the alewife became the dominant forage fish in the lakes.

1918

- ❖ The Great Lakes fishery peaks. After 1918, fish catches decline.
- ❖ The first species of ciscoes to decline are the larger ones, such as the blackfin cisco.

- ❖ Major declines in cisco (lake herring) are seen in Lake Michigan.
- ❖ Northern pike in Lake Erie show significant decline.

The 1920s through 1950s saw the decline—and in some cases the end—of the Great Lakes commercial fishery for several native fish species. For example:

- ❖ Lake trout declined to a catch of less than 1,000 pounds (454 kg) in Lake Erie in 1937.
- ❖ Lake trout catches had already dropped in Saginaw Bay and Green Bay. They declined in Lake Huron in the late 1930s and in Lake Superior in the 1940s.
- ❖ After much fluctuation, the lake trout fishery suffered a dramatic collapse in Lake Superior in the 1950s.
- ❖ Lake whitefish declined in the western basin of Lake Erie in the 1920s, and fishermen there switched to yellow perch.

- ❖ In Lake Michigan, lake whitefish resurged in the 1920s, but the catch dropped again in the 1930s.
- ❖ By the 1930s, Lake Huron fishermen were noticing rapid drops in lake whitefish.
- ❖ Lake Superior continued its reputation as being somewhat isolated from and resistant to negative impacts—a recovery of lake whitefish occurred there in the 1930s and 1940s.

Other native fish species were impacted during this era. In the 1930s, Lake Ontario's total fish production dropped behind that of the historically less-productive Lake Superior. In 1924, sauger in Lake Erie declined. Northern pike in Lake Erie had already declined by 1915, largely due to loss of wetland spawning areas.

PRESERVING FISH

Throughout the Great Lakes, commercial fishing operations kept workers employed during the winter months by harvesting ice off the lakes for both commercial and residential use. Before electric-generated refrigeration was available, ice was delivered in blocks and stored in "ice boxes." There are many traditional techniques for preserving fish, including pickling, salting, canning, smoking, and drying. These preservation methods kept fish safe to eat and allowed for shipping the fish to markets in other areas of the United States and Canada. Many of these preservation methods continue to be used today, with smoked fish a popular consumer product.

ENVIRONMENTAL PROBLEMS AND RECOVERY

ERA: 1950s TO 1980s

After the St. Lawrence Seaway system opened in 1959, the Great Lakes were accessible to oceangoing vessels. The region became a bigger player in the global marketplace, spurring further industrial growth and development. However, with this direct opening came problems. The industrial boom led to new, more insidious environmental degradation. Chemical pollutants, cultural eutrophication, and invasive species continued to negatively influence the ecosystem of the Great Lakes basin.

BETTER LIVING THROUGH CHEMISTRY?

During this period, a vast array of industrial, agricultural, and household chemical products were being produced and used. Point sources of pollution included municipal sewage treatment plants and a variety of new industrial processes, supported by new technologies. Non-point sources of pollution included agricultural runoff, use and disposal of household products with **phosphates**, and use of lawn and garden chemicals. They were used in cities, suburbs, and rural areas of the Great Lakes region. It would take some

1920

First diesel vessels on the Great Lakes.

1924

Passage of the Indian Citizenship Act grants citizenship to all Native Americans. However, a Michigan court case rules that Native Americans have no special fishing or hunting rights under state regulations.

BRANDON SCHROEDER, MISG

1921

❖ Lake trout populations reach final peak.

❖ Sea lampreys are discovered in Lake Erie.

GONE, BUT NOT FORGOTTEN

Like the Arctic grayling, other species of fish have disappeared from the Great Lakes during the last century. It has been more than 40 years since the blue pike (*Sander vitreum glaucum*) was declared extinct, but it is not far from the minds of some Great Lakes anglers. Every few years, rumors of rogue stocking of an inland lake or a catch of a blue-ish walleye pops up, reopening the door to the blue pike mystery.

The blue pike, a native of Lake Erie, Lake Ontario, and the Niagara River was once an important part of the lower lakes' ecosystems and a significant catch for the commercial and recreational fishing industries.

The blue pike was related to the walleye, but had a blue hue rather than yellow coloring and featured larger, more pronounced eyes. It preferred the deeper, colder, and clearer water of the lakes. According to Wisconsin Sea Grant fishery experts, it was a successful fish, providing an annual commercial catch that often exceeded 20 million pounds (an estimated $150 million today). Commercial and sport anglers relentlessly pursued the blue pike, landing 1 billion pounds of the fish between 1885 and 1962. At times, it made up more than 50 percent of the commercial catch in Lake Erie.

The blue pike began to decline because of multiple factors, including pollution, changes in habitat, invasive species, and overfishing. The last successful spawning occurred in 1954 and the fishery collapsed entirely within three years; the blue pike was thought to be extinct by 1970.

However, rumors about stocking in secret inland lakes in the northern Great Lakes region persist, keeping alive the idea that the genetic offspring of the blue pike are swimming around somewhere out there.

OTHER DISAPPEARANCES

At least three other species of fish native to the Great Lakes also disappeared during this time. A deepwater cisco, *Coregonus johannae*, native to Lake Huron and Lake Michigan was eliminated in the 1950s; the blackfin cisco, *C. nigripinnis*, native to all Great Lakes with the exception of Erie, disappeared in the 1960s; and the longjaw cisco, *C. alpenae*, native to Huron, Michigan, and Erie, was extirpated in the 1970s.

BLUE PIKE
Sander vitreum glaucum

1925

- ❖ Lake whitefish recovers in Lake Ontario.
- ❖ Tourism and commercial charter fishing grow as an industry.
- ❖ Fishing fleets convert to diesel engines and steel hulls begin to replace wooden hulls.

- ❖ Total fish catch levels off to less than 120 million lbs. (54.5 million kg) per year.
- ❖ Lake Erie cisco fishery crashes.

time before the impacts of such chemicals were observed throughout the Great Lakes basin.

Several specific chemicals arising from the agricultural and industrial sectors had serious, wide-reaching effects. The main chemicals used in this era were **dichlorodiphenyltrichloroethane (DDT)** and **polychlorinated biphenyl (PCB)**. DDT was used as an insecticide to battle the organisms causing Dutch elm disease and to eradicate mosquitoes. PCBs were one of many chemicals used in electrical insulation and in manufacturing. They were also widely used in plastics, paints, electrical parts and transformers, carbonless copy paper, adhesives, fire retardants and lubricants in industrial machinery, commercial refrigeration units, inks, and carpets.

DDT and PCBs, as well as some other chemicals and chemical by-products of industrial processes, were identified in this era as **persistent chemicals**—substances that bio-accumulate and break down very slowly in the environment over long periods of time. Persistent chemicals influence the food web and environment when the chemicals are passed from one organism to another. Some fish and other aquatic organisms still exhibit high levels of PCBs today, decades later.

Eventually the presence of chemical contaminants became known in the late 1960s and early 1970s when people began to observe their effects on fish and wildlife. Some species, such as the bald eagle, had nearly disappeared from the Great Lakes region. Meanwhile, scientists developed the technology to measure smaller and smaller concentrations of chemical contaminants in water and animal tissue. Some contaminants, like DDT and PCBs, are fat-soluble and are stored in fatty tissue.

ATTENTION-GETTERS

The challenges posed by chemical pollutants were in concert with eutrophication problems of the 1960s and 1970s. Very serious and obvious problems focused public attention on the Great Lakes. Two events stand out.

THE CUYAHOGA RIVER ON FIRE

In June 1969, the Cuyahoga River, a tributary of Lake Erie flowing through Cleveland, Ohio, caught on fire. The high level of contaminants saturating the water sustained the blaze. Surprisingly, this was not the first time the river—or other rivers—had caught on fire because of chemical contaminants. However, this particular event proved to be a catalyst for those who had been increasingly concerned about the impact of pollutants on water quality to rally the general public. The public reacted strongly, and

---

THE USE OF DDT AND PCBs

The use of DDT was banned in individual Great Lakes states between 1969 and 1971 and subsequently banned by the United States and Canada in 1972. The use and manufacture of the insecticides aldrin and dieldrin were banned in 1974. Voluntary control of PCBs began in 1971, and their manufacture was banned in 1977.

PCBs, however, still enter the environment through improper disposal of products containing PCBs, and airborne PCBs from geographically distant sources. DDT and its derivatives continue to be deposited into the Great Lakes from air masses picking up material from countries where DDT is still used.

Toxic quantities of legacy contaminants, such as DDT and PCBs, still remain in bottom sediments where the non-water-soluble chemicals settled. Disturbance of sediments by dredging, shipping activity, storms, and burrowing organisms can bring these contaminants back into the food chain. Ironically, since use and deposition of these contaminants has been on a gradual decline, the lakes themselves now act as a source for these contaminants.

1928

Deep trap nets are introduced on Lake Huron to catch lake whitefish in their summer habitats.

1929

The U.S. stock market crashes, forcing many fish wholesalers out of business.

1930s

❖ The bull net is banned in most areas of the U.S. Great Lakes; pound and trap nets become more common.

❖ Lake trout decline to a catch of less than 1,000 lbs. (454 kg) in Lake Erie.

❖ Widespread acknowledgment that the fishery is in trouble, although Lake Superior seems to have been spared.

---

the Cuyahoga became an example of how polluted many waterways in the Great Lakes region had become.

LAKE ERIE DECLARED "DEAD"

Although news media reported the "death" of Lake Erie in the 1960s, the lake was actually too alive. As covered in the "Ecology" section, the eutrophication process caused by excess nutrients in the lake resulted in overenriched productivity. Algae bloomed, consumed oxygen, and died. Increased plant life meant more decay, particularly at the lake bottom. This decay led to lower oxygen levels in the hypolimnion, the bottom, coldest layer of water. With the oxygen demands from the boost in production and decay, little was left for other plants and organisms, causing what today we call "dead zones."

Lake Erie was the most affected of the lakes due to a multitude of factors, including shallow depth, warmth, population density, pollution, and location (acting as a drainage basin for the upper lakes). Yet the other lakes were beginning to experience some of the same serious changes, particularly in the bays. Shallow, nearshore areas were the first to be affected by both high levels of nutrients and chemical contaminants. Great Lakes nearshore areas are critical for fish and birds, drinking water supplies, and tourism.

Non-native species continued to exert their influence in the Great Lakes. The effects of the sea lamprey worsened in the 1950s until the first control efforts with lampricides began in 1958. Alewife numbers had also increased greatly. Massive die-offs of alewives began in the late 1950s and increased substantially in the 1960s, causing aesthetic problems on beaches. A new wave of invasions began in the 1980s and this time the hitchhikers—notably the spiny water flea, zebra and quagga mussels, Eurasian ruffe, and invasive aquatic plants—arrived aboard transoceanic vessels.

ENVIRONMENTAL EFFECTS ON FISH

In the central basin of Lake Erie, warming water temperatures, a notable decrease in oxygen levels at the lake bottom in summer months, and the lack of burrowing mayflies and other benthic foods were serious warning signs. With the loss of oxygen in Lake Erie's central basin, walleye lost their important summer habitat, and commercial catches in Lake Erie declined by 1969 because of habitat loss and overfishing. Another problem—**stunting** or slow growth—of yellow perch occurred in Green Bay on Lake Michigan and Saginaw Bay on Lake Huron, partly due to crowding from a lack of large predators consuming perch. Also, the perch's food source, burrowing

A Native American fisher with nets.

mayflies, were absent likely due to contaminants or low oxygen in the lake sediments.

Throughout the lakes, the decline of lake trout populations hit catastrophic levels. In 1964, the Lake Ontario lake trout catch dropped to less than 1,000 pounds (454 kg). In Lake Superior, long thought to be immune from environmental and fishing pressures influencing the other lakes, the lake trout declined dramatically in the 1960s. The effects of predation by the sea lamprey and intensive fishing pressure with nylon gill nets were too much for populations to withstand. The only fish left to support the Great Lakes

1930s

❖ The Great Lakes basin population is close to 23 million, an increase of 30 percent in 20 years.

❖ United States and Canada enter World War II and demand for fish is high.

1932

Sea lampreys are discovered in Lake Huron.

1936

Sea lampreys are discovered in Lake Michigan.

---

commercial fishery by the 1960s were smelt, yellow perch, and bloaters. White perch, an invasive species that arrived in the 1950s, supported a small fishery in the Bay of Quinte on Lake Ontario.

FISHING RIGHTS CHALLENGED

The multitude of changes in the Great Lakes environment and resulting impact on fisheries populations led to tremendous change in the social policies concerning tribal fishing in the region. States increased restrictions on tribal fishing operations that had purchased state commercial fishing licenses. In 1972, the Gurnoe decision of the Wisconsin State Supreme Court reaffirmed fishing rights originally specified in the Treaty of 1842 for the Red Cliff, Bad River, and Keweenaw Bay bands. This led to the establishment of 10-year fishing agreements negotiated between the tribes and the state of Wisconsin to establish fishing zones, harvest quotas, fishing effort, and types of gear that may be used. In addition, the agreements also require the exchange of biological information between the state and the tribes.

Widespread conflict occurred over tribal fishing rights in the Treaty of 1836 waters of Lake Huron, Lake Michigan, and eastern Lake Superior, as sportfishing began to expand in the 1970s. In some communities, violence and vandalism between the Native American fishers and state-licensed fishers occurred.

FIGHTING FOR RIGHTS

From 1971 to 1979, a Native American fisherman named Abe LeBlanc set gill nets in an effort to challenge the restriction of treaty fishing rights in 1836 treaty waters. By 1979, the issue had reached both the state and federal courts; the federal circuit court judge decided in favor of tribal fishing rights in treaty-ceded waters of Lakes Huron, Michigan, and Superior. The U.S. Court of Appeals subsequently upheld the decision. While the tribal fishing rights were under consideration by the courts, a "racehorse" fishery existed—where fishermen harvested as much as they could as quickly as they could. Activities by all parties went unchecked for years.

Further controversy arose over the use of tribal fishing equipment, specifically gill nets. Tribal, federal, and state governments, as well as sportfishing organizations, participated in further court action about tribal fishing rights. In 1980, the U.S. court of appeals agreed with the judge's decision that

the state could not interfere with tribal fishing unless it could be shown that the fishery was in jeopardy. The U.S. Supreme Court agreed with this decision by declining to review it. This process assured the tribes' right to self-regulation of fishery resource use.

In 1981, the tribes in the upper Great Lakes region established an intertribal regulatory body called the Chippewa Ottawa Treaty Fishery Management Authority (COTFMA). This organization was responsible for establishing and enforcing fishing regulations for tribal members. In cooperation with other fisheries management agencies and on the advice of the Inter-Tribal Fisheries and Assessment Program, the intertribal management established harvest quotas, and conducted fisheries research, enhancement projects, and long-term studies on contaminants in fish. Another important organization is the Great Lakes Indian Fish and Wildlife Commission, which supports fishery

---

NAVIGATION AND RESEARCH

Along with the changes in shipping and global economies came other technological changes. The computer age began, allowing more accurate navigation and data processing. Fish finders and Loran-C navigation (using radio signals) soon became commonplace.

1940s

❖ Nylon, invented in the 1930s, replaces cotton and linen in gill nets.

❖ Wooden floats or "corks" are replaced by plastic or aluminum float.

❖ Radar, depth-finders, radios, and refrigerated trucks are invented and are used to catch and transport fish.

❖ Fisheries managers adopt a strategy of maximum sustainable yield (MSY).

conservation efforts conducted by tribal groups in the Lake Superior region.

CHANGES HERE TO STAY

By the 1950s, the cumulative impact of human population growth and technological changes had forever changed the Great Lakes fisheries. Many of these changes had occurred over a relatively short time. In fact, some had their roots in the earliest technological changes at the beginning of European settlement and commercial fishing in the area. Social, technological (including overfishing), and environmental changes (e.g., forest cutting and settlement, invasions by aquatic species, and cultural eutrophication) had profound impacts. Great Lakes fisheries changed in two major ways between 1950 and 1980:

1. Invasive species such as smelt and alewives replaced native species in their food web niches, thus altering the forage base for the larger fish in the lakes; and

2. There was a general and widespread decline of lake whitefish and of large predators such as lake trout, walleye, and burbot, resulting in big changes to relatively stable fish populations.

Lakes Ontario and Erie and deepwater regions of Lakes Superior, Huron, and Michigan showed the greatest changes.

CLEVELAND PRESS COLLECTION, CLEVELAND STATE UNIVERSITY LIBRARY, VAN DILLARD

The students and faculty of Cleveland State University held an Earth Day march on April 21, 1970. More than 1,000 people marched from campus to the Cuyahoga River to protest pollution and environmental degradation.

THE PUBLIC REACTS

The United States and Canada experienced a social reawakening in the 1960s. Environmental quality had become so poor that the environmental movement—hand in hand with other social movements of the time—gathered strength.

Awareness of the Great Lakes' vulnerability increased when Rachel Carson's book *Silent Spring* told of the newest threats to the environment: pesticides and other chemical contaminants. Environmental groups formed and the first Earth Day was held in 1970. People spoke up for laws to make water "fishable, swimmable, and drinkable."

By the end of this era, the public supported broad-ranging legislative initiatives to control some of these obvious sources of pollution. The Great Lakes Water Quality Agreement was signed by the United States and Canada in 1972. The Federal Clean Water Act was also revised and signed into legislation in 1972 because of the polluted state of rivers and lakes across the country. The Great Lakes, including Lake Erie, began to recover from both chemical contaminants and nutrient overenrichment.

1941

Japanese attack Pearl Harbor and the United States enters World War II.

1946

❖ Sea lampreys are discovered in Lake Superior.

❖ Commercial fishing operations increase fishing effort: people fish harder but catch less.

GREAT LAKES FISHERY COMMISSION

1950s

❖ Nearly all gill nets, as well as pound and trap nets, are now nylon.

❖ The chemical TFM is applied to some Great Lakes streams in an attempt to control sea lampreys.

CLEVELAND STATE UNIVERSITY: MICHAEL SCHWARTZ LIBRARY

The Cuyahoga River—described by Time magazine as a river that oozes instead of flows—caught fire in June of 1969. Though it had caught fire many times before, this fire sparked a new movement in environmental awareness.

Sea lamprey control, pollution control, and new directions for fisheries management were initiated throughout the region.

Environmental action in the basin was spurred by the losses of fisheries due to the sea lamprey. In 1955, in one of the most important developments in Great Lakes fisheries management, the Great Lakes Fishery Commission was formed under a convention between the United States and Canada. The Fishery Commission was established for three reasons:

❖ To coordinate and facilitate fisheries research programs, which would help in the sustained productivity of fish, particularly the native lake trout.

❖ To develop a program to eradicate or minimize sea lamprey in the lakes.

❖ To establish working arrangements among governments, accomplished today through the Joint Strategic Plan.

POLLUTION CONTROL

New water quality standards established in the 1970s went a long way toward controlling the factors that had so altered fish habitats in the Great Lakes. The governments of Canada and the United States signed the first Great Lakes Water Quality Agreement in 1972. Under this agreement, each government committed to reduce the inputs of phosphorus, which had caused cultural eutrophication in the lakes.

The International Joint Commission was charged with overseeing progress of implementing the agreement. In the United States, pollution control and cleanup were carried out by several states in conjunction with the Environmental Protection Agency under the Federal Clean Water Act (1972). In Canada, the Province of Ontario's Ministry of the Environment joined forces with Environment Canada and many other governmental agencies to implement the agreement. As a result:

❖ New wastewater treatment plants were constructed. Phosphates in detergents were reduced or banned.

❖ Beginning in 1987, the United States and Canada identified areas of the Great Lakes basin severely affected by pollution.

❖ Each of the 43 **areas of concern** identified has a **remedial action plan**, which is intended to take a comprehensive, ecosystem approach to

DON SIMONELLI

❖ Starting in the mid-1950s, scientists note reproductive failures in fish-eating birds, including the almost total reproductive failure of some species, such as double crested cormorants, bald eagles, and herring gulls in Lake Ontario. This is later attributed to toxic chemicals, including the insecticide DDT.

1955

The International Convention on Great Lakes Fisheries establishes the Great Lakes Fishery Commission to focus on sea lamprey control.

1959

The St. Lawrence Seaway is opened, allowing medium-sized, international, oceangoing vessels to travel the Great Lakes.

restoring the area's beneficial uses, such as fishing and swimming. These action plans allow many different agencies, communities, and individuals to work together to solve serious water quality problems within the areas of concern.

❖ Water quality in the Great Lakes greatly improved and additional agreements to limit other pollutants in the basin were enacted.

SHIFT IN FISHERIES MANAGEMENT

A third set of strong actions further influenced the direction of Great Lakes fisheries in the modern era. New fisheries management goals were needed to address low native fish populations, new forage fish, and changing market demands. In 1966, the Michigan Department of Natural Resources (MDNR) began to take bold steps in changing the course of fisheries management, moving toward a primary goal of establishing recreational fisheries. Over the next few years, the MDNR

❖ Prohibited the commercial harvest of lake trout and walleye in certain Michigan waters;

❖ Regulated the commercial fishing effort by designating fishing zones and depths, banned gill nets for many state-licensed fishermen, limited the number of licensed commercial businesses, and established catch and effort quotas;

❖ Shifted the commercial fishery to the species less valued by sport anglers such as whitefish; and

❖ Introduced Pacific salmon (Coho salmon in 1966 and Chinook salmon in 1967) and built hatcheries to continue these stocking efforts.

FROM MAXIMUM TO OPTIMUM

Similar changes by state regulatory agencies were soon made throughout the region. For example, the New York State Department of Environmental Conservation also reduced commercial fishing through programs like the buyout of Lake Erie fishermen. This shift in basic approach benefited millions of Great Lakes residents by giving them a chance to experience the Great Lakes through recreational fishing.

The alterations also reflected a change in fisheries management strategy from maximum sustainable yield to **optimum sustainable yield**. Optimum sustainable yield blends biological, ecological, social, economic, and political information and values in developing unique management goals for various fisheries to produce the optimum—most favorable or acceptable—benefits to society from fish stocks.

There was much discussion and controversy throughout the region as these sweeping changes were made. The Province of Ontario did not agree

with the strategy of introducing non-native species (e.g., the Pacific salmon) to manage invasive species (e.g., alewife and smelt) in the Great Lakes. Instead, provincial Great Lakes fisheries management goals targeted native fish like lake trout and their habitats. Some states shared those goals, but eventually other Great Lakes states and the Province of Ontario also began stocking Pacific salmon to varying degrees.

OUT OF BUSINESS

The new orders restricting commercial fisheries quickly put some commercial fishing operations out of business. It was already an enterprise diminishing in the Great Lakes region due to declining lake trout and other cold-water species. Yet the loss of small-scale family fishing in the region can be compared to the loss of small family farms. Family members converted to other enterprises, leaving the Great Lakes fishery—along with their heritage and institutional knowledge—behind. Fewer young people were willing to accept the personal and business risks of their parents.

A few families were permitted to carry on their fishing activities in certain areas of the Great Lakes, including urban areas, under fisheries assessment programs established by resource management agencies. These fishers continued a tradition of stewardship by collecting

1960s

❖ The decline of lake trout reaches catastrophic levels. In Lake Ontario, the lake trout catch in 1964 drops to less than 1,000 lbs. (454 kg).

❖ After the loss of the lake trout as a large predator, alewife populations increase. The alewife begins to have influence on the Great Lakes ecosystem.

1969

The Cuyahoga River in Cleveland, which empties into Lake Erie, is so contaminated that it catches on fire. It also caught fire in 1936 and 1952.

GREAT LAKES FISHERY COMMISSION

1962

❖ Alewife die-offs litter the beaches.

❖ Lake Erie is proclaimed "dead" due to eutrophication from sewage, and industrial and agricultural runoff. It is one of the biggest environmental stories in North America.

---

age, growth, and reproductive data to help agencies with management decision-making. Over time, however, more people left the fishery and the commercial fishing industry was reduced significantly throughout the Great Lakes.

ADAPTIVE, COLLABORATIVE ECOSYSTEM MANAGEMENT

ERA: 1980s TO 2000s

By the 1980s and 1990s, it became clear that the cumulative impact of change over the centuries would require new approaches to fisheries management. State, provincial, and tribal managers recognized a need to reach across varied stakeholder groups and through binational organizations, such as the International Joint Commission and the Great Lakes Fishery Commission.

New, more flexible management strategies emerged that would allow state, provincial, and federal agencies and tribal organizations to improve and sustain fisheries and the Great Lakes ecosystem. Ongoing controversy over fishing rights—tribal, recreational, and commercial—was a driving force in management changes. An important question remained unanswered: how should the overall Great Lakes fishery resources be allocated among all users?

FISHING RIGHTS

In 1985, the state of Michigan, the tribes, and the U.S. federal government arrived at a 15-year negotiated settlement called the Entry of Consent Order, mandated by the federal courts. In this arrangement, the tribes agreed not to fish in certain treaty waters that were important for sportfishing and regained exclusive commercial fishing rights in certain other waters. Great Lakes waters were divided into three distinct zones: tribal fishing zones, zones for state-licensed commercial and sportfishing, and lake trout refuges or rehabilitation zones. In the trout refuges, neither gill netting nor sportfishing for lake trout was allowed. The order also established a mechanism for resolving disputes.

The agreement turned out to be generally effective for both sport and tribal fisheries. Primarily, it allowed a 50-50 tribal-sport allocation of the fishery resources; however, more importantly, it eased some social conflicts and tensions by segregating the lakes into zones. The agreement ended the racehorse exploitation of the fishery that started decades before and created an atmosphere in which all parties work together on resource management.

THE 2000 CONSENT DECREE

The 1985 Consent Order expired in 2000, and after several years of negotiation,

the Consent Decree under which 1836 tribes in Michigan regulate their treaty fishery was signed in August 2000. As part of the decree, a Technical Fishery Review Committee was established. The committee was composed of the tribes (represented by the Chippewa Ottawa Resource Authority [CORA]), the U.S. Fish and Wildlife Service, and the Michigan Department of Natural Resources. The committee studied and established the total allowable catch levels, population levels of fish, catch and effort statistics for sport and commercial fisheries, and other important management data.

In 2001, the Chippewa-Ottawa Treaty Fishery Management Authority (COTFMA) officially changed over to the Chippewa Ottawa Resource Authority (CORA), gathering all tribes involved in the 1836 treaty into one organization.

Although current management structures have settled some of the major, emotional disputes, Great Lakes fisheries and user group issues are an ongoing challenge.

EVOLUTION OF FISH ADVISORIES

The legacy of the Great Lakes industrial strength is unfortunately reflected in the persistence of toxic chemicals. To address the contamination of fish and possible resulting human health risks, Great Lakes states and the Province of Ontario began to issue fish consumption advisories in

1971

Fish consumption warnings issued for Lake Michigan trout because of PCBs in the fish.

1979

For years, Native American fisherman Abe LeBlanc sets gill nets in an effort to challenge the restrictions of treaty fishing rights. Courts rule in favor of tribal self-management.

1972

U.S. and Canadian governments sign the first Great Lakes water quality agreement to protect and improve Great Lakes water quality.

the 1970s to guide consumers in their choices about eating fish. To establish these advisories, managers use the science of **risk assessment**, a procedure used to estimate the probability of negative health effects from a specific source and at a particular exposure level.

Risk assessments are conducted in many different ways. For example, methods developed by the U.S. Environmental Protection Agency use estimates of increased cancer risks associated with specific amounts of contaminated fish consumed. In this safe-level approach, fish over a given action level, those with more than 2 ppm (parts per million) of PCBs, for example, are not to be sold in interstate commerce. Other agencies, such as the U.S. Food and Drug Administration, use a different approach and focus more on assessing the risk of commercially caught fish harboring foodborne pathogens. Each state then uses different assumptions about this risk assessment information to develop its own **risk management** plan, a step that incorporates social, economic, and political information to decide how to reduce or eliminate the potential health risks to humans.

A VARIETY OF ADVICE

Thus, a mosaic of fish consumption advisories exists for the Great Lakes region. In order to learn about the current fish consumption advisories for a given

MANAGEMENT PAYS OFF

Over time, the Great Lakes Fishery Commission has become an umbrella organization for collaborative fisheries management in the region through its system of technical and lake committees involving a wide array of government, tribal, and university scientists, agency managers, and engaged stakeholders. The commission provides a forum through which state, provincial, and tribal agencies can achieve consensus on management issues.

The establishment of the commission allowed fisheries managers to enter into a new era of international, broad-scale management. For example, the commission facilitated coordination on sea lamprey management. Several years of extremely intensive research—much of this work performed at what is now the U.S. Geological Survey Hammond Bay Biological Station in northeast Michigan—led to the discovery of a chemical lampricide called TFM in 1957. The lampricide works effectively to eliminate larval sea lampreys that live in sediments in Great Lakes tributaries, while minimizing impacts on other life in the streams and rivers. As a result, by the 1960s and 1970s, many Great Lakes tributaries had been treated. The sea lamprey problem has come under control to a large degree, allowing agencies to stock fish for restoration and recreational purposes.

Lampricide treatment in the St. Louis River near Duluth, Minn.

DAVID RIECKS

1980s

❖ Large oceangoing vessels travel into the Great Lakes, especially from Eastern Europe and western Russia, introducing non-native species.

1980

Several groups and the Great Lakes Fishery Commission develop a joint strategic management plan.

MISG ARCHIVES

❖ The total economic impact of the Great Lakes sport fishery reaches $2–$4 billion per year and the recreational fishery creates more than 60,000 jobs in the region.

❖ About 32 million people live in the Great Lakes basin, creating a major population and industrial center.

CAROL SWINEHART, MISG ARCHIVES

jurisdiction of the Great Lakes, one must consult its fishing regulation information. The advisories provide information on species and sizes of fish to avoid or minimize consuming for specific bodies of water. Advisories also provide information on which groups of people (such as pregnant women or children under 15 years of age) should minimize or avoid consumption of fish and how to prepare fish to reduce risk.

Since many contaminants, including PCBs, are fat-soluble, trimming fatty tissue in the belly flap and cooking the fish by broiling or grilling so that fat drains away, are recommended ways to reduce exposure. Since the 1980s concentrations of contaminants in fish flesh have declined in most areas of the lakes.

Studies are inconclusive about the effects eating contaminated fish has on humans.

Some research has demonstrated a potential link between contaminated fish consumption and low birth weights or delayed early childhood development. However, further research on the possible links between contaminants in many foods, not just fish, and effects on humans and animals is needed. Long-term, more complex studies will provide scientists and managers with more accurate information.

INTERNATIONAL TRADE: MORE THAN BARGAINED FOR

After an economic decline in the 1980s, business and industry were on the rise again by the 1990s. International trade agreements and other economic forces brought more and larger oceangoing vessels into the region. Particularly noteworthy were the vessels traveling to and from the Ponto-Caspian region of Europe—which includes the Black, Caspian, and Azov Seas. Changing technologies led to increased trade and shipping, which in turn increased the risk of introducing non-native species.

An alarming number of non-native species entered the Great Lakes during this era. The increased introduction of non-native species posed additional management challenges. In some areas of the Great Lakes, for example northern Lake Huron, sea lamprey numbers and wounding rates (number of sores) on lake trout and salmon increased in the

GREAT LAKES FISHERIES HERITAGE TRAIL

PEOPLE, FISH, AND FISHING

The Great Lakes Fisheries Heritage Trail offers opportunity to explore the past, present, and future of the lakes through the lens of fish and fishing. From lighthouses to shipwrecks, the Great Lakes are rich in maritime heritage and tradition. Great Lakes fisheries—fish and people who fish—have significantly benefited coastal communities, the Great Lakes region, and the nation throughout history and still today.

The Great Lakes Fisheries Heritage Trail network represents a partnership among museum, maritime heritage, and fisheries partners cooperating across Michigan to promote our fisheries heritage. The collective efforts of these partners are helping to preserve and interpret historical artifacts, enhancing local communities and heritage-based tourism, and offering educational opportunities focusing on Great Lakes literacy and stewardship.

This trail includes museum exhibits and educational opportunities, fish towns and markets, research and science centers, events and experiences that highlight our fisheries heritage as it has defined Great Lakes coastal communities. Visitors are offered unique opportunities to explore the dynamic social, technological, and environmental changes that have shaped today's fisheries. View an interactive map of Great Lakes Fisheries Heritage Trail sites online.

To learn more visit: greatlakesfisheriestrail.org

1981

Tribes in the upper Great Lakes region set up the Chippewa-Ottawa Treaty Fishery Management Authority, later renamed to the Chippewa Ottawa Resource Authority (CORA) to establish and enforce fishing regulations for tribal fishers.

1984

A new invasive species, the spiny water flea (a type of zooplankton) arrives in Lake Huron and spreads throughout the Great Lakes.

1982

❖ Canada protects tribal fishing rights on the Great Lakes under the Canadian Constitution Act of 1982.

❖ The International Joint Commission identifies 43 contaminated areas of concern around the Great Lakes.

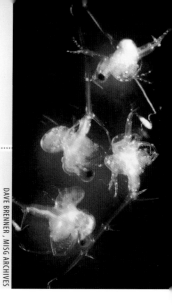

DAVE BRENNER, MISG ARCHIVES

late 1980s. Reasons for this resurgence of sea lampreys probably included improved water quality in spawning areas, recovery of a key prey species, and a lack of funding for sea lamprey control treatments due to high costs.

Meanwhile, an increasing number of non-native species were introduced through ballast water—many from the Eastern Baltics—with the potential to negatively impact the fisheries more than lampreys.

ZEBRA AND QUAGGA MUSSELS

The invasion by zebra and quagga mussels has been linked to significant ecosystem alterations and has caused much concern about impacts on Great Lakes fisheries. Researchers have found that zebra and quagga mussels filter out very large amounts of phytoplankton and nutrients from the water column. As a result, water clarity increases but less food is available for the base of the food web. In Lake Erie, the result has been that water clarity increased for a period, giving the mistaken impression that the mussels were beneficial. However, clearer water is not necessarily an advantage to the ecosystem. In shallow water areas, increased water clarity has increased the amount of lake bottom area exposed to sunlight, changing the habitat by encouraging plant growth and decreasing oxygen levels.

It is clear that Great Lakes food webs are altered when zebra and quagga mussels filter and trap many, if not a great majority, of phytoplankton in a lake. Less phytoplankton means less food available to zooplankton. These smaller animals are important foods preferred by many smaller forage and juvenile predator fish species. With less food available for fish and other organisms, these invasive species have undoubtedly affected the Great Lakes food web. What is not yet clear is what additional impact the invasive mussels may have on the Great Lakes ecosystem.

LAKE HURON EXAMPLE

The Lake Huron sport fishery has recently undergone dramatic changes related to modifications of the ecosystem. The changes are thought to be a result of invasive zebra and quagga mussels. Starting around the year 2000, biologists from the NOAA Great Lakes Environmental Research Laboratory began noting an alarming decline in the density of *Diporeia*, a small benthic animal that feeds on plankton as it settles out of the water column. Similarly, during this same period, U.S. Environmental Protection Agency research and monitoring efforts indicated depleted numbers of zooplankton in the offshore waters of Lake Huron. By 2004, the Great Lakes Science Center's Lake Huron Prey Fish Survey documented

sharp reductions in abundance of forage fish, accented by the near total collapse of the lake's alewife population.

Lake Huron fishery managers witnessed large changes across the range of predator sport fish species they monitor, including severe reductions in Chinook salmon. They also saw some native species, such as walleye and lake trout, benefit, likely because of less competition with alewives

IMPOSSIBLE TO ELIMINATE

Once certain non-native species arrive in the Great Lakes and begin to thrive, complete eradication of these biological pollutants is likely impossible. However, some measures can be taken to slow the rate of invasions. For example, ships are now required to exchange their fresh ballast water in the salt water of the high seas before entering the St. Lawrence Seaway. This increases the chance that freshwater species sensitive to saltwater will be killed prior to ship entry into the system. Voluntary guidelines for Canadian and U.S. waters established in 1989 became mandatory in U.S. waters in 1992.

1985

❖ Zebra mussel arrives in the Great Lakes and soon spreads to inland lakes and rivers.

❖ Entry of Consent Order grants the tribes exclusive fishing rights in designated Great Lakes waters. In exchange, the tribes agree not to commercially fish in certain sport fish areas or those used to re-establish lake trout populations.

DAVE JUDE

and an increasing ability to capitalize on another invasive species—the round goby—as a food source. Regardless, the total productivity of fish, or biomass, that Lake Huron is able to produce is diminished because fewer nutrients are now available to move up through the food web to larger fish species. More research is required in order to know with more certainty; however, preliminary results link the onslaught of invasive species—like zebra and quagga mussels as well as water fleas—with the ongoing changes to Lake Huron's food web.

NATIVE MUSSELS SUFFER

Zebra mussels negatively impact populations of native mussels in the Great Lakes. They occupy habitats required by native mussels and out-compete them for food. Zebra mussels also kill native mussels by attaching to their shells, preventing feeding and smothering them. In the 1990s, researchers began investigating whether any control measures could effectively and appropriately manage the zebra mussel in nearshore areas. The quagga mussel presents additional concerns because it tolerates colder, deeper water and can colonize on softer substrate than zebra mussels.

Some fish have the type of tooth or mouth structures necessary to prey on both zebra and quagga mussels. These

fish include freshwater drum, red ear sunfish, pumpkinseed, lake sturgeon, and river and copper redhorse suckers. However, the zebra and quagga mussels' best predator might be yet another non-native species—the round goby. Gobies coevolved with zebra and quagga mussels in the Ponto-Caspian Sea region. Biologists acknowledge that gobies, which are a prolific forage fish, serve as an abundant food source for some shallow water predators. Therefore, through an altered food chain, gobies readily absorb the nutrients in zebra mussels, and predator fish absorb the nutrients from consuming gobies, reintroducing the potentially lost nutrients back to the food web.

A native mussel covered with invasive zebra mussels.

BRANDON SCHROEDER, MISG

Despite adaptation, researchers, biologists, and managers fear what is yet to come if native food webs and ecosystems continue to be affected by non-native species from other parts of the world. Another big concern is establishing a new pathway for the bioaccumulation of persistent toxic contaminants from sediments throughout the Great Lakes. Zebra mussels concentrate these contaminated sediments, passing them to forage fish (e.g., gobies), which then pass the contaminants to predator fish, including popular sport fish (e.g., walleye).

SMALL INVADERS, BIG IMPACT
EURASIAN RUFFE

Another invasive species from the era is the Eurasian ruffe, a perch-like, non-native fish that was discovered in 1986 in Lake Superior near Duluth, Minnesota, and soon after in Thunder Bay, Ontario. Scientists are following this fish's populations and studying its effects on other species. It may prey on lake whitefish and cisco eggs, impacting their populations. To try to prevent its spread, Great Lakes managers and shippers agreed to avoid the discharge of ballast water from the Duluth and Thunder Bay areas into other parts of Lake Superior.

1990s

❖ Bacterial kidney disease (BKD) reduces Pacific salmon populations.

❖ By 1990, the Great Lakes basin population exceeds 33 million, 8 percent more than in 1970.

1991

More than 2.5 million anglers spend upwards of 25 million days per year fishing in the Great Lakes.

❖ Licensed commercial catch in the Great Lakes is 105 million lbs. (47.7 million kgs) of mostly lake whitefish, yellow perch, and alewife. The catch is larger in Canada.

❖ Concentrations of PCBs, DDT, and other contaminants in fish have declined by more than 90 percent from 1970 levels.

1992

The International Joint Commission recommends that Canada and the United States eliminate the use of chlorine and chlorine-containing compounds as industrial feedstocks.

WATER FLEAS

Not all potentially damaging invaders are larger animals. A species of zooplankton, the spiny water flea (*Bythotrephes longimanus*), also arrived in the 1980s and quickly spread throughout the Great Lakes. It was closely followed by another similar zooplankton, the fishhook water flea (*Cercopagis pengoi*), which began working its way through the Great Lakes after arriving in the late 1990s.

These invasive species are believed to have made their way into the Great Lakes in the ballast water of oceangoing vessels. The spiny water flea and the fishhook flea are relatively large for water fleas (total length about 0.3 inches or 8 mm) and have long barbed spines, making them difficult for small predators and forage fish to ingest, although larger fish have been known to eat them. More importantly, both invasive water fleas are predators of other zooplankton. Researchers began to investigate the effects of the spiny and fishhook fleas on the entire Great Lakes food web. They found that invasive zooplankton reduce the availability of smaller zooplankton (such as *Bosmina* or *Daphnia*) that are important to young, native fish and comprise the base of the native food web.

FISH DISEASES

In the late 1980s, bacterial kidney disease was found in large numbers of Chinook salmon and has been proposed as a cause of declining stocks, particularly in Lake Michigan. Fish with this disease show signs of bloating, internal bleeding, and susceptibility to other parasites and diseases. Bacterial kidney disease, or BKD as it is sometimes called, has always been present in low levels in Great Lakes salmon. Certain environmental conditions trigger the disease and appear to have greater impacts on fish populations.

Researchers have investigated ways of controlling or limiting the occurrence of bacterial kidney disease in hatchery-reared fish. This disease and its impacts have caused managers to rethink the role of hatcheries in sustaining fish populations in the basin. Some managers believe that a reduced reliance on hatchery fish for stocking will lead to more viable and resilient populations of wild-produced fish, more resistant to diseases like bacterial kidney disease. Hatcheries also take steps to monitor and prevent diseases.

CAUSE FOR CONCERN: FORAGE FISH

By the mid-1980s, the status of forage fish became of great concern for fisheries managers throughout the Great Lakes basin. Some of the indicators included the decline of two non-native species in various lakes. For example:

❖ Alewife populations declined sharply in Lake Michigan and Lake Huron.

ADVANCED TECHNOLOGIES

Within the Great Lakes, both sport and commercial fisheries benefited from boat designs, motors, engines, and fishing equipment improvements that continued through the 1990s. Advanced "fish finding" technologies, GPS (Global Positioning System) technologies and real-time monitoring of water temperatures using satellites were among the newest technologies that sport and commercial fishers used then and continue to use to find fish more quickly and efficiently.

These same advances in technology—along with more advanced computers and software—contributed significantly to fisheries research and management work. Using these, fisheries researchers and managers have greater abilities to monitor and collect data on fish populations and to better understand and manage more complex ecosystem interactions.

1993

Flooding introduces cryptosporidium, a protozoan parasite, into the drinking water system of Milwaukee, Wisconsin. The outbreak affects about 400,000, hospitalizes 4,000, and kills 111 people.

1994

Collingwood Harbour on Georgian Bay in Lake Huron is the first area of concern to be declared restored and is delisted.

1997

Canada and the United States sign the Great Lakes Binational Toxics Strategy.

ROBERT BURNS, DETROIT RIVERKEEPER

2000s

Environmental stewardship grows. Citizen science is on the rise.

❖ The threat of an Asian carp invasion brings invasive species issues to the forefront.

❖ Restoring the Great Lakes becomes a national priority.

❖ In Lake Superior, rainbow smelt declined and ciscoes, particularly C. artedi, increased; however, both of these fish species tend to have populations that fluctuate, possibly due to climate variations from year to year.

❖ In Lake Ontario, older and larger alewives and rainbow smelt waned, contributing to a decline in overall forage biomass between 1991 and 1993.

Alewives in poor condition may be especially susceptible to die-offs during cold winters and other extreme weather.

Researchers and managers discovered that high levels of stocked salmonids also played a role in reducing the forage base.

While any one of these issues alone could have significantly impacted the Great Lakes fishery, in reality they came in overlapping waves, so their effects were multiplied, and management efforts that had worked in the past were not as

---

A SLIPPERY PROBLEM: SEA LAMPREY

After invading the Great Lakes in the early 1900s, sea lampreys, along with overfishing and habitat degradation, devastated the Great Lakes fishery and ecosystem. In response, the governments of Canada and the United States formed the Great Lakes Fishery Commission to develop and implement a sea lamprey control program. GLFC scientists developed selective pesticides called lampricides that target sea lamprey larvae in their birth streams before they can damage fish. Through the use of lampricides and barriers that block migrating adults and reduce the availability of larval habitat, the GLFC reduced sea lamprey populations in most of the Great Lakes by 90 percent. Annual applications of lampricides and the use of barriers continue to keep sea lamprey populations in check, and binational efforts to rehabilitate the fish community and ecosystem are succeeding. The Great Lakes fishery is

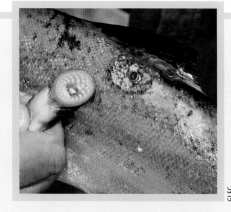

GLFC

now valued at over $7 billion.

Although relatively selective, lampricides can impact certain nontarget species, and barriers impede native fish migrations. Therefore, the GLFC continues to study the effects of lampricide on both sea lampreys and nontarget species, such as lake sturgeon. GLFC researchers seek to maximize toxicity to sea lampreys while minimizing the impacts to nontarget species. They also study sea lamprey and nontarget fish migratory behavior to develop tactics and technologies that allow desirable species to pass above barriers while restricting sea lamprey access.

Alternative designs such as electrical, seasonal, and velocity barriers are being explored.

Additional control tactics include reducing sea lamprey reproduction by trapping and removing adults, disrupting pheromones that enable lampreys to attract mates, and releasing sterilized males that compete with fertile males for mates. Scientists with GLFC also study pheromones, migratory cues, and alarm cues in an effort to modify sea lamprey behaviors and potentially concentrate reproduction in areas where egg survival is low or where lampricides are very effective.

Overall, the pursuit of additional control tactics is important to the GLFC, considering the social challenges associated with the use of lampricides and barriers. The potential for lampricide resistance may also become a concern in the future and further highlights the need for an integrated pest management approach.

2001

❖ The United States and Canada release a State of the Great Lakes Report; 25 percent of the 33 health indicators show good or improving trends; 50 percent are mixed; and 25 percent are poor.

❖ By 2001, water levels in Lakes Huron, Michigan, St. Clair, and Erie reach lowest levels since mid-1960s.

2016

Lake Michigan cisco catch recovers to 14,000 with no help from hatcheries. Stocking options are considered for fostering cisco restoration in Lake Huron.

2008

The total commercial harvest of Great Lakes fish from U.S. and Canadian waters is 49,591,700 lbs., valued at more than $43,770,000.

GREAT LAKES COMMISSION

2010

The Great Lakes Restoration Initiative is the largest environmental investment in the Great Lakes in decades. $475 million is appropriated for GLRI projects during the first years (2010–2013).

---

successful. The decline in forage stocks combined with the increase of invasive species and diseases likely contributed to a reduction in salmon in many areas of the lakes, especially Lake Michigan. In turn, recreational salmon fishing and catches decreased dramatically in the late 1980s. Managers concluded that stocking programs for salmonids had reached their limits; most states and the Province of Ontario reduced stocking levels to a more sustainable level in relation to the lakes' forage base.

EFFORTS TOWARD NATIVE FISH RESTORATION

Recent years have seen increased interest and investment toward efforts to restore native fish species.

For lake trout in particular, long-term investments seem to be paying off. Along with diminishing alewife populations, restoration efforts such as habitat improvements, stocking, sea lamprey management, and tighter fishing regulations have contributed to significant natural lake trout reproduction in Lake Huron and, to a lesser degree, in Lake Michigan. Lake Huron's 2018 stocking numbers were significantly lower than in previous years as a result of natural reproduction and growing adult lake trout populations. Lake Superior's lake trout are now considered rehabilitated.

Other native fish species have benefited from similar efforts. In 2000, the Great Lakes Fishery Trust brought together researchers, managers, and community stakeholders from around the region to advance the restoration of lake sturgeon in the Great Lakes. This effort ignited collaborations, conversations, and restoration efforts that continue today. Supported by the Great Lakes Fishery Commission, state and federal agencies have also coordinated to research and begin restoration for cisco populations in the Great Lakes. Most recently, stocking and restoration efforts have begun in Lake Huron, while Lake Michigan has witnessed some limited recovery of cisco populations even without hatchery support.

SUMMARY

HISTORY OF THE GREAT LAKES

The history of the Great Lakes is a long and varied one. Starting with the first people who lived in the region, the fisheries helped guide and shape the culture that developed around the lakes. This chapter reviewed the development of the Great Lakes region, the advances made through time, and how the fishery responded.

To summarize:

❖ Drawn by the abundance of natural resources, people found the region to be prosperous and appealing. The Great Lakes were thought to be inexhaustible resources.

❖ With European settlement came increasing pressure, exploitation of Great Lakes resources, and degradation of the environment.

❖ The introduction of industry, particularly logging in the 1800s–1900s, then manufacturing and the eventual use of chemicals, led to negative impacts on water quality and the Great Lakes fishery.

❖ The turning point for management and environmental regulation hit in the 1950s and 1960s, when several fisheries collapsed and major environmental problems, such as the cultural eutrophication of Lake Erie, surfaced.

❖ Overfishing and increasing stress on the Great Lakes ecosystem drove the continuing need for smart resource management, stewardship, and legislative collaboration.

❖ Today's Great Lakes fisheries are quite different than they were thousands of years ago. In the last century, and particularly in recent decades, the pace of change has accelerated.

FUTURE
of the
GREAT LAKES
FISHERIES

The past, current, and emerging issues affecting the Great Lakes will ultimately define the future of the Great Lakes fisheries. That future will include a variety of challenges such as new and existing invasive species, changes in the status of certain fisheries, changes to and rehabilitation of habitats, lingering and new contamination, and continued joint management of a vast international resource.

Managers, stakeholders, and researchers will continue to confront these issues—amid uncertainty and increasing complexity. As we move forward, advances in research and technology will help improve understanding of the ever-changing Great Lakes ecosystem. The collaborative efforts among managers and users will continue to be essential to achieving broader **ecosystem management** goals.

This section explores three primary areas related to the future of the Great Lakes fishery.

UNDERSTANDING AND ADAPTING TO HABITAT AND ECOSYSTEM CHANGES

The Great Lakes are comprised of very large, diverse, and dynamic ecological systems. These ecosystems are always changing; and particularly so when human activities result in altered habitats or introductions of new non-native species. There are limits to what we know and understand about these ecosystems. Even with the management tools of stocking, harvest regulation, and habitat restoration, managers have only so much control over the broad ecological processes. In the end, how we use and manage the Great Lakes fishery is dependent upon our understanding of these ecosystems and on how we adapt to change.

POLICY, MANAGEMENT, AND MAKING DECISIONS RELATED TO FISHERY ISSUES

Resource managers often have to make decisions using imperfect information. They have to approach complex issues, sometimes without a complete understanding of ecosystem functions or stakeholder values regarding a particular resource. Making management decisions is not simply about how one piece of the puzzle will affect the rest of the ecosystem. It is also understanding how people use a resource and gauging how they will respond to a management action. Part of the management challenge is providing decision-makers and the public with science-based education resources about the fisheries. Creating opportunities for public involvement in Great Lakes management is equally important.

STAKEHOLDER AND USER GROUP ENGAGEMENT

Stakeholders play an important role in fisheries management. This role will only grow in the future. While it may feel like natural resources decisions—or most policy decisions, really—are made at a distinctly high level, users of the Great Lakes may have more authority than they realize. User groups have significant influence on how decisions are made. However, stakeholder needs vary, and balancing conflict is not simple. Because there is such a demand placed on our natural resources, it is all the more important for resource managers to have a strong understanding of users, as well as the policy and ecological sides of decision-making.

UNDERSTANDING AND ADAPTING TO CHANGES

THE CHALLENGES OF ECOSYSTEM MANAGEMENT

Fisheries researchers and managers have shifted from managing individual species and localized areas of the Great Lakes, to managing fish communities on an ecosystem scale. Ecosystem management is a holistic approach. For instance, in the Great Lakes this approach to fisheries management is based on fish interactions and interrelationships within the Great Lakes ecosystem.

The challenge will be to continue making progress toward sustainability, while responding to emerging issues and continual ecological changes in these ecosystems. Many different issues—including the impacts of non-native species, restoration of native

fish populations, changing habitats, and management and allocation of harvestable predators and their prey—must all be considered in relationship with each other. To do this will require increased cooperation among researchers, managers, user groups, the public, and decision-makers. For example, Great Lakes Sea Grant outreach experts provide on-the-ground services to facilitate this cooperation, and ensure that decision-makers have access to science-based information.

As part of the overall ecosystem management strategy, many habitat- and ecology-related issues and challenges are identified individually, but are considered collectively.

Future fisheries-specific management considerations include
- ❖ Sustainability and harvest of fisheries
- ❖ Natural reproduction, stocking, and genetics
- ❖ Biodiversity and restoration of native species
- ❖ Predicting and managing the forage base
- ❖ Influence of fish consumers
- ❖ Invasive species management
- ❖ Fish health and diseases

Future habitat- and ecosystem-specific considerations include
- ❖ Habitat protection, restoration, and accessibility to fish
- ❖ Water quantity and water levels
- ❖ Water quality and environmental contaminants
- ❖ Climate change

Cohesive management methods require that all of these important issues are considered in order to achieve a sustainable future for the Great Lakes fisheries.

FOCUS ON THE FISH

UNDERSTANDING SUSTAINABILITY AND NATURAL CHANGES

Sustainability of Great Lakes fisheries, in the context of the future, means the long-term health and stability of fish populations, predominantly species targeted and harvested by sport anglers and commercial operations. Managing Great Lakes fish communities for sustainability includes reducing the introduction and the spread of invasive species and restoring and rehabilitating native species.

CHINOOK SALMON
Oncorhynchus tshawytscha

© EMILY S. DAMSTRA

NATURAL CYCLES

Not all changes in the fishery are negative or need to be managed. Long-term trends show that fishery fluctuations are part of a natural cycle. Populations experience highs and lows based on habitat and environmental changes, predator-prey interactions, and other, sometimes unknown, factors. Stakeholders and managers will likely have to monitor, predict, manage, and adapt to these continually fluctuating populations. Managers will also consider whether each new change in a fish population is the result of a natural cycle or an indicator of fishery health issues, habitat alterations, overfishing, or other manageable factors.

Understanding sustainability of fish communities—including the diversity of species, the structure of communities, the functional characteristics of fish within these communities, and the food web supporting them—will continue to be critical.

PREDATORS: MANAGING HEALTHY RELATIONSHIPS

In addition to individual species, researchers and managers are working to better understand the relationships between predator and prey species. For instance, the carrying capacity for predator fish in relation to available forage fish is an important consideration when making management decisions.

Predators such as lake trout, salmon, walleye, pike, and largemouth and smallmouth bass are among the more popular fish sought. Calculating stocking rates, enhancing natural reproduction, and understanding genetic diversity of species are just a few of the concerns managers juggle. Managers also contemplate appropriate predator habitats and ecological niches. The goal is to maintain healthy predator-prey relationships within the Great Lakes ecosystem while balancing the diversity and number of fish available for harvest.

STOCKING VERSUS NATURAL REPRODUCTION

Historically, stocking predator fish in the Great Lakes was thought to be a main goal for fisheries management. Some resource managers believed that more fish stocked equated to more fish caught. Today, many managers know this is not true; they recognize that stocking too many fish increases risks to the forage base and fish health. Habitat improvements to enhance natural reproduction will be important in the future, but it is possible that natural reproduction alone may never meet the current and increasing demands on the Great Lakes fishery resource. Future stocking of predators should focus on supplementing—not replacing—natural reproduction. Stocking decisions should also take into account the appropriate mix of predators and their genetics in relation to Great Lakes habitats, fisheries communities, management, and user values and goals.

UNKNOWN FACTORS

Natural reproduction of fish, which most natural resource managers consider preferable to stocking, is more difficult to monitor, and reproduction rates are challenging to predict. The health and recruitment of new fish into the fisheries is also unpredictable. Managers weigh the relative investment in hatchery rearing and fish stocking, versus protecting and improving habitats for naturally reproducing fish populations. A future management challenge for some sought-after species will be to complement natural reproduction and environmental variability with stocking—

FISHERIES SCIENCE AND MANAGEMENT

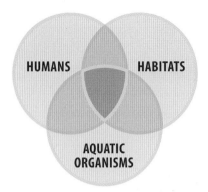

Effective fisheries management takes place when consideration of humans, animals, and environment overlap.

all while regulating fisheries to achieve sustainable harvests. Little is known about the combined impacts of stocked and naturally reproduced predators on forage fish populations.

Future challenges for managing predator fish populations will also include meeting the needs of many different user groups. Recently, Great Lakes fishery managers involved user groups in decision-making on managing salmon stocking based on the best scientific information about natural reproduction rates and available forage fish abundance. In light of increased natural reproduction and declining populations of alewife—the salmon's primary forage—salmon stocking in both Lake Michigan and Lake Huron was reduced. It was predicted that, without stocking reductions, both lakes faced potential collapse in predator species because of too many predators and not enough food. Scientists and managers believe that these reductions will help create healthier fish populations. The goal is to provide more sustainable harvests over time and to avoid fish population extremes or "boom and bust" periods.

Fish ladders are used to allow fish to migrate upstream around dams. Fish species such as trout and salmon that need to migrate to spawning grounds are particularly affected by obstructions like dams. Effective passages, like this ladder, can be critical for fish populations.

PREY: MANAGING THE FORAGE SPECIES

Fisheries management is more than simply assessing and understanding the predator species at the top of the food chain. Tracking and managing popular sport and commercial fish populations based on the status of forage fish is an important aspect of Great Lakes fishery management. Forage fish are preyed upon by predator species higher up the food chain. Humans have a stake in prey fish because we harvest them directly and because other fish we find desirable are reliant upon them. Forage fish also have a broader food web value, and changes to their populations can have far-reaching effects on many species within the Great Lakes ecosystem. While some forage fish species are declining, other populations are increasing, and many species of forage fish are expected to continually be in flux into the future. Forage fish populations can be affected by

❖ Amount of food available
❖ Competition for food resources
❖ Non-native species interactions
❖ Predator feeding pressures
❖ Reproductive cycles
❖ Climate variations

In turn, forage fish impact other parts of the lower food web, such as quantities and types of zooplankton that affect the feeding habits and growth rates of juvenile fish of various species. As prey, forage stocks contribute to the overall health and status of Great Lakes predators, for example lake trout. Scientists and managers are now sorting out the implications of changes in the forage base for the management of all Great Lakes fisheries. New sampling techniques and technologies will allow for more accurate population estimates. However, variables such as difficulties in accurately measuring, estimating, and making decisions about forage fish populations will continue to present challenges in estimating populations.

BALANCING HUMAN, FISH, AND ECOSYSTEM NEEDS

Many forage fish, such as bloater and cisco, are harvested commercially. Managers will continue to be challenged to balance the commercial harvest with the predatory needs of popular sport fish. Many of these smaller forage species also reflect ecological values beyond human use, contributing to biodiversity and playing important roles in a broader, functioning ecosystem.

Understanding the allocation of prey fish resources will continue to be critical in the future given the complex, important ecological and human significance of these species. Managers might ask the following questions:

❖ Which predator species should be favored based on existing forage populations? How will predators respond?
❖ What factors do we need to know about prey consumption, harvest, environmental conditions, and reproduction to better predict forage fish populations?
❖ What management tools or options exist by which we might manage particular forage fish populations?
❖ How can we effectively communicate the complexity of these decisions to our stakeholders and the public?
❖ What are the best methods for gathering stakeholder input to assist in decision-making?

Regardless of specific answers, prey species are becoming a focal point of management discussions. In the future, managers may concentrate more efforts on prey species as part of ecosystem-wide management activities.

OTHER FISH CONSUMERS

Many birds, including eagles, loons, mergansers, and cormorants consume Great Lakes fish. In the past, habitat degradation and health problems caused by pesticides reduced the populations of these birds. Since then, we have reduced or eliminated the use of certain harmful chemicals and are using more ecologically friendly products and production methods. A measure of success has been the resurgence of Great Lakes fish-eating birds.

However, with the resurgence of some fish-eating bird populations comes a contentious discussion. Specifically, fisheries managers have been discussing the population growth of double-crested cormorants and the impact on the Great Lakes. The rising numbers of cormorants could pit humans against birds for harvest of fish. The increasing harvest pressure by multiple consumers could have negative consequences for fish communities—another management consideration. The Les Cheneaux Islands yellow perch fishery of northern Lake Huron is one well-studied area where the impacts of growing cormorant populations on fish populations have been considered. Here, cormorant populations have been monitored and reduced as a management measure to help protect locally impacted fish populations.

The recovery of fish-eating birds like the cormorant is complicated because it creates additional competition, yet humans value fish-eating birds like eagles as part of a healthy Great Lakes ecosystem. How do we best allocate available fishery resources among birds, people, fish, and ecosystem? Ecosystem management efforts to balance the increasing demands of diverse human and wildlife fish consumers will remain vital to a healthy Great Lakes fishery.

NUANCES

The bottom line is that it is important to consider interactions of the fisheries community—from predators to forage fish, to humans and other consumers. It is also important to understand life cycles, population trends, and general health of individual species. Grasping the interconnectedness of these issues

© EMILY S. DAMSTRA

THE INVASIVE ALEWIFE

"Make yourself irreplaceable" is an age-old piece of advice for how to succeed in the work world, and it is one the invasive alewife has accomplished in the Great Lakes. The alewife, an invasive species, is now a crucial part of Great Lakes fisheries, as introduced non-native salmon are dependent on this prey species.

When alewife populations declined, biologists responded by reducing salmon stocking to match the reduction in forage fish. Alewife populations affect the productivity of salmon in the Great Lakes, which in turn, impacts the region's economy and angler satisfaction. Yet, managing alewife populations may present a different set of challenges for the health of native fish such as the lake trout, due to the effects of high levels of the enzyme thiaminase found in alewives. Alewives also prey upon the eggs and larvae of native species, such as lake trout, yellow perch, and walleye, further increasing pressure on native species populations.

What does this tell us? Managing forage fish populations for multiple uses, for example, by supporting both a non-native salmon fishery and the recovery of native fish populations, will continue to be complex.

BRAD MACNEILL

Populations of double-crested cormorants, the dark birds pictured here, were devastated in the Great Lakes during the 1960s and 70s due to chemical pollution. Today, the fish-eating bird populations have reached historic highs in the region. While the resurgence is a positive sign, there has been controversy about the effects the cormorants may have on stocks of fish species.

Inset: A 6-month old lake sturgeon raised at the Great Lakes WATER Institute in Milwaukee. Above: Sturgeon spawning in river shallows. Before spawning, sturgeon exhibit behaviors such as "porpoising" (raising their heads out of the water) and sometimes leaping out of the water entirely. The males gently slap their tales against a female's abdomen to indicate a readiness to spawn. They also emit what some call "sturgeon thunder" during spawning, a low-frequency sound similar to the drumming of a grouse.

PHOTOS: BOB RASHID

is critical to understanding the larger fishery community. Additionally, many concerns remain about the long-term impacts of non-native species introductions, the decline of certain key native benthic zooplankton populations such as *Diporeia*, and the resurgence of fish-eating birds..

NATIVE SPECIES RESTORATION

As stated previously, today's Great Lakes fishery is vastly different than the Great Lakes fishery of the past. And it will likely be quite different in the future. Supporting native species,

however, will continue to be imperative to fisheries management. Emphasizing the rehabilitation and maintenance of native species in the Great Lakes will be important in sustaining populations. Rehabilitating a species involves attaining a sufficient number of adults of reproductive age to produce enough young to maintain a robust population.

CONSIDER THE TROUT: LAKE TROUT CASE STUDY

Lake trout is one native species that has been targeted for rehabilitation. The work is challenging and costly. Since the early 1960s, attempts to achieve self-

sustaining and harvestable stocks of lake trout in the Great Lakes have been mostly unsuccessful, except in Lake Superior. In Lake Michigan and Lake Huron, lake trout stocking and management continues with some recent, but limited, success. For example, documentation of naturally occurring lake trout in Lake Huron demonstrates advances in lake trout population rehabilitation.

MODELING: A RESTORATION TOOL

Biologists working for state and federal agencies, universities, and the tribes have collaboratively developed computer models to estimate current and predict future lake trout populations. These models allow biologists to predict how lake trout populations will respond to changes in fishing pressure from tribal, state, and provincial fishers; reduced lampreys; and various stocking strategies.

For example, based on these models, size limit changes were made in certain areas of the Great Lakes to protect spawning lake trout from sportfishing mortality. They can also help forecast a reduced rate of lamprey-induced mortality because of increased lampricide treatment of the St. Marys River, a primary lamprey spawning area. Mortality from tribal commercial fishing was reduced significantly through a combination of harvest quotas, reduction in use of gill nets, and the conversion to trap net gear by some tribal fishers. The results created a steadier supply of larger lake trout, while simultaneously improving the likelihood of naturally reproducing or even self-sustaining lake trout populations.

OTHER NATIVE SPECIES RESTORATION

COASTER BROOK TROUT

Coaster brook trout is another native species that has been a focus of rehabilitation efforts. Researchers have

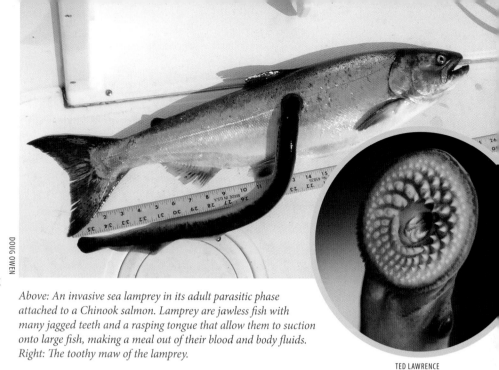

Above: An invasive sea lamprey in its adult parasitic phase attached to a Chinook salmon. Lamprey are jawless fish with many jagged teeth and a rasping tongue that allow them to suction onto large fish, making a meal out of their blood and body fluids. Right: The toothy maw of the lamprey.

identified several remnant stocks and are implementing a rehabilitation plan that involves hatchery rearing for stocking, tightened regulations, and habitat improvements. The U.S. Fish and Wildlife Service, state agencies, tribes, universities, and national and state-level user groups have invested in a rehabilitation effort that focuses on historically important stream and river systems that are best suited for improving coaster brook trout populations. As with other species, enhancing coaster brook trout populations may mean tightening regulations and adjusting stocking or management strategies in ways that may conflict with management or use of other Great Lakes species.

STURGEON

The lake sturgeon, once abundant throughout the Great Lakes, is another depleted native species drawing increased attention with rehabilitation efforts. Among the issues involved in lake sturgeon rehabilitation are habitat degradation, historic overharvest, and poaching of reproducing adults. Researchers and managers have invested a great deal to understand lake sturgeon populations, genetic diversity of stocks, habitat restrictions such as dams blocking sturgeon passage to river spawning grounds, and fishery conflicts, such as whether or not to allow minimal harvest of protected populations.

REHABILITATION ISSUES

However, issues do arise when rehabilitating species. Some experts express concerns that larger and older fish, like those seen as a result of lake trout rehabilitation efforts, accumulate more contaminants over time, increasing risks associated with fish consumption. In addition, the Great Lakes historically hosted different genetic strains of fish species, which may have been more successful in specific habitats.

Consequently, understanding the characteristics of specific genetic strains, hybridizing stocks, and decisions about what and where to stock are all part of the complexity associated with the use of stocking as a rehabilitation tool.

An additional challenge is that the solution to one fishery health issue might be the cause of another problem. For example, managing for healthy non-native salmon might depend on a healthy stock of alewives. However, current research indicates that alewives are very high in thiaminase, an enzyme that destroys thiamine (vitamin B1). Young lake trout are susceptible to thiamine deficiency complex (TDC) due to their parents' alewife consumption. Symptoms of TDC include loss of equilibrium, swimming in a spiral pattern, and lethargy, and it can result in premature death.

It is cyclical—scientists predict that more alewives in the Great Lakes means that lake trout consume more alewives, possibly increasing the mortality of young lake trout. Many fisheries experts are concerned that managing for non-native salmon inhibits native lake trout rehabilitation efforts, yet both species are important within the Great Lakes fishery.

INVASIVE SPECIES MANAGEMENT

The sea lamprey is one historic "poster fish" for invasive species in the Great Lakes. They have been in the Great Lakes basin for almost 200 years, and significant time and money has been spent on controlling their populations and mitigating the damage they cause to the Great Lakes fishery. Scientists doubt we will ever completely eradicate sea lampreys from the Great Lakes; however, the combination of control techniques is effective in keeping populations in check.

Since the invasion of sea lampreys, many more non-native species have been introduced, including zebra and quagga mussels, round and tubenose gobies, Eurasian ruffe, and spiny and fishhook water fleas. Each new non-native species—past, present, and future—alters the Great Lakes ecosystem by changing or competing for habitat and food and preying on native species. Similar to the sea lamprey, many invasive species have become integrated into the Great Lakes and are unlikely to be eliminated by human control. As the total number of non-native species increases, the complexity and expense of control methods also increases.

EFFECTS OF INVADERS

SEEN AND UNSEEN

The arrival of sea lampreys was evident when they first invaded because of the large wounds they inflicted on fish. However, the consequences associated with invaders that are more recent have not been as obvious. The suspected impacts of these alterations have led to significant research on food web dynamics of the Great Lakes ecosystem. For example, invasive zebra and quagga mussels have expanded their range and increased in density. The mussels are filter feeders; by filtering and consuming food, they have depleted the water column of nutrients, leading to changes in how energy is transferred within the ecosystem. Thus, the effect of the invasive mussels on fish communities is indirect and not entirely clear, yet potentially substantial. Managers will continue to study the long-term alterations associated with these and other invasives and develop strategies to mitigate those changes.

ALTERED HABITAT

Invasive species have altered habitats throughout the Great Lakes, and scientists are still learning the extent to which this has affected native species. Rocky shoals that have traditionally been important spawning areas for native species are now likely to be completely covered with invasive quagga and zebra mussels. The rock crevices that once protected eggs from waves and predators are now filled with waste from the mussels, rendering the habitat less suitable. Also, round gobies are efficient egg predators and are common among beds of dreissenid (i.e., zebra and quagga) mussels. The mussels have also changed water clarity by filtering out much of the material that reduced visibility, which additionally affects lower food web dynamics—but again, the full impact on the ecosystem is not yet understood.

PRECIPITOUS DECLINE

This dramatic change to the benthic habitat of the lakes is believed to have had serious consequences for important invertebrates such as *Diporeia*. Once a major food and energy source within Great Lakes food webs, the abundance of *Diporeia* has declined precipitously since the early 1990s. Filtration by dreissenid mussels has caused nutrients to be concentrated in the benthos, a process referred to as benthification. The increased water clarity has negatively impacted a variety of aquatic species and both nearshore and offshore habitats.

FUTURE INVADERS: WHO WILL IT BE?

It will be very difficult to prevent new non-native species from entering the Great Lakes. Shipping technologies that support a global economy increase opportunities for non-natives to arrive from around the world. The Ponto–Caspian Sea region, the origin of many species that have arrived in the Great Lakes, has been identified as a high-risk "donor region." Researchers have identified other species from this region that are suited for survival in the Great Lakes, given amenable vectors, or means of introduction, and timing.

A NEW POSTER FISH

Today, it is difficult to discuss invasive species without mentioning silver and bighead carp. Asian carp reflect a "new face" of invasive species because they exhibit the all-too-common risks, unknowns, and concerns that come with new invasive species introductions. The possible introduction of silver and bighead carp has garnered public, political, and legal attention.

Bighead carp, Hypophthalmichthys nobilis

RYAN HAGERTY, USFWS

WHAT'S THE HARM?

These fish reproduce at incredible rates, grow to large sizes, and can reach very high densities—as they do this, they feed voraciously on the smallest elements of the food web, plankton. The combination of their sheer biomass and ability to feed on large volumes of zooplankton and phytoplankton suggests they will have a profound effect on the ecosystems they inhabit.

Recent research suggests that Asian carp will be able to survive in all five Great Lakes. Lake Erie and warm, nutrient-rich bays and river mouths will likely suffer the worst effects. Asian carp typically spawn in long stretches of undammed rivers, but new findings suggest that suitable spawning habitat is more abundant in the Great Lakes region than previously thought. The grass carp, an Asian carp species that feeds on rooted plants, has already spawned successfully in a tributary of Lake Erie.

Preventing the spread of Asian carp is crucial to protecting the Great Lakes basin from additional invasive species that could alter or cripple the ecosystem. Chicago's waterways have been clearly identified as the pathway of highest risk, and commercial trade in live fish is another known pathway for invasion.

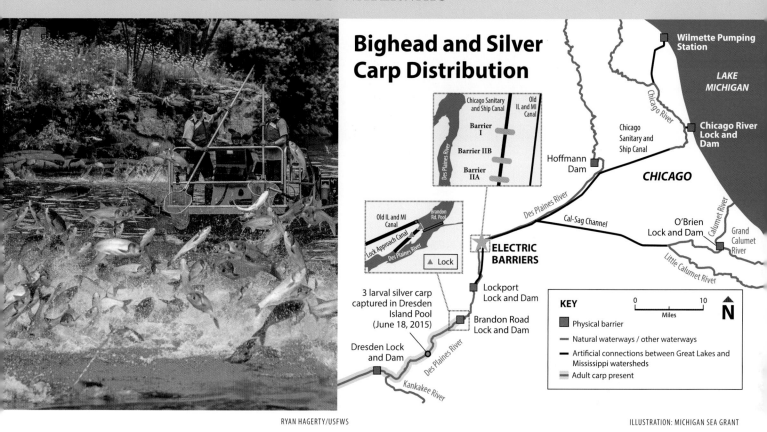

RYAN HAGERTY/USFWS

ILLUSTRATION: MICHIGAN SEA GRANT

Silver carp can leap out of the water when disturbed by vibrations like those caused by boat motors.

Man-made waterways are another way invasive species can reach the Great Lakes. In the "History" section, we explained how the development of the Welland Canal opened the Great Lakes to the introduction of many non-native species, including the invasive sea lamprey. More recently, another man-made waterway has come under scrutiny as one more possible vector of introduction—the Chicago Sanitary and Shipping Canal. This waterway connecting the Great Lakes basin and the Mississippi River watershed—two very large and very different ecosystems—may now serve as a passage for Asian carp.

Asian carp species, including the grass, silver, and bighead carp, have flourished within the Mississippi River basin. As these species move north, they present a new threat to the Great Lakes. These large fish are efficient at feeding on the lower end of the food chain, which could negatively impact habitat and reduce food for native Great Lakes species.

CHALLENGES

Recent attention has also focused on baitfish harvest, aquaculture, and pet trades as potential vectors for importing and transporting various non-native species into the Great Lakes. Some Great Lakes states have banned species of fish that might be cultivated for sale in the basin, such as the snakehead, because it can survive in Great Lakes waters as an aggressive predator and would compete with native species. A future challenge will be to continue to identify and prevent the movements or accidental releases of high-risk species such as the snakehead.

HOW CAN YOU HELP?

WHEN YOU LEAVE A BODY OF WATER:

❖ Remove any visible mud, plants, fish, or animals before transporting recreational equipment.

❖ Drain water from equipment (boat, motor, trailer, live wells) before transporting.

❖ Clean and dry anything that comes into contact with water (equipment, clothing, dogs, etc.).

❖ Never release plants, fish, or animals into a body of water unless they came out of that body of water.

See: stopaquatichitchhikers.org

Large tankers and bulk cargo carriers sometimes use ballast water to stabilize and make the ship easier to navigate. Ballast is taken on in coastal waters in one region after a ship unloads cargo, and then the water is discharged at the next port of call when more cargo is loaded. Ballast water has introduced many invasive species into the Great Lakes.

INDUSTRY PROTOCOLS

Recall from the "Today's Great Lakes Fishery" section that proactive educational efforts resulted in effective AIS-HACCP protocols. These protocols are aimed at preventing introductions from aquaculture, bait industry, and pet trades. However, pet owners or anglers using live bait also carry responsibility for preventing new introductions and limiting the spread of existing invasive species.

PREVENTION METHODS

Once certain invasive species arrive in the Great Lakes and become established, complete eradication is impossible. However, some measures can be taken to slow the rate of new invasions. Ships are now required to exchange their ballast water at sea before entering the St. Lawrence Seaway and the Great Lakes. However, ships entering the Great Lakes

A gizzard shad with VHS, Viral Hemorrhagic Septicemia, a disease that has been introduced into the Great Lakes.

carrying cargo in place of ballast can declare "no ballast on board," referred to as NOBOB. These NOBOB ships still have small amounts of sediment and water in the bottoms of ballast tanks—enough to allow the continued movement of non-native species throughout the Great Lakes and the world.

Researchers are working to find methods, such as chemicals, ultraviolet radiation, and screen structures, that might filter and eliminate non-native species from ballast tanks. The most economical solutions may be chemical biocides, such as glutaraldehyde or minute doses of chlorine. Yet many people are reluctant to resort to chemicals. Currently, no mandates exist requiring the shipping industry to implement chemical treatments, nor is there any way to enforce treatment.

New research is exploring biological control opportunities through use of pheromones. For example, researchers are experimenting with pheromones as a means of manipulating sea lamprey movement and spawning to control populations. Managers and decision-makers may ask, How and at what cost will it be possible to manage invasive species already established in the Great Lakes, while limiting new introductions? Unfortunately, such questions are not easy to answer.

Other methods, including localized education and legal and legislative efforts, have been employed to restrict the transportation and spread of invasive species. However, the interconnected nature of the Great Lakes demands binational and multijurisdictional solutions.

FISH HEALTH AND DISEASES

Research and technology are allowing scientists to better understand disease and fish health issues of the Great Lakes fishery. Future challenges will include new diseases and health issues that arise through non-native introductions and other pathways. Yet the largest challenge may be correcting fishery health issues within the contexts of the larger ecosystem. For example, biologists better understand bacterial kidney disease (BKD) and its effects on salmon. They see that overpopulation of predators and poor health due to an inadequate forage base may be related to increased epidemics of the disease. The challenge is to better understand forage stocks and manage predator stocking in relation to natural reproduction to create a healthy mix of predators and prey.

Viral hemorrhagic septicemia (VHS) is a disease that is not native to the Great Lakes. Fish infected with VHS exhibit red sores on the skin and on internal organs. This disease is often fatal and has caused large die-offs of freshwater drum, muskie, round gobies, gizzard shad, white bass, and yellow perch. Other species have been noted to carry the virus, yet mortalities have not been reported for those species. It is important that both commercial operations and anglers continue to use extreme caution and help prevent the spread of non-native species and diseases by following the protocols and guidelines established by state, provincial, and tribal resource management agencies.

DAMS

Dams on Great Lakes tributaries sever the connection between river, wetland, and nearshore and create other fishery habitat issues.

LIMITED ACCESS

Dams limit fish access to rivers, cutting them off from spawning habitat and blocking juvenile fish that use inland wetlands as nursery areas before migrating into the lakes. Managers contend that dam removal could greatly increase the natural reproduction of many Great Lakes fish. **Fish passages** or fish ladders are often used to allow fish to navigate around dams to move up and down rivers, but even these may be designed only for specific species such as salmon or trout. Species such as suckers, walleye, or sturgeon are far less able to navigate fish passages. Dams are also physical barriers to anglers, particularly limiting their access to migrating Great Lakes fish while fishing inland rivers.

ALTERED FLOW

Dams alter the natural flow of biological nutrients in rivers and alter fish habitat simply by changing the

BRANDON SCHROEDER, MISG

flow rate of water or increasing the temperature of pooled water behind dams. Vast fluctuations in the amount of water in dammed rivers has had a negative impact on the fisheries, boating, and other activities related to the Great Lakes ecosystem and economy.

In a free-flowing tributary, these nutrients are ultimately transported downstream and enhance production, for example, energy and available food, of the Great Lakes. Management decisions and agreements with operators of dams, primarily hydroelectric structures, have resulted in compensation for fish damages such as habitat loss and fish mortalities. Maintaining a constant or "run of river" flow of water past dams, as well as upholding water quality standards,

has vastly improved fish production. However, there is room for better practices that focus on protecting habitat, fish, and other species.

REMOVAL NOT SO SIMPLE

Simply removing dams to increase Great Lakes fish production or fish health is a costly venture with some negative implications. Dams also impede many invasive species, such as sea lampreys, from moving upstream, to find additional habitat suitable for reproduction. Dams also protect populations of threatened or endangered fish from having to compete with invasive species.

Some dam removal projects are complicated by the fact that the sediment load built up behind the dam contains harmful chemicals. Removing dams could cause contaminants to be re-released into the water column and downstream into the Great Lakes. The sediment load that is washed downstream could also compromise the habitat quality in the lower reaches of the tributary, at least for a time. Using science-based information is important in making sound dam management decisions that are ecologically sound and economically feasible.

HABITAT: A NECESSITY FOR FISH AND PEOPLE

HEALTHY ENVIRONMENTS, CONTAMINATION, AND WATER USE

Resource managers recognize that healthy relationships among nearshore, river, and wetland habitats are all critical to healthy Great Lakes fish communities. These areas provide vital spawning habitat and nursery areas for juvenile fish. Many managers now understand that these habitats can yield an abundant and

sustainable production of fish—without the costs and management of hatcheries.

In the recent past, for example, Great Lakes tributaries were estimated to yield nearly 30 percent of the salmon production in the Great Lakes. Updated studies indicate that the population of naturally produced salmon may be even higher; in Lake Huron, studies indicate that 80 percent of salmon in the lake are wild. Some salmon species, such as pink salmon, are not stocked at all. Catches of pink salmon in the upper Great Lakes are exclusively from natural reproduction.

Native fish such as walleye, yellow perch, pike, suckers, and sturgeon also depend on Great Lakes tributaries, wetlands, and nearshore habitats for successful reproduction. From an ecosystem management perspective, understanding, protecting, enhancing, and increasing access to spawning and nursery areas will be important for fish production and future fisheries. However, protecting and managing nearshore and inland waters, particularly those associated with lake shoreline, riverfronts, and wetlands will likely become increasingly difficult

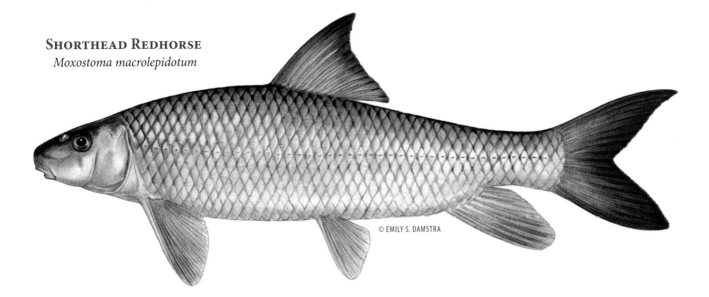

SHORTHEAD REDHORSE
Moxostoma macrolepidotum

© EMILY S. DAMSTRA

with expanding development and the encroachment of human populations.

LAND-BASED DECISIONS

Researchers and resource managers also work beyond the Great Lakes, taking into consideration inland tributaries, wetlands, and a multitude of smaller watersheds that feed into the larger Great Lakes basin. Land-use practices, erosion that results in sedimentation of waterways often with attached nutrients, and **point source pollution** are also concerns.

The implications of such land-based issues are just as complex as water-based issues and vary across regional, agricultural, and urban settings. Some of the more obvious impacts have been addressed using greenbelts and waterway corridors and controlling point source pollution, but problems such as **non-point source pollution** remain and likely will continue to influence water quality.

LAKE LEVELS AND WATER USE

Lake levels and the direct and indirect use of Great Lakes water are also a factor in the overall health of the Great Lakes. One common concern, when looking at fluctuating lake levels, is considering the impact of climate change. During the past 30 years, Great Lakes water levels have been at record highs and near-record lows. Trend analysis of Great Lakes water levels suggests that changes can be seen on as little as a yearly basis and that, over a long time (e.g., a decade or longer) changes can be as great as a meter in either direction compared with the long-term average. Since we cannot predict high or low water levels in relation to climate with certainty, planning for ongoing fluctuations in water levels is recommended for all coastal communities. Recently, many communities have experienced more frequent and severe storm events that result in flooding for both coastal and inland areas. Scientists predict that the long-term dynamics of water levels will change as the climate changes.

Strategies for identifying, protecting, and managing nearshore habitats may need to be altered as water levels change. User groups may need to adapt to changing water levels. For instance, dredging and development to maintain coastal access during low water levels is a critical issue for boater safety, and also important for charter fishing and other coastal-dependent businesses. However, minimizing impacts on fish habitat as people alter ecosystems to adapt to changing water levels is equally important.

GREAT LAKES COMPACT

The Great Lakes–St. Lawrence River Basin Water Resources Compact is a legally binding interstate compact among the states of Illinois, Indiana, Michigan, Minnesota, New York, Ohio, Pennsylvania, and Wisconsin. The compact details how the states will manage the use of the Great Lakes basin's water supply and builds on the 1985 Great Lakes Charter and its 2001 annex. The compact is the means by which the states implement the governors' commitments under the Great Lakes–St. Lawrence River Basin Sustainable Water Resources Agreement. The agreement is a nonbinding, good-faith agreement between the U.S. states on one side and the Canadian provinces of Ontario and Quebec on the other.

Another consideration in the future of fisheries is water demand. Many communities have experienced an increase in demand for water, particularly in the western and southern regions of the United States. The freshwater of the Great Lakes is coveted by many and could be subject to water withdrawals. As part of a regional compact, the Great Lakes–St. Lawrence River Basin Water Resources Compact, Michigan, and the other states and provinces in the Great Lakes have enacted laws that require major water users to report water withdrawals made within the Great Lakes basin. This information provides a baseline for managing water resources in a more integrated manner and strengthens the legal basis for opposing diversions of Great Lakes water.

In Michigan and other states, the Water Use and Withdrawal Program is responsible for collecting annual water use data, making determinations on the potential impacts to water resources as a result of a proposed withdrawal,

and issuing water withdrawal permits. Generally only those who withdraw more than 3 million gallons of surface or ground water during a consecutive 30-day period from the Great Lakes basin are required to file a permit.

While protections are currently in place, increasing scarcity of water along with increased population and industrial demands may put additional pressure on the freshwater resources of the Great Lakes.

AREAS OF CONCERN

Pollution and contaminant loadings into the Great Lakes have been reduced, yet a pollution-free Great Lakes is not envisioned in the near future. Point source pollution, that is, pollution from a single, identifiable source, is not as widespread as it was when the Cuyahoga River repeatedly caught fire in the 1960s. However, it is still a major concern and requires strict oversight because not all industries agree with regulations.

As part of cleaning up legacy pollution in the Great Lakes, leadership has turned to remedial action plans to identify specific problems in severely degraded Great Lakes areas of concern (AOCs) and to describe methods for addressing critical issues. The U.S. and Canadian governments have identified 43 such areas; 26 in U.S. waters, 17 in Canadian waters—five of which are shared between the United States and Canada on connecting river systems. Collingwood Harbour in Ontario was the first of these 43 sites to be delisted in the mid-1990s. In recent years, several others have been delisted or designated as areas of recovery in acknowledgment that everything (currently) economically feasible has been done to address the challenges, and time will be required to fully restore impaired beneficial uses. Clean-up efforts in the Great Lakes have been admittedly

Students performing fisheries research.

slow due to the complexity and expense of remediating degraded AOCs.

However, the Great Lakes Restoration Initiative (GLRI) that began in 2010 is focused on Great Lakes AOCs. Many researchers, outreach experts, natural resource managers, nongovernmental organizations, industries, and businesses are collaborating on projects focused on improving water quality and on habitat and coastal business best practices. As a result of GLRI funding, the Great Lakes region has received attention and resources to address AOCs and to better inform the public about why this effort is a critical part of economic recovery and resource sustainability. The GLRI is similar to other federally funded restoration projects, such as those in the Florida Everglades and the Chesapeake Bay.

WASTE WATER TREATMENT

Another major concern within the Great Lakes is the treatment of wastewater before it is released back into the lakes. The sewerage infrastructure of the oldest parts of the region's largest cities combines raw, domestic sewage and stormwater runoff. During periods of heavy rain, water treatment facilities do not have the

WHY DO LAKE LEVELS FLUCTUATE?

Lake levels are determined by the combined influence of precipitation—which is the primary source of natural water supply to the Great Lakes— upstream inflows, groundwater, surface water runoff, evaporation, diversions into and out of the system, consumptive uses, and water level regulation. The interplay among human activities, such as consumptive uses, in and out of basin diversions, wetland reduction, urbanization and agriculture, and the ecology of the lakes is highly complex.

ANN HRUSKA

Through the Clean Boats, Clean Waters program, volunteers organize and conduct boater education on invasive species in their communities. Teams educate boaters about where they are most likely to find invasives on their recreational watercraft and how to remove them.

capacity to treat all of the wastewater and, thus, divert it to overflow pipes. It is not uncommon for raw sewage, industrial wastewater, and other pollutants to be funneled directly into the lakes when the systems are overwhelmed. While many solutions have been developed, including some major infrastructure investment to intercept stormwater and provide primary treatment or at least disinfection prior to release, it is critical that we continue to educate about this issue and advocate for the appropriate water treatment facilities.

ACCUMULATION OF CONTAMINANTS

Environmental contaminants will continue to be a complex and challenging issue. Recall that contaminants accumulate within Great Lakes food webs and fish, raising concern about how contaminants might affect human health through fish consumption. Alternatively, Great Lakes fish are a valuable food resource for people, providing many

health benefits. There are also emerging contaminants such as hormones, caffeine, flame-retardants, and pharmaceuticals that will likely become more of a concern as we learn more about them.

Given the dangers, the simplest way of eradicating contaminants from the environment is to not introduce them in first place.

OUR CHANGING CLIMATE

The effects of a changing climate add yet another layer of variability to fisheries management and the future of the Great Lakes. In recent decades, we have seen more severe and frequent extreme events, increasing intensity and duration of heat waves such as those experienced in the Great Lakes during summers of 2006 and 2010, and the harmful algal bloom in western Lake Erie in 2011. Scientists anticipate that these extreme weather trends will continue. Whether or not they do, considering both climate variables and lake levels fluctuations will continue to be important.

Temperature changes to the Great Lakes could have a significant impact on fish, habitat, and wildlife. For example, surface temperatures of all of the Great Lakes have been increasing. As discussed in the "Ecology" section, warmer water creates a different habitat and supports a different ecosystem than colder water. Consider Lake Erie, which is the warmest and shallowest of the Great Lakes, and how it differs from the deeper, colder lakes, especially Superior. Although the specific implications of climate change on the Great Lakes fisheries are not known, we can anticipate that fish communities will change in response to climate-related habitat changes. Resource managers will likely consider how to adapt plans and management strategies based on model predictions as well as trend data.

PEOPLE IN THE MIX

POLICY, MANAGEMENT, AND DECISIONS

People interact with ecosystems and influence biological change, yet—good or bad—management actions are only one influence in the mix of many. There are limits to what we know about ecosystems and how they function, and our best understanding of these ecosystems drives our resource management, policies, and decision-making processes. The sheer size, ecological complexity, and diverse uses of the Great Lakes ecosystem make it difficult for researchers, managers, and decision-makers to think holistically about the Great Lakes basin.

Consider this: management and care for the Great Lakes basin includes two different countries, many states and provinces, tribes, multiple agencies, a multitude of special interest organizations, overlapping political jurisdictions, many cultures, and millions of users. Within that wide pantheon of stakeholders, imagine the different goals each country, each state/province, each group, and each person might have for the Great Lakes fishery. Even when goals are common, the necessary research or information to generate action or informed decisions may be lacking. Trade-offs between short-term and long-term benefits are often the results.

There is hope. Many efforts, agreements, and organizations have been successfully designed to overcome these multijurisdictional barriers. Coordinated management is a best practice that will continue in the future. The strategic efforts of binational organizations, such as the Great Lakes Fishery Commission and the International Joint Commission, have aided in bridging the gaps and coordinating fishery management activities among a multitude of different agencies and organizations responsible for Great Lakes management. For example, the Great Lakes Fishery Commission has traditionally organized agencies to work as lake-wide management committees with stakeholder input. These committees share information, create joint management objectives, and work cooperatively to achieve results and evaluate them. Binational organizations will continue to be a factor in the ultimate success of ecosystem, basin-wide, or watershed management initiatives.

Binational groups encourage collaboration, but the ultimate management authority for fisheries in U.S. waters of the Great Lakes falls to each respective state, tribal, or provincial agency. On a local level, some state agencies, such as the Michigan Department of Natural Resources, have restructured their fisheries management units to coincide with watershed boundaries.

MANAGEMENT STRATEGIES

By now we know that fisheries resource managers often have to make decisions using limited information. How the public or ecosystem will react to management decisions or outcomes is uncertain. The equation is further complicated by that fact that what is known about an ecosystem and its users can change at any time.

Fluctuations in a fish population, outbreaks of disease, the introduction of a new aquatic invasive species, modified habitat, and angler attitudes are examples of very real changes that can happen quickly. Yet they still must be considered now and in the future. So, how is that accomplished? Different approaches to natural resource management have been developed, including adaptive and risk-based.

ADAPTIVE

Many managers are advocating the implementation of **adaptive management** as a more effective management approach. The concept of adaptive management is to allow management decisions to be flexible in response to the unknowns of a constantly changing environment.

For example, adaptive management principles might apply to the harvest regulations for a particular fish. In this scenario, management decisions are made with the best possible research and available data/information. Managers closely monitor and evaluate the impacts of their decisions in relation to the goals for the fish species in question, then adjust as needed to continue to meet goals or objectives for that fishery. The strength in adaptive management lies in allowing the managers flexibility to react and change approaches in response to ecological changes. The challenge is that, while it is easy to commit to adaptive management principles on paper, in reality they can be difficult to implement.

Challenges to implementing adaptive management occur at many levels. Both at the federal and state/provincial decision levels, it may take several months to years—in addition to the time it takes to collect crucial public

Muskellunge
Esox masquinongy

© EMILY S. DAMSTRA

Students help with Detroit River fish restoration project, releasing lake sturgeon within a former Area of Concern EPA clean-up site near Trenton, Mich.

TODD MARSEE, MISG

input—to accomplish policy or regulatory changes. Examples include changing size limits on fish or more complicated issues such as regulating the introduction of invasive species, such as blocking Asian carp through the Chicago Sanitary Canal or ballast water regulation. Adaptive management requires a tremendous amount of ongoing planning and the ability to coordinate rapidly among many involved decision-makers. All of this takes time, especially efforts to engage stakeholders in early decision-making stages. The payoff is stakeholders that are informed, involved, and active in management changes.

A lack of resources can sometimes be a barrier to effective management, too. Management agencies may not have the money, experience, or capacity to develop or implement a tool, take action, or respond to an issue.

RISK-BASED

Risk-based decision-making is another method in the management toolbox. Although it may not be possible to understand Great Lakes ecosystems perfectly, risk-based decision-making allows decisions to be made within an acceptable range of risk. Managers and users calculate what kind of risks they are willing to take based on what information is known and the estimated unknowns. How is risk calculated? Some of the information can be based on experience and institutional knowledge. Fisheries scientists often use models to simulate unexpected results because of uncertainty, allowing them to gain a greater appreciation and better understanding of the complexity of the Great Lakes. This approach depends on the technology of fish population and fish community modeling. Using computers to model ecosystem dynamics, researchers run management scenarios or options and statistically assess the risks related to the uncertainty of the biological aspects of the fishery.

PAYING FOR IT

Finding funding for fisheries research and management will continue to be a major test for management agencies into the future. Agencies will remain challenged to accomplish more with less and to find more efficient ways to learn about, protect, and manage Great Lakes fisheries.

In light of declining revenue from decreasing angler participation and license sales, some Great Lakes states have explored alternative funding scenarios and opportunities, such as through state taxes. Often, stakeholder organizations provide volunteer hours and financial resources directly to fishery research or management efforts important to their respective organizational interests. Students, both recreational and commercial fishery stakeholders, and fishery-related businesses are increasingly called upon to serve as "citizen scientists" and contribute to fishery research efforts.

USER GROUPS AND OVERLAPPING NEEDS

Imagine being a manager faced with this decision—you can choose to manage for either large catch rates at the expense of size or you can grow trophy-size fish at the expense of losing harvestable fish to natural mortality. How to allocate fisheries and make decisions that impact various sport and commercial user groups is challenging. Many questions arise:

❖ Should a manager choose one type of management strategy over the other?

❖ Who decides how to manage a public resource when conflicting values exist?

❖ Who decides when to manage only for trophy fish?

❖ How should decisions about sport and commercial gear use and regulations on the fishery be made?

❖ What types of commercial nets are appropriate for harvesting fish?

❖ Should sport anglers be allowed to utilize live bait or artificial baits only?

❖ If gear should be restricted, which waters are affected? Who decides?

❖ How can we effectively balance decision-making to ensure sustainable Great Lakes fish populations for future generations in light of pressures today?

The complexity of the questions and difficulty in finding mutually acceptable answers are likely to increase in the future.

SPECIAL INTEREST

Special interest groups and organizations that focus on particular fish species or specific interests are also in the stakeholder mix. Many of these groups invest resources and energy in advocating for increased or decreased regulation of, or management attention to, particular species, such as lake sturgeon. Some are professional associations that advocate for charter and commercial fishing interests. The tribes also invest considerable resources speaking for and protecting the interests of tribal fishers, whether they are sport, subsistence, or commercial. Other groups may be interested specifically in the protection and enhancement of fish habitat or watersheds. The mission of these watershed organizations typically involves developing linkages and partnerships between government agencies, fishing organizations, water quality entities, other public organizations, and citizens to tackle challenges involved with issues on a watershed scale.

A future fishery challenge—and opportunity—lies in engaging citizens beyond the most directly involved anglers and water-interested stakeholders. The Great Lakes ecosystem and fishery is a shared public resource with many overlapping community values. That includes economic values resulting from coastal tourism, historic and cultural values intrinsically connected with coastal fishing communities and festivals, and ecological values of clean water and vibrant, functioning ecosystems.

All Great Lakes communities are ultimately affected by and benefit from the value of Great Lakes fisheries. Similarly, everyday actions of citizens have important implications for the future of the Great Lakes fishery;

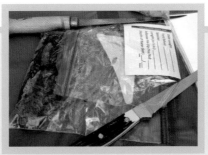

ANGLER CITIZEN SCIENCE

Fishery businesses are important management partners, as charter captains systematically report catches to management agencies. Commercial fishers often help by providing catch reports and, more directly, by setting research nets or collecting large quantities of fish for marking and movement studies.

Many anglers are asked to look for and report marked or tagged fish in their catch. They may also be among the first to observe and report invasive species introductions and spread. For example, volunteers with the Salmon Ambassadors program have been measuring and reporting fin-clipped and unclipped Chinook salmon since 2013. This provides important information on how stocked and wild salmon are contributing to fisheries around Lake Michigan and northern Lake Huron.

BRANDON SCHROEDER, MISG

Students learn about fish anatomy as well as how to clean them at 4-H Great Lakes Natural Resources Camp hosted in northeast Michigan.

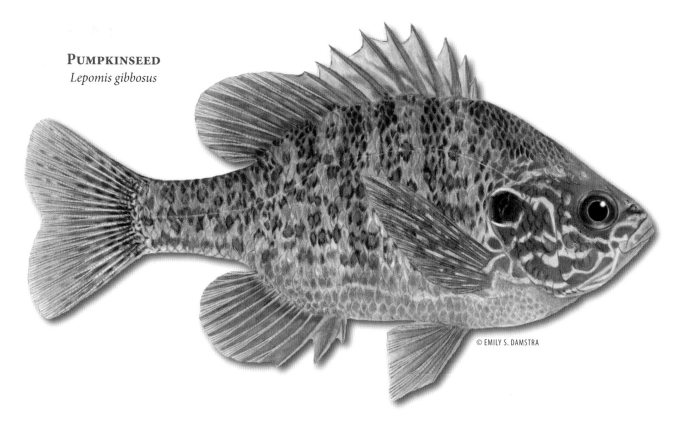

PUMPKINSEED
Lepomis gibbosus

© EMILY S. DAMSTRA

practices on private property that can affect habitat (e.g., eliminating the use of fertilizers) are enhancing coastal landscapes for better habitat. Also, advocating for the Great Lakes fisheries by electing public officials who are prepared to handle the complexity of issues like aquatic invasive species management is important.

Therefore, involving the general public through dialogue and decision-making processes is an opportunity. Advancing internet and communication technologies provide better tools by which to share information and gather input. Tapping into online and social networking resources to raise awareness, share information, and educate will help natural resource professionals more effectively engage new and broader audiences.

VALUING ANGLER PARTICIPATION

In recent years, most Great Lakes states have reported relatively stable trends in fishing license sales. National sport-fishing surveys suggest similar—or

slightly increasing—trends for fishing participation. However, this recent trend has not always been the case.

National surveys conducted by the U.S. Fish and Wildlife Service showed a significant decline in anglers fishing in U.S. waters of the Great Lakes from 1991 to 2006. During that time, angler numbers fell from nearly 2.6 million to roughly 1.4 million. Today, participation

numbers remain low, but recent surveys show more stable and even slightly increasing trends, with 1.7 million Great Lakes anglers in 2011 and 1.8 million in 2016.

Across the Great Lakes states, nearly 8 million people bought fishing licenses in 2016. License sales have remained relatively stable, hovering around 8 million each year for the past decade.

TOTAL LICENSED ANGLERS, BY STATE

State	2016
Illinois	696,656
Indiana	477,680
Michigan	1,148,869
Minnesota	1,423,502
New York	906,545
Ohio	819,880
Pennsylvania	1,042,651
Wisconsin	1,399,323
TOTAL	**7,915,106**

SPORT FISH RESTORATION FUND, BY STATE

State	2016
Illinois	$6,423,169
Indiana	$4,281,315
Michigan	$10,637,433
Minnesota	$11,953,143
New York	$7,582,086
Ohio	$6,688,840
Pennsylvania	$8,097,836
Wisconsin	$11,005,470
TOTAL	**$66,669,292**

License sales by state, as reported by USFWS.

Yet, this trend also reflects a longer-term decline of 18 percent decline in license sales since 1990. Canadian officials note similar trends in Canadian Great Lakes waters. Yet demands on fisheries management efforts continue to increase to meet the challenges of ecosystem or basin-wide management, as well as the demands of a more diverse set of fishery user groups. Because fishing license dollars and taxes on fishing equipment provide the primary source of funding for fisheries management personnel, programs, and activities, the decline in angler numbers and license sales presents a serious challenge. It raises an increasingly important question—who will pay for fisheries management, research, and education if angler participation and revenue generated from this participation does not increase?

In the United States, for example, a significant portion of fisheries management is supported directly from fishery user groups. In 2016, Great Lakes anglers in the United States spent nearly $158 million purchasing fishing licenses, tags, and permits. This funding is earmarked for fisheries management activities by state agencies. That same year, the federal Sport Fish Restoration Fund—money collected through excise sales taxes on fishing gear and equipment—provided nearly $67 million to state agencies in the Great Lakes. These two sources, generated by those who use the fishery, combine to form the primary financial foundation for Great Lakes management activities. Public support may also help pay for additional programs, such as sea lamprey control programs, from other budget resources within the state, provincial, or federal governments.

Developing exact figures about the use of the fishery and relating sport and commercial harvest to management decisions is difficult. Managers estimate how many sport anglers or commercial fishing licenses exist and how many people are using the fishery. This analysis of funding is not conducted on a regular basis and may not be accurate. Complicating matters is the fact that not all sport anglers or commercial fishers may fish for the same amount of time, target the same species or areas of the lakes, or make the same decisions about how they use the resource (e.g., for harvest or catch-and-release). The challenge is to develop management decisions that are based on scientific estimates of effort and harvest by sport and commercial fishers.

GETTING HOOKED ON FISHING

More precise, timely information, measurements, and predictions regarding recruitment, retention, and involvement of those who use the fishery resource could help improve opportunities and management of fishery resources. Increasing efforts toward recruiting and retaining anglers will become a more important issue in the years to come. Many education efforts are underway throughout the region to introduce new anglers to the Great Lakes fishery. While some fear that too many anglers will increase pressure on the fishery, possibly leading to overfishing or angler conflicts, a reality remains that angler participation is a necessary element of the fishery. A more realistic and pressing concern may be a future with too few anglers.

As previously mentioned, without angler investment, financing fisheries management activities will become a serious challenge. More important than sales is the realization that public interest and involvement in the conservation of a healthy, usable fishery resource could greatly diminish.

SUMMARY

THE FUTURE OF THE GREAT LAKES FISHERY

The key to managing for the future is to remember that the Great Lakes are a dynamic and resilient ecosystem. Amid the complexity of that ecosystem, environmental changes, shifting stakeholder expectations and involvement, and changing agency structures and objectives will always occur. The following elements are at the core of keeping the Great Lakes vibrant into the future:

❖ State, provincial, tribal, and federal agencies will have an even greater need to work with each other and with citizens to formulate and implement a common vision for the Great Lakes fisheries.

❖ The fisheries will continue to serve as indicators of the Great Lakes system's health and quality.

❖ Today, managers recognize that using different approaches is key in achieving sustainable resources. This will need to continue.

❖ Management goals and outcomes will still need to reflect an appreciation for diverse resources, stakeholders, and fisheries.

❖ Maintaining and restoring Great Lakes habitats is a key component to a healthy fishery.

❖ User groups and the public have an opportunity to shape the Great Lakes, becoming active participants in the life of the lakes.

❖ Learning about and respecting the Great Lakes and the resources that they provide is essential.

We've come to the end of the book, but this isn't where the tale of the life of the lakes ends! We're all characters in this story—which means we all play a role in shaping its next chapter.

What will your contribution be?

"*When you put your hand in a flowing stream,
you touch the last that has gone before
and the first of what is still to come.*"

— Leonardo da Vinci

GLOSSARY

abiotic: (AY-BYE-ah-tick) Nonliving.

adaptation: The adjustment or changes in physiology, structure of an organism, or behavior to become better suited to an environment.

adaptive management: A style of decision-making allowing fisheries management decisions to be flexible in response to the unknowns of a constantly changing Great Lakes environment.

algae: (AL-gee) Simple, photosynthetic plants that lack true roots, stems, or leaves.

algal bloom: A large growth of algae in a body of water.

anadromous: (a-NAD-ra-muss) Fish that migrate up river to spawn, but live in lakes (or oceans) as adults.

aphotic zone: Deepest portion of a lake where light energy cannot penetrate. Also called the profundal zone.

aquaculture: The cultivation of aquatic plants or animals.

area of concern (AOC): A severely polluted area of the Great Lakes that has been designated by the International Joint Commission for clean-up effort upon recommendation by state and provincial officials.

ballast water: Water held in a boat or large vessel to help balance it.

benthic: Refers to animals and plants that live in or on the bottom of a lake or sea.

bioaccumulation: The buildup of a substance in a plant or in an animal's body.

biomagnification: The process by which concentrations of contaminants in plants and in animals are increased along a food chain; organisms (e.g., consumers) at higher trophic levels have higher concentrations.

biomass: The total mass of all living things in a given area.

biotic: Living.

carrying capacity: The maximum number of individuals of a species that can be supported in a given area or habitat over an extended period of time.

common property resource: A resource owned not by individuals but by the general public and managed by the government on the public's behalf.

community: An interacting group of different plants and animals.

competition: An interaction between two or more individuals or species that require the same limited resource to survive; this interaction can be harmful to one or more of the organisms.

consumer: Organisms that eat other organisms or plants for nourishment.

contaminant: A chemical substance that is not naturally found in the environment, usually made by humans.

coregonines: (kor-eh-GO-neens) A genus (Coregonus) of fish that includes freshwater whitefish such as lake whitefish and cisco species.

DDT: Dichlorodiphenyltrichloroethane; a chemical contaminant, used as an insecticide, that can build up in living organisms and cause health problems. Banned by the United States and Canada in 1972.

detrital rain: Dead algae and zooplankton that sink down to lower levels from upper layers of water.

detritivore: (deh-TRY-ti-vore) A small animals that feeds on decomposing matter and organic debris.

detritus: (deh-TRY-tus) Organic material that is either waste material from an organism or decomposing plants and animals.

diatom: (DYE-uh-tom) A single-celled plant with a hard "shell" of silica.

downrigger: A weighted device that allows a lure to be trolled at a given depth.

downwelling: As a result of temperature changes and/or wind, water on the surface becomes denser than the water beneath it and sinks.

ecology: The study of the interrelationships between organisms and their environment.

ecosystem: All the animals, plants, and environmental factors that interact within a system; the living and nonliving parts of the environment that interact.

ecosystem management: The holistic understanding and manipulation of the Great Lakes fisheries in relation to their interactions and interrelationships within the entire Great Lakes ecosystem.

epilimnion: (EP-i-LIM-nee-on) The warmer, buoyant top layer of water in a lake during summer stratification.

eutrophic: (yoo-TRO-fik) A water body that is rich in nutrients and has high productivity—often turbid, with algal blooms and periodic decreases in dissolved oxygen.

eutrophication: (yoo-TROF-i-KAY-shun) The process through which waters become eutrophic.

fishery: The complex interactions between fish population(s) being used, the humans using it, and the environment of each.

fisheries management: The manipulation of people, aquatic populations, and/or habitats in an effort to obtain the goals desired for that aquatic population or ecosystem by its human members.

fisheries science: The scientific study of aquatic (water-related) living resources of the world; the study of the structure, dynamics (or changes), interactions of habitat, aquatic organisms, and humans in order to achieve the goals set for that resource by humans.

fish passage: A fish ladder or other mechanism intended to allow fish to navigate around dams in order to move up and down rivers or waterways.

fish production: The amount of new biomass of a given fish species in a given area over a given period of time.

food chain: The chain of organisms that feed, in turn, on each other and through which energy is passed on from one organism to another.

food web: A set of food chains intersecting and overlapping each other.

forage fish: Small fish that are preyed upon by larger fish; for example, bloaters, lake herring, sculpins, alewives, smelt, and the juveniles of larger fish.

fry: Newly hatched young fish.

habitat: An area that provides life requirements such as appropriate food, water, shelter, and space for a particular organism.

hypolimnion: (hi-poh-LIM-nee-on) Colder, denser water located at the bottom of a lake during summer stratification.

introduced: A non-native species intentionally introduced into an ecosystem for a reason, for example Pacific salmon in the Great Lakes.

invasive species: An animal or plant that is not native to an ecosystem and that has a profound and negative impact upon it.

landed value: Price paid to fishers for fish prior to processing, wholesaling, or retailing.

limnetic zone: Area of a lake where light can penetrate. Also called the photic zone.

limnology/limnologist: (lim-NOL-uh-gee) The study of, or a person who studies, freshwater bodies/ecosystems (ponds, lakes, and streams) and the relationships between their inhabitants and their environment.

littoral: (LIT-ah-rahl) The area near the shore that is shallow enough for light to be able to penetrate the water, reach the lake bottom, and allow rooted plants to grow.

macroinvertebrate: A small animal, able to be seen with the naked eye, that does not have a backbone.

macrophyte: A large, rooted, aquatic plant that grows in areas where light reaches the lake bottom.

maximum sustainable yield (MSY): To produce the greatest number of pounds of fish over a given time with a given level of fishing effort; this is done by determining the requirements of fish and the productivity of the environment.

mesh size: The size of the open spaces between the cords of a net.

mesotrophic: A water body that has a moderate amount of nutrients and moderate production of organic matter; midway between oligotrophic and eutrophic.

metalimnion: (met-uh-LIM-nee-on) Water layer between epilimnion (warm, top layer) and hypolimnion (cold, bottom layer), where temperature drop-off is greatest.

non-native: Species that are living outside of the area where they evolved, usually introduced through human actions either intentionally or accidentally.

non-point source pollution: Pollutants that do not enter the lakes at a single confined source, but rather from diffuse multiple sources such as agricultural runoff, road salt, and acid rain.

oligotrophic: (ah-li-guh-TRO-fik) Waters that are low in nutrients and in productivity and are often cold and deep.

optimum sustainable yield (OSY): Harvest level for a species that achieves the greatest benefit, economically, socially, and biologically.

parasite: An organism that lives in or on another living organism (host) and receives nourishment from it, but gives nothing to the host organism in return.

PCB: Polychlorinated biphenyl; a type of persistent hydrocarbon that is toxic to some organisms and bioaccumulates.

pelagic: (puh-LAJ-ik) Referring to the open water area of a lake.

percids: Members of the perch family including yellow perch, walleye, and sauger.

persistent chemical: A chemical that is not decomposed in the environment. Many persistent chemicals accumulate in the tissues of animals as they eat contaminated prey.

phosphate: Chemical nutrient containing phosphorus that can be found in agricultural or industrial runoff, household wastewater, and stormwater and that accelerates the eutrophication of a body of water.

photic zone: Area of a lake where light can penetrate. Also called the limnetic zone.

phytoplankton: (FYE-toe-PLANK-ton) Small, free-floating plants, including algae, diatoms and cyanobacteria.

piscivorous: (puh-SIV-er-us) Fish-eating.

planktivorous: Plankton-eating.

plankton: Plants or animals that inhabit lake or sea and drift with the currents; they may have some abilities to move; they range in size from single-celled plants or animals to large jellyfish.

point source pollution: Pollution that has a distinct and identifiable source; it usually comes from a single pipe or series of pipes.

pollutant: A contaminant or natural substance present in large enough quantities to cause a problem.

predator: A species that lives by killing and eating other prey species.

processed value: Value of a commercial fish harvest after processing.

producer: Converts and stores the sun's energy and nonliving materials into living biomass (tissue), which is then available to other organisms in the food chain.

profundal zone: Deepest portion of a lake, where light energy cannot penetrate. Also called the aphotic zone.

reef: A ridge of rock or sand at or near the surface of the water that provides habitat for many aquatic plants and animals.

rehabilitation: The repair of degraded aquatic ecosystems to increase their ability to sustain aquatic communities and provide benefits to society.

remedial action plan: A plan to restore water quality in a severely polluted area of concern (AOC).

restoration: To return to nearly a former condition or status.

risk assessment: Procedure used to estimate the probability of negative effects from a specific source of a contaminant and at a particular exposure level.

risk-based decision-making: A strategy of accounting for and eliminating risk factors involved with fisheries management decisions, allowing for decisions to be made within the acceptable risk range that managers and users are willing to take, based on what information is known and the estimated risks of unknowns.

risk management: The process of incorporating social, economic, and political information with risk assessment information to decide how to reduce or eliminate potential risks for humans or fish populations.

scientific method: A systematic way of gathering and evaluating information by posing specific research questions, designing experiments, making observations and measurements, and compiling and interpreting results to answer the questions.

sediment: The deposited material, both organic and inorganic, at the bottom of water bodies.

spawn: To breed and deposit eggs.

species: Individuals that share similar genetics and that can successfully reproduce.

stock: (noun) A group or population of a fish species that is different from other groups of the same species (for example, spawns in a different habitat, at a different time).

stocking: The act of artificially introducing a group or population of a fish species into waters, particularly to introduce new or supplement existing fish populations or stocks.

stunting: Reduced growth due to lack of adequate food.

thermal stratification: Vertical layering of water of different densities that results from water temperature.

toxic: Refers to a substance that is poisonous and present in sufficient quantity to cause death or serious injury to an organism.

treaty: A tool and process used by one government to give its word to another government. The intention of a treaty is to protect a particular intergovernmental agreement over a long period of time.

tributary: (TRIH-bew-tair-ee) Stream or river flowing into a larger body of water.

trophic level: Any of the feeding levels that energy passes through as it continues through the ecosystem.

turbidity: (tur-BID-i-tee) The condition where sediment and/or other particles are stirred-up or suspended in the water, giving it a muddy or cloudy appearance.

upwelling: A mass of water that has moved to the surface of a lake or the ocean.

watershed: A region or area that is drained by a river system.

weir: (WEER) Small dam that may be used for taking spawning fish.

wetlands: Areas that contain a lot of soil moisture, can support vegetation that needs wet soil, and have standing water for some part of the year; these areas include swamps, marshes, bogs, coastal areas, and estuaries.

zooplankton: (ZOH-uh-PLANK-ton) Tiny or even microscopic and floating or free-swimming animals.

REFERENCES

ECOLOGY AND MANAGEMENT

Bails, J. D. 1986. "Waters of Change." *Michigan Natural Resources* 55(3): 45–55.

Baldwin, N.A., Saalfeld, R.W., Dochoda, M.R., Buettner, H.J., Eshenroder, R.L., and O'Gorman, R. 2018. Commercial Fish Production in the Great Lakes 1867-2015 [online]. Available from www.glfc.org/great-lakes-databases.php [Accessed August 2018].

Becker, G. C. 1983. *Fishes of Wisconsin.* Madison: University of Wisconsin Press.

Beeton, A. M., and D. C. Chandler. 1966. "The St. Lawrence Great Lakes." In *Limnology in North America*, ed. D. G. Frey. Madison: University of Wisconsin Press.

Bolsenga, S. J., and C. E. Herdendorf, eds. 1993. *Lake Erie and Lake St. Clair Handbook.* Detroit: Wayne State University Press.

Botts, L., and B. Krushelnicki. 1988. *The Great Lakes: An Environmental Atlas and Resource Book.* Chicago: Great Lakes National Program Office, U.S. Environmental Protection Agency.

Christie, W. J., J. M. Fraser, and S. J. Nepszy. 1972. "Effects of Species Introductions on Salmonid Communities in Oligotrophic Lakes." *Journal of Fisheries Research Board of Canada* 29(6): 969–973.

Claudi, R., and J. H. Leach. 2000. *Nonindigenous Freshwater Organisms: Vectors, Biology, and Impacts.* Boca Raton, FL: Lewis Publishers.

Colby, P. J., G. R. Spangler, D. A. Hurley, and A. M. McCombie. 1972. "Effects of Eutrophication on Salmonid Communities in Oligotrophic Lakes." *Journal of Fisheries Research Board of Canada* 29(6): 975–983.

Coon, T. G. 1999. "Ichthyofauna of the Great Lakes Basin." In *Great Lakes Fisheries Policy and Management: A Binational Perspective*, ed. W. W. Taylor and C. P. Ferreri. East Lansing: Michigan State University Press.

Decker, D. J., R. A. Howard Jr., W. H. Everhart, and J. W. Kelley. 1980. *Guide to Freshwater Fishes of New York.* Ithaca, NY: Distribution Center, Cornell University.

Edwards, C. J., and R. A. Ryder, eds. 1990. *Biological Surrogates of Mesotrophic Ecosystem Health in the Laurentian Great Lakes.* Report to Great Lakes Science Advisory Board of the International Joint Commission. Detroit.

Everhart, W. H., and W. D. Youngs. 1981. *Principles of Fishery Science.* 2nd ed. Ithaca, NY: Cornell University Press.

Fisheries Learning on the Web: Project FLOW. 2008. Michigan Sea Grant College Program, Ann Arbor. www.miseagrant.umich.edu/lessons

Goode, George Brown. 1884. *The Fisheries and Fishery Industry of the United States.* Section 1: *Natural History of Useful Aquatic Animals.* Washington, DC: Government Printing Office.

Great Lakes Basin Map. 2011. Michigan Sea Grant College Program, Ann Arbor. MICHU-11-705.

Great Lakes Fishery Commission. 2000. The Great Lakes Fishery Commission—Established by Treaty to Protect Our Fishery. Fact sheet. Ann Arbor, MI.

4-H Youth Programs. Great Lakes Fishes 4-H Fact Sheets, MSU Extension. Michigan State University, East Lansing, MI.

Hartman, W. L. 1988. "Historical Changes in the Major Fish Resources of the Great Lakes." In *Toxic Contaminants and Ecosystem Health*, ed. M. S. Evans. New York: John Wiley & Sons.

Hesselberg, R. J., J. P. Hickey, D. A. Nortrup, and W. A. Willford. "Contaminant Residues in the Bloater (*Coregonus hoyi*) of Lake Michigan, 1969–1986." *Journal of Great Lakes Research* 16(1): 121–129.

Hubbs, C. L., and K. F. Lagler, revised by Gerald R. Smith. 2004. *Fishes of the Great Lakes Region.* Rev. ed. Ann Arbor: University of Michigan Press.

Hubert, W. A., and M. C. Quist. 2010. *Inland Fisheries Management in North America.* 3rd ed. Bethesda, MD: American Fisheries Society.

Kapuscinski, A., and L. Miller, L. 2007. *Genetic Guidelines for Fisheries Management.* 2nd ed. Duluth: University of Minnesota–Duluth.

Keller, M., K. D. Smith, and R. W. Rybicki, eds. 1990. Review of Salmon and Trout, *Management in Lake Michigan.* Fisheries Special Rep. No. 14. Charlevoix Fisheries Station, Michigan Department of Natural Resources.

Kuchenberg, T. 1978. *Reflections in a Tarnished Mirror: The Use and Abuse of the Great Lakes.* Sturgeon Bay, WI: Golden Glow Publishing.

Michigan Department of Natural Resources, Fisheries Research Division. 1992. "Status Report on the Arctic Grayling in Michigan Waters." Lansing.

Mills, E. L., J. H. Leach, J. T. Carlton, and C. L. Secor. 1993. "Exotic Species in the Great Lakes: A History of Biotic Crises and Anthropogenic Introductions." *Journal of Great Lakes Research* 19(1): 1–54.

Ohio Sea Grant. 2002. "Entering the Zone: Aquatic Nuisance Species, Combined Sewers, Agricultural Run-Off and Low Water Levels May Be to Blame for Dead Zone Frequency in Lake Erie." *Twineline* 24(5) (September–October): 1–5.

Page, L. M., and B. M. Burr. 1991. *A Field Guide to Freshwater Fishes.* Peterson Field Guild Series. Boston: Houghton Mifflin.

Read, J. 2003. *Institutional Arrangements for Great Lakes Fisheries Management.* Great Lakes Fisheries Leadership Institute Curriculum. East Lansing, MI.

Regier, H. A., and K. H. Loftus. 1972. "Effects of Fisheries Exploitation on Salmonid Communities in Oligotrophic Lakes." *Journal of Fisheries Research Board of Canada* 29(6): 959–968.

Reid, G. K. 1987. *Pond Life.* New York: Golden Press.

Robins, C. R., R. M. Bailey, C. E. Bond, J. R. Brooker, E. A. Lachner, R. N. Lea, and W. B. Scott. 1991. *A List of Common and Scientific Names of Fishes from the United States and Canada.* 5th ed. Bethesda, MD: American Fisheries Society.

Ryder, R. A. 1972. "The Limnology and Fishes of Oligotrophic Glacial Lakes in North America (about A.D. 1800)." *Journal of Fisheries Research Board of Canada* 29(6): 617–628.

Ryder, R. A., and L. Johnson. 1972. "The Future of Salmonid Communities in North American Oligotrophic Lakes." *Journal of Fisheries Research Board of Canada* 29(6): 941–949.

Scott, W. B., and E. J. Crossman. 1973. *Freshwater Fishes of Canada.* Bulletin 184. Ottawa: Fisheries Research Board of Canada.

Smith, C. L. 1987. *The Inland Fishes of New York State.* Albany: New York State Department of Environmental Conservation.

Smith, G. R. 2010. *Guide to Great Lakes Fishes.* Ann Arbor: University of Michigan Press.

Smith, P. W. 1979. *The Fishes of Illinois.* Urbana: University of Illinois Press.

Smith, S. H. 1972. "Factors of Ecologic Succession in Oligotrophic Fish Communities of the Laurentian Great Lakes." *Journal of Fisheries Research Board of Canada* 29: 717–730.

Snyder, F.L. and David, W.G., 1997. *Zebra mussels in North America.* Ohio Sea Grant College Program. National Oceanic and Atmospheric Administration. http://ohioseagrant.osu.edu/archive/_documents/publications/FS/FS-045%20Zebra%20mussels%20in%20North%20America.pdf

Spiny Tailed Bythotrephes in the Great Lakes. 1991. MICHU-SG-90-700-FS. Michigan Sea Grant, Ann Arbor, Michigan.

Teaching Great Lakes Science, Lessons and Data Sets. 2019. Fisheries, Dead Zones, and Seiches lessons and activities. Michigan Sea Grant College Program, Ann Arbor, MI. www.greatlakeslessons.com

Tomelleri, J. R., and M. E. Eberle. 1990. *Fishes of the Central United States.* Lawrence: University Press of Kansas.

Trautman, M. B. 1981. *The Fishes of Ohio.* 2nd ed. Columbus: Ohio State University Press.

Underhill, J. C. 1986. "The Fish Fauna of the Laurentian Great Lakes, the St. Lawrence Lowlands, Newfoundland and Labrador." In *The Zoogeography of North American Freshwater Fishes*, ed. C. H. Hocutt and E. O. Wiley. New York: John Wiley & Sons.

Water on the Web (WOW). 2004. "Monitoring Minnesota Lakes on the Internet and Training Water Science Technicians for the Future; Lessons on Thermocline and Water Density". University of Minnesota–Duluth. www.waterontheweb.org

TODAY'S GREAT LAKES FISHERIES

American Sportfishing Association. 2016. *Sportfishing in America: An Economic Force in Conservation.* Statistics prepared by R. Southwick of Southwick and Associates. Alexandria, VA: American Sportfishing Association, Alexandria, Virginia. https://asafishing.org/wp-content/uploads/Sportfishing-in-America-Revised-November-2018.pdf

Baldwin, N. A., R. W. Saalfeld, M. R. Dochoda, H. J. Buettner, and R. L. Eshenroder. 2002. Commercial Fish Production in the Great Lakes 1867–2000. August. www.glfc.org/commercial/old_commerc.php

Bence, J. R., and K. D. Smith. 1999. "An Overview of Recreational Fisheries of the Great Lakes." In *Great Lakes Fisheries Policy and Management: A Binational Perspective*, ed. W. W. Taylor and C. P. Ferreri. East Lansing: Michigan State University Press.

Boat Owners Asssociation of tje United States. 2001. 2001 Great Lakes State Boating Facts. Alexandria, VA: Boat Owners Association of the United States, www.boatus.com/gov/lake_facts.htm

Brown, R. W., M. Ebner, and T. Gorenflo. 1999. "Great Lakes Commercial Fisheries: Historical Overview and Prognosis for the Future." In *Great Lakes Fisheries Policy and Management: A Binational Perspective*, ed. W. W. Taylor and C. P. Ferreri. East Lansing: Michigan State University Press.

Dawson, C. P., F. R. Lichtkoppler, and C. Pistis. 1989. "The Charter Fishing Industry in the Great Lakes." *North American Journal of Fisheries Management* 9: 493–499.

Gile, S. R. 2009. Lake Huron Commercial Fishing Summary for 2008. Ontario Ministry of Natural Resources, Upper Great Lakes Management Unit, Lake Huron, Report TR-LHA-2009-1.

Great Lakes Fishery Commission, Great Lakes Water Quality Board, and University of Windsor. 1999. *Addressing Concerns for Water Quality Impacts from Large-Scale Great Lakes Aquaculture.* East Lansing: Department of Fisheries and Wildlife, Michigan State University.

Great Lakes Indian Fish and Wildlife Commission. *Masinaigan.* Newsletter supplement.

Hudson, J. C. and Ziegler, S. S. .2014. Environment, Culture, and The Great Lakes Fisheries. Geographical Review, 104: 391–413. doi: 10.1111/j.1931-0846.2014.12041.x View article online: https://commons.nmu.edu/cgi/viewcontent.cgi?article=1107&context=facwork_journalarticles

International Joint Commission, Great Lakes Regional Office. Brochures: *Remedial Action Plans for Areas of Concern; The Great Lakes: A Vital Resource Worth Protecting* and *The IJC: What It Is; How It Works.*

Moccia, R. D., and D. J. Bevan. 2017. Aquastats: Ontario Aquacultural Production in 2016. University of Guelph. Ontario, Canada. Order No. 01-017.Online here: http://animalbiosciences.uoguelph.ca/aquacentre/files/aquastats/Aquastats%202016%20-%20Ontario%20Statistics%20for%202016.pdf

O'Keefe, D., and S. R. Miller. 2011. "2009 Charter Fishing Study." Michigan Sea Grant and the Michigan State University Center for Economic Analysis, East Lansing.

O'Keefe, D., and S. R. Miller. 2011. "2009 Lake Michigan Tournament Fishing Study." Michigan Sea Grant and the Michigan State University Center for Economic Analysis, East Lansing.

Ontario Ministry of Natural Resources. 2009. *2005 Survey of Recreational Fishing in Canada: Selected Results for Ontario Fisheries.* Peterborough: Fish and Wildlife Branch, Ontario Ministry of Natural Resources.

Ontario Ministry of Natural Resources and Forestry. 2016. *2010 Survey of Recreational Fishing in Canada: Selected Results for the Great Lakes Fishery, 2010.* Species Conservation Policy Branch, Ontario Ministry of Natural Resources and Forestry, Peterborough, Ontario. 29 p. + Appendices.

Talhelm, D. R. 1988. *Economics of Great Lakes Fisheries: A 1985 Assessment.* Technical Report No. 54. Ann Arbor, MI: Great Lakes Fishery Commission.

U.S. Army Corps of Engineers. 2008. Great Lakes Recreational Boating Report. John Glenn Great Lakes Basin Program Report, In response to Public Law 106-53, Water Resources Development Act of 1999, Section 455(c), Washington DC https://www.lre.usace.army.mil/Portals/69/docs/PPPM/PlanningandStudies/JohnGlenn/boating.pdf

U.S. Department of Agriculture, National Agricultural Statistics Service. 2014. *2014 Census of Aquaculture.* Volume 3, Special Studies, Part 2 (AC-12-SS-2) https://www.nass.usda.gov/Publications/AgCensus/2012/Online_Resources/Aquaculture/

U.S. Department of Interior, Fish and Wildlife Service and U.S. Department of Commerce. 2006, 2011. *2006 and 2011 National Survey(s) of Fishing, Hunting and Wildlife-Associated Recreation.* Washington, DC: Government Printing Office. https://www.census.gov/prod/2012pubs/fhw11-nat.pdf

U.S. Department of Interior, Fish and Wildlife Service and Great Lakes Fishery Commission. 2016. Great Lakes Fish stocking database. Washington DC. Database source: http://www.glfc.org/fishstocking

U.S. Department of Interior, U.S. Geological Survey. 2015. *Commercial Fish Production—Pounds and Value, 2015.* USGS Great Lakes Science Center, Ann Arbor, MI.

HISTORY OF THE GREAT LAKES FISHERIES

Bogue, M. B. 1985. *Around the Shores of Lake Michigan: A Guide to Historic Sites.* Madison: University of Wisconsin Press.

Bogue, M. B. 2000. *Fishing the Great Lakes: An Environmental History 1783–1933.* Madison: University of Wisconsin Press.

Bogue, M. B., and V. A. Palmer. 1979. *Around the Shores of Lake Superior: A Guide to Historic Sites.* Madison: University of Wisconsin Sea Grant Institute.

Bronte, C., D. Bunnell, S. David, R. Gordon, D. Gorsky, M. Millard, J. Read, R. Stein, and L. Vaccaro. 2017. *Report from the Workshop on Coregonine Restoration Science.* Conference proceedings, U.S. Fish and Wildlife Service and U.S. Geological Survey. Report 2017-1081. Available online: https://pubs.usgs.gov/of/2017/1081/ofr20171081.pdf

Chippewa-Ottawa Resource Authority. 1999. Michigan's 1836 Treaty Fishery Guide. Public Information and Education Office, CORA, Sault Ste. Marie, MI.

Cleland, C. E. 1982. "The Inland Shore Fishery of the Northern Great Lakes: Its Development and Importance in Prehistory." *American Antiquity* (Society for American Archaeology) 47(4): 761–783.

Cleland, C. E. 1992. *Rites of Conquest: The History and Culture of Michigan's Native Americans.* Ann Arbor: University of Michigan Press.

Clifton, J. A., G. L. Cornell, and J. M. McClurken.1986. *People of the Three Fires: The Ottawa, Potawatomi and Ojibway of Michigan.* Grand Rapids, MI: Grand Rapids Inter-Tribal Council.

The 2000 Great Lakes Consent Decree. 2000. U.S. District Court, Western District of Michigan, Southern Division: Kalamazoo, MI. Documents can be located at Michigan Department of Natural Resources website.

Cox, E. T. No date. *A Chronology of Events in the Development and Administration of Commercial Fishing on Lake Erie.* Lake Erie Assessment Unit, Ontario Ministry of Natural Resources, Wheatley.

Danziger, E. J., Jr. 1979. *The Chippewas of Lake Superior.* Norman: University of Oklahoma Press.

Gearhart, C. R. 1987. *Pity the Poor Fish, Then Man: C. R. (Cliff) Gearhart Reflects on Fifty Years in Michigan's Commercial Fish Industry.* Au Train, MI: Avery Color Studios.

Great Lakes Indian Fish and Wildlife Commission. 2007. A joint strategic plan for management of Great Lakes fisheries (adopted in 1997 and supersedes 1981 original). Great Lakes Fish. Comm. Misc. Publ. 2007-01. Available online: http://www.glfc.org/fishmgmt/jsp97.pdf

Great Lakes Indian Fish and Wildlife Commission. No date. *Lake Superior Indian Fishery.* Odanah, WI: GLIFWC.

Holey, M., E. Baker, T. Thuemler, and R. Elliott. 2000. *Research and Assessment Needs to Restore Lake Sturgeon in the Great Lakes.* Conference Proceedings. Great Lakes Fishery Trust, East Lansing, MI. Available online: https://www.glft.org/documents/cms/cms_file?path=/29/2000_lake_sturgeon_workshop.pdf

Larson, G., and R. Schaetzl. 2001. "Origin and Evolution of the Great Lakes." *Journal of Great Lakes Research* 27(4): 518–546.

Lloyd, T. C., and P. B. Mullen. 1990. *Lake Erie Fishermen: Work, Identity, and Tradition.* Urbana: University of Illinois Press.

McCullough, A. B. 1989. *The Commercial Fishery of the Canadian Great Lakes.* Hull, Quebec: Canadian Government Publishing Centre, Supply and Services Canada.

Michigan Department of Natural Resources. 1994. *State of the Great Lakes: 1993 Annual Report.* Lansing: Office of the Great Lakes, MDNR.

Oikarinen, P. 1979. *Island Folk: The People of Isle Royale.* Houghton, MI: Isle Royale Natural History Association.

Oikarinen, P. 1991. *Armour: A Lake Superior Fisherman.* Calumet, MI: Manitou Books.

Ontario Ministry of National Resources. 1992. *Strategic Plan for Ontario's Fisheries: SPOF II—an Aquatic Ecosystem Approach to Managing Fisheries.* Toronto: OMNR.

Rakestraw, L. 1968. *Commercial Fishing on Isle Royale.* Houghton, MI: Isle Royale Natural History Association.

Reinert, R. E., B. A. Knuth, M. A. Kamrin, and Q. J. Stober. 1991. "Risk Assessment, Risk Management, and Fish Consumption Advisories in the U.S." *Fisheries* 16(6): 5–12.

Schroeder, B. 2000. *Great Lakes fishing pact stresses science.* Michigan Out-of-Doors, 54(10): 82-83.

Sivertson, H. 1992. *Once upon an Isle: The Story of Sighing Families on Isle Royale.* Mount Horeb: Wisconsin Folk Museum.

Strategic Vision of the Great Lakes Fishery Commission for the Decade of the 1990s. 1992. Ann Arbor, MI: Great Lakes Fishery Commission.

Tanner, H. H., ed. 1987. *Atlas of Great Lakes Indian History.* Norman: University of Oklahoma Press.

Time Magazine. 1969. "American's Sewage System and the Price of Optimism." August 1.

White, R. and S. Tainter. 1977. *Seines to Salmon Charters: 150 Years of Michigan Great Lakes Fisheries,* Michigan Sea Grant/Michigan State University Extension Bulletin E-1000 (MICHU-T-77-003), East Lansing, MI. Available online: https://eos.ucs.uri.edu/seagrant_Linked_Documents/michu/michut77003.pdf

Wild Caught and Close to Home: Selecting and Preparing Great Lakes Whitefish. 2010. East Lansing: Michigan Sea Grant College Program and Michigan State University Extension Program.

Williams, C. H., and W. Neubrech. 1976. *Indian Treaties: American Nightmare.* 3rd ed. Seattle: Outdoor Empire Publishing.

FUTURE OF THE GREAT LAKES FISHERIES

Dinse, K., J. Read, and D. Scavia. 2009. *Preparing for Climate Change in the Great Lakes Region.* Report and series of fact sheets. Ann Arbor: Michigan Sea Grant.

Eshenroder, R. L., M. E. Holey, T. K. Gorenflo, and R. D. Clark Jr. 1995. *Fish-Community Objectives for Lake Michigan.* Spec. Pub. 95-3. Ann Arbor, MI: Great Lakes Fishery Commission.

Fish-community Objectives for Lake Huron. 1995. Spec. Pub. 95-1. Ann Arbor, MI: Great Lakes Fishery Commission.

Fishery Division, Michigan Department of Natural Resources. 1994. *Current Issues in Fishery Management in Michigan.* Spring. Lansing: MDNR.

Great Lakes Fishery Commission. 1997. *A Joint Strategic Plan for Management of Great Lakes Fisheries.* Ann Arbor, MI: GLFC.

Great Lakes Fishery Commission. 2001. *Strategic Vision of the Great Lakes Fishery Commission for the First Decade of the New Millennium.* Ann Arbor, MI: GLFC.

Great Lakes Fishery Commission. 2011. *Strategic Vision of the Great Lakes Fishery Commission, 2011-2020.* Ann Arbor, MI: GLFC.

Great Lakes Restoration Initiative. 2018. https://www.glri.us

Horns, W. H., C. R. Bronte, T. R. Busiahn, M. P. Ebener, R. L. Eshenroder, T. Gorenflo, N. Kmiecik, W. Mattes, J. W. Peck, M. Petzold, and D. R. Schreiner. 2003. *Fish-Community Objectives for Lake Superior.* Spec. Pub. 03-01. Ann Arbor, MI: Great Lakes Fishery Commission.

Leach, J. H., E. L. Mills, and M. R. Dochoda. "Non-indigenous Species in the Great Lakes: Ecosystem Impacts, Binational Policies, and Management." In *Great Lakes Fisheries Policy and Management: A Binational Perspective,* ed. W. W. Taylor and C. P. Ferreri. East Lansing: Michigan State University Press.

Madenjian, C. P. et. al. 2002. "Dynamics of the Lake Michigan Food Web, 1970–2000." *Canadian Journal of Fisheries and Aquatic Sciences* 59: 736–753.

McGinn, N. A. 2002. *Fisheries in a Changing Climate.* Bethesda, MD: American Fisheries Society.

Ryan, P. A., R. Knight, R. MacGregor, G. Towns, R. Hoopes, and W. Culligan. 2003. *Fish-Community Goals and Objectives for Lake Erie.* Spec. Pub. 03-02. Ann Arbor, MI: Great Lakes Fishery Commission.

Stewart, T.J., Todd, A., and LaPan, S. 2017. *Fish community objectives for Lake Ontario* [online]. Available from: www.glfc.org/pubs/FisheryMgmtDocs/Fmd17-01.pdf

Taylor, W., A. Lynch, and N. Leonard, eds. 2012. Great Lakes Fisheries Policy and Management: A Binational Perspective. East Lansing: Michigan State University Press.Online here: http://msupress.org/books/book/?id=50-1D0-3C61#.XBCRzG4vxpg

U.S. Fish and Wildlife Service. 2016. Final Apportionment of Dingell-Johnson Sport Fish Restoration Funds for Fiscal Year 2016, Sport Fish Restoration Program. wsfrprograms.fws.gov/Subpages/GrantPrograms/SFR/SFR_Funding.htm

U.S. Fish and Wildlife Service. 2016. National Fishing License Data, Sport Fish Restoration Program, 2016 license sales data Available online: https://wsfrprograms.fws.gov/subpages/licenseinfo/fishing.htm

Whitehouse Council on Environmental Quality et al. 2010. Great Lakes Restoration Initiative Action Plan. Washington DC.

ACKNOWLEDGEMENTS

PATRICK KENNEDY

SPECIAL THANKS

We are grateful to those who served as reviewers and contributors at various times supporting development and updates for *The Life of the Lakes*. Any errors are solely those of the authors, not reviewers or contributors. Affiliations listed may have changed.

Ray Argyle, U.S. Geological Survey Great Lakes Science Center

Stephanie Ariganello, Michigan Sea Grant

Helen Ball, Ontario Ministry of Natural Resources and Forestry

Ted Batterson, Department of Fisheries and Wildlife, Michigan State University

Kieth W. Brickley, Statistical Services, Fisheries and Oceans Canada

Charles Bronte, U.S. Fish and Wildlife Service

David "Bo" Bunnell, U.S. Geological Survey Great Lakes Science Center

Dennis Cartier, Ontario Commercial Fisheries Association

Richard Clute, Besser Museum for Northeast Michigan

Tom Coon, Department of Fisheries and Wildlife, Michigan State University

Alan Crook, Ontario Ministry of Natural Resources

Jennifer Dale-Burton, Chippewa Ottawa Resource Authority

Sally DeRoo, Educational Consultant

John Dettmers, Illinois Natural History Survey / Great Lakes Fishery Commission

James Diana, Michigan Sea Grant Director and Professor, University of Michigan, School of Natural Resources and the Environment

Doug Dodge, Ontario Ministry of Natural Resources, retired

Chad Dolan, Illinois Natural History Survey

Sandra Enness, Michigan Sea Grant Extension

Randy L. Eshenroder, Great Lakes Fishery Commission

Jim Fenner, Ludington Charter Boat Association

Carlos Fetterolf, National Sea Grant Review Panel

Rosanne Fortner, Ohio Sea Grant

Marc Gaden, Great Lakes Fishery Commission

Don Garling, Department of Fisheries and Wildlife, Michigan State University

Neal Godby, Michigan Department of Natural Resources

Chris Goddard, Great Lakes Fishery Commission

Robert Graham, Ontario Commercial Fisheries Association

David Greene, New York Sea Grant

Denny Grinold, Michigan Charter Boat Association

Todd Grischke, Fisheries Division, Michigan Department of Natural Resources

Jeff Gunderson, Minnesota Sea Grant

John Halsey, Michigan Department of History, Arts and Literature

Dale Hanson, U.S. Fish and Wildlife Service

James Haynes, Department of Environmental Science, State University of New York, Brockport

Michael Hermann, Fisheries Division, Michigan Department of Natural Resources

David Jude, School of Natural Resources and Environment, University of Michigan

Robert Kavetsky, U.S. Fish and Wildlife Service

Kevin Kayle, Ohio Department of Natural Resources

Ronald Kinnunen, Michigan Sea Grant

Elizabeth LaPorte, Michigan Sea Grant

Jesse Lepak, New York Sea Grant

Frank Lupi, Department of Fisheries and Wildlife, Michigan State University

Abigail Lynch, PhD candidate, Michigan State University

David MacNeill, New York Sea Grant

Christin Manninen, Great Lakes Commission

Todd Marsee, Michigan Sea Grant

Brian Matchett, Science Educator

Alastair Mathers, Ontario Ministry of Natural Resources

Nathanial Matthews, Outdoor/Environmental Writer

Jared Myers, Department of Fisheries and Wildlife, Michigan State University

Philip Moy, Wisconsin Sea Grant

Daniel O'Keefe, Michigan Sea Grant

Bruce Patterson, Educator

Charles Pistis, Michigan Sea Grant

Mike Quiqley, Great Lakes Environmental Research Laboratory

Jennifer Read, Michigan Sea Grant

Bev Ritchie, Ontario Ministry of Natural Resources

Edmund Sander, Great Lakes Fisheries Commission, New York Fisheries Advisory Board

Mike Siefkes, Great Lakes Fishery Commission

Gerald R. Smith, University of Michigan, retired

Fred Snyder, Ohio Sea Grant

Rochelle Sturtevant, Great Lakes Sea Grant Network

Trent Sutton, Purdue University

Carol Swinehart, Michigan Sea Grant, retired

James Thannum, Great Lakes Indian Fish & Wildlife Commission

Gary Towns, Fisheries Division, Michigan Department of Natural Resources

Thomas Trudeau, Illinois Natural History Survey